Dhyan Manik

Mastering Thai Grammar and Tenses

with

เเรียน แล้ว

Book I

Dolphin
BOOKS
www.dolphinbooks.org

22 Secrets of Learning Thai

Copyright © Dhyan Manik and Dolphin Books 2023

Cover design, layout: Uri Hautamki, Data Graphics

Drawings: Tone Artist

Audio spoken in MP3 format by native speakers can be downloaded from the following address:
www.thaibooks.net
Thai voices: Ms. Waree Singhanart
                 Ms. Jiraporn Buasuk
English voice: Ms. Jiraporn Buasuk

Publisher:
Dolphin Books
info@dolphinbooks.org
www.dolphinbooks.org

ISBN 978-952-6651-44-6

Acknowledgement

I would like to thank the following people for valuable guidance on Thai syntax and grammar, and assistance with editing and proofreading the text to reflect standard spoken Thai:

Ms. Duangmon Loprakhong, Thai Teacher, Duke Language School, Bangkok

Ms. Waree Singhanart, Thai Teacher, Bangkok

Mr. Watit Pumyoo, Chiang Mai University, Chiang Mai

I am also grateful to Mr. Walter Kassela and Mr. Lloyd Tuchman for editing and proofreading the English text. Additionally, Ms. Tuija Turpeinen and Ms. Mirka Venäläinen have contributed by editing and suggesting various improvements to the text.

With the help of the above people, the clarity of the written Thai and English text has been significantly improved.

Special thanks to Duke Language School for kind co-operation.

Table of Contents

Book I, Secrets 1–7

Secret 1 11
   A. lɛ́ɛu แล้ว and two word expressions................................. 12
   B. How the language works
   – five different kinds of verbs.. 13
   C. Language hints 26
   D. Conclusion 36
   E. Simple advice 41

Secret 2 43
   A. The present time and lɛ́ɛu แล้ว..................................... 44
   B. How the language works
   – lɛ́ɛu แล้ว and basic sentences 45
   C. Language hints 57
   D. Conclusion 61
   E. Simple advice 65

Secret 3 67
   A. lɛ́ɛu แล้ว and the present time words and tense markers..... 68
   B. How the language works
   – tɔɔn-níi ตอน นี้, yùu อยู่, kamlang กำลัง 69
   C. Language hints 87
   D. Conclusion 91
   E. Simple advice 95

Secret 4 97
   A. lɛ́ɛu แล้ว and the duration of time................................. 98
   B. How the language works
   – naan-lɛ́ɛu นาน แล้ว, tsèt-wan-lɛ́ɛu เจ็ด วัน แล้ว 99
   C. Language hints 118
   D. Conclusion 124
   E. Simple advice 126

Secret 5 129
   A. lɛ́ɛu แล้ว and the past times words and tense markers..... 130
   B. How the language works
   – mûua-kɔ̀ɔn เมื่อ ก่อน, khəəi เคย, phûŋ เพิ่ง 131
   C. Language hints 147

D. Conclusion		155
E. Simple advice		159

Secret 6 163
    A. lέεu แล้ว and future time words and tense markers 164
    B. How the language works
    – khráng-nâa ครั้ง หน้า, yàak-tsà อยาก จะ, kamlang-tsà กำ ลัง จะ.... 165
    C. Language hints 183
    D. Conclusion 194
    E. Simple advice 198

Secret 7 199
    A. Review of the Thai time aspect 200
    B. How the language works – **Present, past and future** 203
    C. Language hints 220
    D. Conclusion 249
    E. Simple advice 252

Book II, Secrets 8–11

Mastering Thai Grammar and Conjunction words

Thai employs numerous linking words, often incorporating **lέεu** แล้ว, to convey special meanings when connecting words and sentences.

Examples

lέεu	แล้ว	*and, and then*
lέεu-kɔ̂ɔ	แล้ว ก็	*and, and then*
lέεu-lăng-tsàak-nán	แล้ว หลัง จาก นั้น	*after that*
lέεu-lăng-tsàak-níi	แล้ว หลัง จาก นี้	*after this*
lέεu-ləəi	แล้ว เลย	*and then, after that*
lέεu-kɔ̂ɔ-ləəi	แล้ว ก็ เลย	*and then, after that*
lέεu-trong	แล้ว ตรง	*then directly*
lέεu-yang	แล้ว ยัง	*and in addition*
lέεu-ìik-yàang	แล้ว อีก อย่าง	*something more...*
lέεu-nɔ̂ɔk-tsàak-nán	แล้ว นอก จาก นั้น	*apart from that*

sèt-lέεu	เสร็จ แล้ว	*when finished*
lέεu-thǔng	แล้ว ถึง	*after finished*
tsòp-lέεu	จบ แล้ว	*when finished*
phrɔ́ɔm-lέεu	พร้อม แล้ว	*when ready*
lέεu-khôi	แล้ว ค่อย	*and then, after a while*
lέεu-dǐiau	แล้ว เดี๋ยว	*soon, in a moment*
lέεu-ìik-mâi-naan	แล้ว อีก ไม่ นาน	*and then, soon*

Book III, Secrets 12–22

Mastering Thai Language and Grammar

In Book III (Secrets 15–22), there will be many more interesting expressions with **lέεu** แล้ว.

Examples

dâai-lέεu	ได้ แล้ว	*placing extra emphasis*
yùu-lέεu	อยู่ แล้ว	*anyway*
dâai-yùu-lέεu	ได้ อยู่ แล้ว	*of course, to be able to*
kɔ̂ɔ-lέεu-kan	ก็ แล้ว กัน	*That is fine! Agreed!*
kɔ̂ɔ-lέεu-ngai-lâ	ก็ แล้ว ไง ล่ะ	*So what? Then what?*
tòk-long-lέεu	ตกลง แล้ว	*Agreed!*
lέεu-ngai	แล้ว ไง	*Then what? So what?*
tsai-tsing-lέεu	ใจ จริง แล้ว	*really, honestly, truly*
sǐia-lέεu	เสีย แล้ว	*to be bad, to be broken*
sám-lέεu-sám-ìik	ซ้ำ แล้ว ซ้ำ อีก	*again and again*
wâa-lέεu-tʃiiau	ว่า แล้ว เชียว	*I knew it, that's it*
tson-lέεu-tson-rɔ̂ɔt	จน แล้ว จน รอด	*until the end*
hâi-rúu-lέεu-rúu-rɔ̂ɔt	ให้ รู้ แล้ว รู้ รอด	*must get over something*

This may come as a surprise to you that **lέεu** แล้ว has so many meanings and grammatical functions.

Introduction

Thai people use the adverb **lɛ́ɛu** แล้ว daily in different ways. Learn to use this word well, and you will be surprised. **lɛ́ɛu** แล้ว is a fascinating and important word.

Basically, **lɛ́ɛu** แล้ว is used grammatically in two ways. When it is used as a *time indicator* (Book I), it is placed at the end of the sentence. When it is used as a *linking word* (Book II), sometimes also called a *conjunction word,* to link words, phrases or sentences, it is placed as a first element in the second clause.

lɛ́ɛu แล้ว is used very much in an *intuitive way* in a variety of situations to express feelings, wishes, and particular nuances. Whenever you see **lɛ́ɛu** แล้ว in a sentence, it always brings something of herself into the meaning. Once you know how to use **lɛ́ɛu** แล้ว well, your Thai language skills will take a quantum leap to the next level.

As a *time indicator,* **lɛ́ɛu** แล้ว refers to a certain *state* that has been *reached, obtained* or *achieved*. **lɛ́ɛu** แล้ว creates a bridge between the *present state* and the *previous state* or *future state*.

The real meaning of **lɛ́ɛu** แล้ว is always understood from the *context* and from the *other words* it is used with.

When we translate Thai sentences into English, several English tenses are used. Do not let the names of English tenses put you off. They are just used in order to maintain the focus.

You may ignore the names of the English tenses if you wish and concentrate only on understanding the Thai sentences and the *Thai time aspect*. The English tense structure is quite complicated compared to the Thai way, which is normally concerned only with the *present, past* or *future time*.

All this becomes clear in the following Secrets. We have carefully chosen specific sentences to illustrate the fact of how to express the *Thai time aspect* with **lɛ́ɛu** แล้ว in spoken Thai.

The title of the book is *Mastering the Thai Tenses and Grammar with* **lɛ́ɛu** แล้ว. The term *Thai tenses* is used in the title since everybody understands it. However, in the book, the term *Thai time aspect* is normally used instead of *Thai tenses*. The English tense system is totally different compared to the Thai way. That way we can keep the *English tenses* separate from the *Thai time aspect*.

Thai does not have any *verb conjugation* as English does. Everything in Thai is in *basic form*. Therefore, the choice of words and word order is important.

How to use this book

Much depends on your level of Thai language skills and your preferences. If you are an intuitive person, then concentrate more on the spoken and written sentences. Listen to the audio and read Thai sentences and get into the flow. If you are a grammatically oriented person and wish to understand how the Thai language works, then also concentrate on the explanations, grammatical rules and the Thai time aspect.

You must know many words and how to put them together in the sentence in order to speak any language fluently. It is as simple as that. We have made it easier for you to learn new Thai words by giving a "word-for-word" translation into English of Thai sentences. Every sentence is also explained in grammatical terms.

You will learn nuances and subtle points which are not always easy to translate into English since it uses a different syntax.

There are many grammatical explanations. You may choose any of the following sections and read them separately or start from the Secret 1 and continue chronologically from the beginning to the end. You can always go back and review what you have already learned.

A. *Sentences* section includes spoken sentences which are structured according to the Thai grammar.

B. *How the language works* section includes English translations of the spoken Thai sentences, transliterations, grammatical explanations, tone marks, etc.

C. *Language hints* section goes deeper into the structure of Thai language and gives many more example sentences and explanations.

D. *Conclusion* section sums up the subject of the Secret in question. It also includes some examples, which may sound unnatural or may be commonly used wrongly by foreigners.

E. *Simple advice* section gives you some advice of how to simplify your expression. All languages have endless possibilities. However, sometimes, it is better to rely on a simple expression that everybody can understand easily. This is quite important in Thai.

The aim of this book is to demystify the Thai language. Once you know the secret, it is no longer a secret.

แล้ว แล้ว and the Thai time aspect
Secrets 1–7

In this Book I, in Secrets 1–7, **แล้ว แล้ว** is used as a *time indicator* together with *time words* and *tense markers*.

The major difference between the Thai way to express the *time aspect* and English *tenses* is that the English tenses are used in a much more complex way; there may be only a subtle difference, which is not always clear to native speakers either since tenses in English are not used consistently. For example, *he went* or *he has gone* and *he has lived* or *he has been living* may mean for some people the same thing, but for some other people there is a difference depending on the context.

แล้ว แล้ว is often used in the sentences that describe *present time conditions* or *actions*. However, it is also often used for *completed past time actions* and even for *future actions*.

Secret 1

Making things simple!

Focusing on two word expressions.

สวัส ดี ค่ะ – ฉัน ชื่อ แล้ว – แล้ว เป็น ชื่อ เล่น ที่ แม่ ตั้ง ให้ – แล้ว บอก ว่า – ตอน นี้ ฉัน อยาก จะ แนะ นำ เพื่อน ทุก คน ให้ คุณ รู้ จัก – ฉัน แน่ ใจ ว่า – หลัง จาก นี้ คุณ จะ เข้า ใจ ภาษา ไทย และ กาล ใน ภาษา ไทย ดี ขึ้น – แล้ว คุณ จะ สนุก ด้วย – เห็น ด้วย ไหม – มา เริ่ม กัน เถอะ

sàwàtdii khâ – tʃán tʃɯ̂ɯ lɛ́ɛu – lɛ́ɛu pen tʃɯ̂ɯ-lên thîi mɛ̂ɛ tâng-hâi – lɛ́ɛu bɔ̀ɔk wâa – tɔɔn-níi tʃán yàak tsà né-nam phɯ̂ɯan thúk-khon hâi khun rúu-tsàk – tʃán nêe-tsai wâa – lăng-tsàak-níi khun tsà khâu-tsai phaasăa thai lɛ́ kaan nai phaasăa thai dii-khɯ̂n – lɛ́ɛu khun tsà sànùk dûuai – hĕn-dûuai mái – maa rɔ̂əm kan-thə̀

A. lɛ́ɛu แล้ว and two word expressions

Group 1 – Present time with adjectives

   1.1 *phɔɔ-lɛ́ɛu* พอ แล้ว
   1.2 *ìm-lɛ́ɛu* อิ่ม แล้ว
   1.3 *thùuk-lɛ́ɛu* ถูก แล้ว
   1.4 *moo-hŏo-lɛ́ɛu* โมโห แล้ว
   1.5 *too-lɛ́ɛu* โต แล้ว

Group 2 – Present time with non-action verbs

   2.1 *khâu-tsai-lɛ́ɛu* เข้า ใจ แล้ว
   2.2 *rúu-lɛ́ɛu* รู้ แล้ว
   2.3 *wái-tsai-lɛ́ɛu* ไว้ ใจ แล้ว
   2.4 *tsam-dâai lɛ́ɛu* จำ ได้ แล้ว
   2.5 *mii-lɛ́ɛu* มี แล้ว

Group 3 – Ongoing actions with general action verbs

   3.1 *rɔ́ɔng-lɛ́ɛu* ร้อง แล้ว
   3.2 *yím-lɛ́ɛu* ยิ้ม แล้ว
   3.3 *nɔɔn-lɛ́ɛu* นอน แล้ว
   3.4 *tham-ngaan-lɛ́ɛu* ทำ งาน แล้ว
   3.5 *fŏn-tòk-lɛ́ɛu* ฝน ตก แล้ว

Group 4 – Completed actions with specific action verbs
   4.1 *kin-léɛu* กิน แล้ว
   4.2 *sèt-léɛu* เสร็จ แล้ว
   4.3 *bɔ̀ɔk-léɛu* บอก แล้ว
   4.4 *tham-léɛu* ทำ แล้ว
   4.5 *rɔ̂ɔm léɛu* เริ่ม แล้ว

Group 5 – Completed actions with direction verbs
   5.1 *pai-léɛu* ไป แล้ว
   5.2 *maa léɛu* มา แล้ว
   5.3 *dâai-ráp-léɛu* ได้ รับ แล้ว
   5.4 *klàp léɛu* กลับ แล้ว
   5.5 *sòng-léɛu* ส่ง แล้ว

B. How the language works
– five different kinds of verbs

The following five exercises have been constructed for you to go deeper into the Thai language with **lɛ́ɛu** แล้ว and to understand how Thai people express themselves by using simple *two word expressions*.

   1. **lɛ́ɛu** แล้ว shares her wisdom
   2. Spoken sentences – *present and past*
   3. **lɛ́ɛu** แล้ว and *two word expressions*
   4. Overall meaning – the *Thai aspect* and *verb groups 1–5*
   5. Spoken sentences translated and grammar explained

It all depends on your personal preferences and your level of the Thai language skills how to use these exercises. You may study the sections in an orderly manner or skip any section and then come back later as you wish.

Sometimes, you may just wish to read Thai sentences only and skip explanations and grammar altogether. That way, you can facilitate your intuitive expression of the Thai language and learn naturally extra words and language skills.

1. lɛ́ɛu แล้ว shares her wisdom

Listen to the audio several times and see if you can make the meaning clear to yourself what **lɛ́ɛu** แล้ว says. There are not any English translations in this section. However, we shall translate some keywords.

This is also an excellent exercise for those who wish to practise reading the Thai script. We have made it easier for you by writing each word separately.

You may wish to skip this exercise for the time being and concentrate on the Sentences section. It is up to you, however!

สวัส ดี ค่ะ – ฉัน ชื่อ แล้ว – แล้ว เป็น ชื่อ เล่น ที่ แม่ ตั้ง ให้ – แล้ว บอก ว่า – ตอน นี้ ฉัน อยาก จะ แนะ นำ เพื่อน ทุก คน ให้ คุณ รู้ จัก – ฉัน แน่ ใจ ว่า – หลัง จาก นี้ คุณ จะ เข้า ใจ ภาษา ไทย และ กาล ใน ภาษา ไทย ดี ขึ้น – แล้ว คุณ จะ สนุก ด้วย – เห็น ด้วย ไหม – มา เริ่ม กัน เถอะ

sàwàt-dii khâ – tʃán tʃɯ̂ɯ lɛ́ɛu – lɛ́ɛu pen *tʃɯ̂ɯ-lên* thîi mɛ̂ɛ *tâng-hâi* – **lɛ́ɛu** bɔ̀ɔk wâa – tɔɔn-níi tʃán yàak tsà né-nam phɯ̂ɯan thúk-khon hâi khun rúu-tsàk – tʃán *nɛ̂ɛ-tsai* wâa – *lăng-tsàak-níi* khun tsà khâu-tsai phaasăa thai lé *kaan* nai phaasăa thai dii-khɯ̂n – lɛ́ɛu khun tsà sànùk dûuai – hěn-dûuai mái – maa rɔ̂əm *kan-thə̀*

Helping words:

tʃɯ̂ɯ-lên	ชื่อ เล่น	*nickname*
tâng-hâi	ตั้ง ให้	*to give,* here *to give me*
nɛ̂ɛ-tsai	แน่ ใจ	*to be sure, confident*
kaan	กาล	*tense, time, period, era**
lăng-tsàak-níi	หลัง จาก นี้	*after this, from now on*
kan-thə̀	กัน เถอะ	*let's, let us...*

* **kaan** กาล *tense* is pronounced the same as the prefix **kaan** การ *job, work, task*, but is written differently in Thai script. The grammatical function of the prefix **kaan** การ is totally different.

2. Spoken sentences – *present* and *past*

Listen to the audio several times. See if you understand all the spoken sentences, and how Thai people express themselves when using the present time and the *natural time aspect*.

In Thai, we can drop a subject, verb or any other word which is not needed for the understanding of the sentence. Then, the correct meaning is understood from the context. Therefore, longer English sentences can be expressed only by two simple word expressions in Thai. This is usually the case when you reply to a question.

Here are some grammatical words and expressions which can be helpful.

Examples

lέɛu แล้ว as a *time indicator*

Group 1 **phɔɔ lέɛu** พอ แล้ว *to be enough already*
(adjective = state verb = *non-action verb*)

Group 2 **khâu-tsai lέɛu** เข้า ใจ แล้ว *to understand already*
(state verb = *non-action verb*)

Group 3 **rɔ́ɔng lέɛu** ร้อง แล้ว *is already crying*
(general action verb = *action verb*)

Group 4 **kin lέɛu** กิน แล้ว *have already eaten*
(specific action verb = *action verb*)

Group 5 **pai lέɛu** ไป แล้ว *has already gone*
(direction verb = *action verb*)

3. lέɛu แล้ว and *two word expressions*

The first thing to understand about **lέɛu** แล้ว as a *time indicator* is that it is often used with *temporary conditions* or *actions*. However, it can be used in sentences which refer to the *present*, *past* or *future* time.

lɛ́ɛu แล้ว is not normally used with *universal truths* or *long-term facts,* which cannot be changed. Good examples are **lôok klom** โลก กลม the *earth is round* and **thúk-khon tʃɔ̀ɔp ìtsàrà** ทุก คน ชอบ อิสระ *everybody likes freedom,* etc.

The nature of the *time indicator* **lɛ́ɛu** แล้ว is easily understood from the simple *two word expressions.* They are often used by Thais when the context is known or when replying to questions.

Word order

When **lɛ́ɛu** แล้ว is used as a *time indicator* (Secrets 1–7), it is placed *at the end* of the sentence.

Thai time aspect

The English tense system is complicated. However, in Thai, we normally talk simply about:

pàt-tsùbanna-kaan	ปัจจุบัน กาล	*present time, now* or *nowadays*
adìitta-kaan	อดีต กาล	*past time, completed actions*
anaakhótta-kaan	อนาคต กาล	*future time, future planning* or *prediction*

In this Secret, the time aspect is understood from the context.

The focus is on the two word expressions and five groups of verbs. **pàt-tsùbanna-kaan** ปัจจุบัน กาล *present time, now* or *nowadays* and **adìitta-kaan** อดีต กาล *past time, completed actions.*

Natural time aspect

The *basic sentences,* which denote the *natural time aspect,* are normally translated into *English in italics.*

Whenever we use the term *natural time aspect,* it means that the *time aspect* is understood *naturally* from the context without *time words* or *tense markers.*

lɛ́ɛu แล้ว makes the natural time aspect clear.

When *non-action verbs* (Groups 1–2) are used, the sentences refer to the *present state,* which is true now.

When the *general action verbs* (Group 3) are used, the sentences refer to the actions, which are happening *now* or *nowadays*.

When the *specific action verbs* or *direction verbs* are used, the sentences refer to *completed actions* in the past (Groups 4–5).

English Tenses

Even though we have used two word expressions in this Secret, several English tenses, such as the *Present Simple,* the *Present Continuous* and the *Present Perfect,* have been used.

If you wish to ignore the names of English tenses, you can do so since they may not help you in understanding how to express the *present, past* or *future* in Thai.

However, reading English translations may be helpful for understanding the Thai sentences.

English translations

Often there is more than one translation into English – one with *time words* or *tense markers* and one without them.

The *basic sentences* denote the *natural time aspect* and are translated into *English in italics*.

In Secrets 1–2, there is only one translation since the *basic sentences* are used.

4. Overall meaning – *the Thai time aspect* and *verb groups 1-5*

Make clear to yourself what overall meaning **lɛ́ɛu** แล้ว plays in this Secret 1 as far as the *natural time aspect* is concerned. Much depends on the context and the type of verbs (Groups 1–5) **lɛ́ɛu** แล้ว is used with.

lɛ́ɛu แล้ว can be translated into English as *already, state* or *condition reached* or *obtained*. Whenever **lɛ́ɛu** แล้ว is used as a time indicator, it connects the *present state* with the *previous state*.

When **lɛ́ɛu** แล้ว is used this way as a *time indicator*, it normally comes at the end of the sentence. When we use a *basic sentence* without *time words* and *tense markers,* **lɛ́ɛu** แล้ว makes the *natural* *time aspect clear.* The statement or sentence refers to the *present time* or to *completed actions* in the past.

There are two types of verbs: *non-action verbs* and *action verbs.* However, we have divided the Thai verbs into *five different groups* in order to show how the *natural Thai time aspect* is affected when **lέεu แล้ว** is used with different verbs. This is very important since Thais normally understand the *time aspect* intuitively from the *context*.

5. Spoken sentences translated and grammar explained

Study the details of each sentence in this Secret and make sure that you understand all the words, and how Thai people express the *Thai time aspect* with *two word expressions* and with **lέεu แล้ว**.

Every sentence is translated into English with grammatical explanations. In addition, "word-for-word" translation is included so that the reader can easily follow the structure of the Thai language and learn extra words.

All the sentences are written with transliterated text. It helps you to get the pronunciation and tones right. Transliterations, which represent how words are pronounced in Thai, can be used alongside the spoken audio file.

Consider the following spoken sentences:

a) Non-action verbs

Group 1 – adjectives used as *non-action verbs*

When **lέεu แล้ว** is placed after adjectives, the English tense is usually the *Present Simple.*

Adjectives are *non-action verbs,* often also called *state verbs,* since they can also play the role of a verb in Thai. *Non-action verbs* express some duration since they are used to describe a state rather than movement.

Examples

1.1 *phɔɔ lɛ́ɛu*
พอ แล้ว
enough already
It is already enough.

1.2 *ìm lɛ́ɛu*
อิ่ม แล้ว
full already
I am already full.

1.3 *thùuk lɛ́ɛu*
ถูก แล้ว
correct already
That is correct now.

1.4 *moo-hŏo lɛ́ɛu*
โมโห แล้ว
angry already
He is already angry.

1.5 *too lɛ́ɛu*
โต แล้ว
big already
You are already a grown-up.

Adjectives as non-action verbs (Group 1)
- The adjectives such as **phɔɔ** พอ *enough*, **ìm** อิ่ม *full*, **thùuk** ถูก *correct*, **moo-hŏo** โมโห *angry* and **too** โต *a grown-up* are followed by **lɛ́ɛu** แล้ว.
- Adjectives in Thai are used as *non-action verbs*, sometimes also called as *state verbs*.
- In all of the above sentences 1.1–1.5, the subject in Thai is understood from the context.
- In English, however, we need to have a *subject* and a *verb* for the sentence to be complete.

Time aspect

- These are basic sentences without *time words* or *tense markers*.

Natural time aspect

- The focus falls *naturally* on the state, which is *true now* since *adjectives* are *non-action verbs* (Group 1).
- The English tense is the *Present Simple.*

Notes

- **lɛ́ɛu** แล้ว makes the *natural time aspect* clear. It emphasises the fact that a certain state or condition has been *reached*, *it is already the case*.
- The correct tense must be used in English while in Thai, the focus is *naturally* understood from the context.
- The English tense is the *Present Simple.*

Group 2 – *State verbs* used as *non-action verbs*

When **lɛ́ɛu** แล้ว is placed after *non-action verbs* also called *state verbs*, the English tense is usually the *Present Simple*. Non-action verbs tend to have some duration since they are used to describe a state rather than movement.

Examples

2.1 *khâu-tsai lɛ́ɛu*
เข้า ใจ แล้ว
enter-heart already
Now, I understand.

2.2 *rúu lɛ́ɛu*
รู้ แล้ว
know already
I already know.

2.3 *wái-tsai lɛ́ɛu*
ไว้ ใจ แล้ว
keep-heart already
Now, I trust him.

2.4 *tsam-dâai lέεu*
จำ ได้ แล้ว
remember-can already
I remember now.

2.5 *mii lέεu*
มี แล้ว
have already
I have it already.

Non-action verbs (Group 2)
- *State verbs* such as **khâu-tsai** เข้า ใจ *to understand,* **rúu** รู้ *to know,* **wái-tsai** ไว้ ใจ *to trust,* **tsam-dâai** จำ ได้ *to remember* and **mii** มี *to have* are followed by **lέεu** แล้ว. *State verbs* are *non-action verbs.*
- In all the above sentences 2.1–2.5, the subject *I*, in Thai, is understood from the context, while in English, it needs to be spoken out for the sentences to be complete.

Time aspect
- These are basic sentences without *time words* or *tense markers.*

Natural time aspect
- The focus falls *naturally* on the *present time* since *state verbs* are *non-action verbs* (Group 2).
- The English tense is the *Present Simple.*

Notes
- The correct tense must be used in English while in Thai, the meaning is *naturally* understood from the context.
- You already know that the Thai language does not have *tenses*. In Thai, we talk about the *Thai time aspect* which can refer to *now* or *nowadays, completed actions* or the *future.*
- Often **lέεu** แล้ว *already* is better translated into English as *now* when a certain state or condition has been *achieved; it is already the case.*

b) Action verbs

Group 3 – Ongoing actions with *general action verbs*

When **lέεu** แล้ว is placed after *general action verbs*, the English tense is normally the *Present Continuous*. General action verbs express some duration since they are used to describe actions which happen *nowadays* or *now* at the time of *speaking*.

Examples

3.1 *rɔ́ɔng lέεu*
ร้อง แล้ว
cry already

The baby is crying.

3.2 *yím lέεu*
ยิ้ม แล้ว
smile already

She is already smiling.

3.3 *nɔɔn lέεu*
นอน แล้ว
sleep already

She is already sleeping.

3.4 *tham-ngaan lέεu*
ทำ งาน แล้ว
do-work already

I am already working.

3.5 *fǒn-tòk lέεu*
ฝน ตก แล้ว
rain-fall already

It is already raining.

General action verbs (Group 3)

- The *general action verbs* such as **rɔ́ɔng** ร้อง *to cry,* **yím** ยิ้ม *to smile,* **nɔɔn** นอน *to sleep,* **tham-ngaan** ทำงาน *to work,* **fǒn-tòk** ฝนตก *to rain* are followed by **lɛ́ɛu** แล้ว. They are *general action verbs* (Group 3).
- In all the above sentence 3.1–3.5, in Thai, the subject such as the *baby, she, I* or *it* is understood from the context, while in English, the subject needs to be spoken out for the sentence to be complete.

Time aspect
- These are basic sentences without *time words* or *tense markers*.

Natural time aspect
- The focus falls *naturally* on *now* since the main verbs are *general action verbs* (Group 3).
- The English tense is the *Present Continuous*.

Notes
- The correct tense must be used in English, while in Thai, the meaning is *naturally* understood from the context.
- A certain state or condition has been *reached, it is already the case*. The action happens at the *time of speaking* or *nowadays*.

Group 4 – Completed actions with *specific action verbs*

When **lɛ́ɛu** แล้ว is placed after some *specific action verbs*, the English tense is normally the *Present Perfect* (when used for completed actions). *Specific action verbs* do not have any duration since they describe actions that have been *completed*.

Examples

4.1 *kin lɛ́ɛu*
   กิน แล้ว
   eat already
   I have already eaten.

4.2 *sèt lɛ́ɛu*
เสร็จ แล้ว
finish already

It has already been finished.

4.3 *bɔ̀ɔk lɛ́ɛu*
บอก แล้ว
tell already

I have already told her.

4.4 *tham lɛ́ɛu*
ทำ แล้ว
do already

It is already done.

4.5 *rə̂əm lɛ́ɛu*
เริ่ม แล้ว
start already

He has already started.

Specific action verbs (Group 4)
- The *specific action verbs* such as **kin** กิน *to eat,* **sèt** เสร็จ *to finish,* **bɔ̀ɔk** บอก *to tell,* **tham** ทำ *to do* and **rə̂əm** เริ่ม *to start* are followed by **lɛ́ɛu** แล้ว.
- In all the above sentences, in Thai, the subject such as *I, it* or *he* is understood from the context, while in English, the subject needs to be spoken out for the sentence to be complete.

Time aspect
- These are basic sentences without *time words* or *tense markers*.

Natural time aspect
- The focus falls *naturally* on the *completed* actions in the past since main verbs are *specific action verbs* (Group 4).
- The English tense is the *Present Perfect*.

Notes
- The correct tense must be used in English while in Thai, the *natural time aspect* is understood from the *context* and **lɛ́ɛu** แล้ว. The action has *happened (recently)*; *it is already the case.*

Group 5 – Completed actions with direction verbs

When **lɛ́ɛu** แล้ว is placed after *direction verbs*, the English tense is normally the *Present Perfect.*

Direction verbs do not have any duration now since they describe actions that have been *completed.*

Examples

5.1 *pai lɛ́ɛu*
ไป แล้ว
go already

He has already gone.

5.2 *maa lɛ́ɛu*
มา แล้ว
come already

He has already arrived.

5.3 *dâai-ráp lɛ́ɛu*
ได้ รับ แล้ว
get-receive already

I have already received it.

5.4 *klàp lɛ́ɛu*
กลับ แล้ว
return already

He has already returned.

5.5 *sòng lɛ́ɛu*
ส่ง แล้ว
send already

I have already sent it.

Direction verbs (Group 5)
- The *direction verbs* such as **pai** ไป *to go,* **maa** มา *to come,* **dâai-ráp** ได้ รับ *to receive,* **klàp** กลับ *to return* and **sòng** ส่ง *to send* are followed by **lɛ́ɛu** แล้ว.
- In Thai, in all the above sentences 5.1–5.5, the subject such as *he* or *I* is understood from the context, while in English, the subject needs to be spoken or written out for the sentence to be complete.

Time aspect
- These are basic sentences without *time words* or *tense markers*.

Natural time aspect
- The focus falls *naturally* on the *completed actions* since the main verbs are *direction verbs* (Group 5).
- The English tense is the *Present Perfect*.

Notes
- The correct tense must be used in English, while in Thai, the *natural time aspect* is understood from the context and **lɛ́ɛu** แล้ว. The action has *happened (recently)*; *it is already the case*.

C. Language hints

What is the real meaning of **lɛ́ɛu** แล้ว when it is used as a time indicator and placed at the end of a statement or a sentence?

Depending on the context, **lɛ́ɛu** แล้ว can be understood as:
- *already*
- *change in state*
- *state reached* or *obtained*
- *it is already the case*
- *as I understand it now*
- *state exists now*
- *it connects the present time with the past*

a) **lɛ́ɛu** แล้ว and non-action verbs

Often, **lɛ́ɛu** แล้ว *state reached* can be replaced with **yùu** อยู่ *state exists* without changing the basic meaning.

We give here some more examples and use the complete Thai sentences in order to gain some more clarity.

When **lέεu** แล้ว is placed after adjectives (state verbs), it commonly expresses *naturally* the *present time* in Thai. It is often fine to replace **lέεu** แล้ว *state reached* with **yùu** อยู่ *state exists,* and the meaning is the same or very similar.

Examples

a) **lέεu** แล้ว and **yùu** อยู่ after *adjectives* as *state verbs – non-action verbs* (Group 1)

1. *sàbàai-dii* สบาย ดี *to be well, to be fine, to be good*

1.1 *sàbàai-dii lέεu*
สบาย ดี แล้ว
well-good already

I am already fine. / I am fine now.

1.2 *sàbàai-dii yùu*
สบาย ดี อยู่
well-good be

I am feeling fine.

1.3 *sàbàai-dii*
สบาย ดี
well-good

I am fine.

2. *nɯ̀ɯai* เหนื่อย *to be tired*

2.1 tʃán mâi yàak tham-ngaan ìik – tʃán *nɯ̀ɯai lέεu*
ฉัน ไม่ อยาก ทำงาน อีก – ฉัน เหนื่อย แล้ว
I no want do-work more – I tired-already

I do not want to work anymore. I am already tired. / I am tired now.

2.2 tʃán mâi yàak tham-ngaan ìik – tʃán *nùuai yùu*
ฉัน ไม่ อยาก ทำงาน อีก – ฉัน เหนื่อย อยู่
I no want do-work more – I tired-be

I do not want to work anymore. I am feeling tired.

2.3 tʃán mâi yàak tham-ngaan ìik – tʃán *nùuai*
ฉัน ไม่ อยาก ทำงาน อีก – ฉัน เหนื่อย
I no want do-work more – I tired

I do not want to work anymore. I am tired.

Adjectives as non-action verbs
- In the sentences 1.1–2.3, the adjectives **sàbàai-dii** สบาย ดี *to be well* and **nùuai** เหนื่อย *to be tired* play also the role of a verb.
- We can replace **lɛ́ɛu** แล้ว *state reached* with **yùu** อยู่ *state exists*, and the English translation is the same or very similar.
- **lɛ́ɛu** แล้ว emphasises the fact that *it is already the case,* and **yùu** อยู่ expresses the fact that a certain state has *some duration.*

Time aspect
- These are basic sentences without *time words* or *tense markers*.

Natural time aspect
- The *natural time aspect* refers to a state, which is true *now* since *adjectives* are *non-action verbs* (Group 1), sometimes also called *state verbs.*
- **lɛ́ɛu** แล้ว connects the *present time* with the *past. Now, I am tired. Before, I was not tired.*
- The English tense is the *Present Simple* or *Present Continuous.*

Notes
- In the last sentences, 1.3 and 2.3, we have dropped both **lɛ́ɛu** แล้ว and **yùu** อยู่. Then, sentences are blank statements without emphasis. The focus still falls *naturally* on the *present time; I am fine* or *I am tired.*

b) **lɛ́ɛu** แล้ว and **yùu** อยู่ after *state verbs – non-action verbs* (Group 2)

3. *tʃɔ̂ɔp* ชอบ *to like*

3.1 tʃán *tʃɔ̂ɔp* kháu *lɛ́ɛu*
ฉัน ชอบ เขา แล้ว
I like he already
I already like him. / Now, I like him.

3.2 tʃán *tʃɔ̂ɔp* kháu *yùu*
ฉัน ชอบ เขา อยู่
I like he be
I like him.

3.3 tʃán *tʃɔ̂ɔp* kháu
ฉัน ชอบ เขา
I like he
I like him.

4. *mii* มี *to have*

4.1 mâi-pen-rai – tʃán *mii* tŭua *lɛ́ɛu*
ไม่ เป็น ไร – ฉัน มี ตั๋ว แล้ว
no-be-anything – I have ticket already
Never mind! I already have the ticket.

4.2 mâi-pen-rai – tʃán *mii* tŭua *yùu*
ไม่ เป็น ไร – ฉัน มี ตั๋ว อยู่
no-be-anything – I have ticket be
Never mind! I have the ticket.

4.3 mâi-pen-rai – tʃán *mii* tŭua
ไม่ เป็น ไร – ฉัน มี ตั๋ว
no-be-anything – I have ticket
Never mind! I have the ticket.

State verbs as non-action verbs
- **tʃɔ̂ɔp** ชอบ *to like* and **mii** มี *to have* are *non-action verbs*. They describe a certain *state* or *condition*.

- We can replace **lɛ́ɛu** แล้ว *state reached* with **yùu** อยู่ *state exists*, and the English translation is the same or very similar.
- **lɛ́ɛu** แล้ว emphasises the fact that *it is already the case,* and **yùu** อยู่ expresses the fact that a *certain state exists* and *has some duration*.

Time aspect

- These are basic sentences without *time words* or *tense markers*.

Natural time aspect

- After *non-action verbs,* sometimes also called *state verbs* (Group 2), the *natural time aspect* normally denotes the *present time* in Thai.
- **lɛ́ɛu** แล้ว connects the *present time* with the *past. Now, I have a ticket. Before, I did not have.*
- The English tense is the *Present Simple*.

Notes

- In the sentences, 3.3 and 4.3, we have dropped both **lɛ́ɛu** แล้ว and **yùu** อยู่. Then, the sentences are blank statements without emphasis. The focus still falls *naturally* on the *present time; I like him* or *I have a ticket*.

c) **lɛ́ɛu** ดี แล้ว and **yùu** ดี อยู่ after *general action verbs* (Group 3)

5. *fǒn-tòk* ฝน ตก *to rain*

5.1 khun mii rôm mái – *fǒn-tòk lɛ́ɛu*
คุณ มี ร่ม ไหม – ฝน ตก แล้ว
you have umbrella "question" – rain-fall-already

Do you have an umbrella? It is already raining. / It is raining now.

5.2 khun mii rôm mái – *fǒn-tòk yùu*
คุณ มี ร่ม ไหม – ฝน ตก อยู่
you have umbrella "question" – rain-fall-be

Do you have an umbrella? It is raining.

5.3 khun mii rôm mái – fǒn-tòk
คุณ มี ร่ม ไหม – ฝน ตก
you have umbrella "question" – rain-fall
Do you have an umbrella? It rains.

General action verbs
- **fǒn-tòk** ฝน ตก *to rain* is a *general action verb* (Group 3).
- **lɛ́ɛu** แล้ว emphasises the fact that *it is already the case*. The action is happening *now* or at the *time of speaking*.
- The *present time indicator* **yùu** อยู่ at the end of the sentence expresses the fact that a *certain state exists* and *has some duration*.

Time aspect
- These are basic sentences without *time words* or *tense markers*.

Natural time aspect
- The *natural time aspect* refers to the *present time* since **fǒn-tòk** ฝน ตก *to rain* is a *general action verb* (Group 3).
- **lɛ́ɛu** แล้ว connects the *present time* with the *past. Now, it is raining. Before, it was not raining.*
- The English tense is the *Present Continuous*.

Notes
- In the last sentence (5.3), we have dropped both **lɛ́ɛu** แล้ว and **yùu** อยู่. Then, the sentence is a blank statement; *It rains.*

d) Completed actions **lɛ́ɛu** แล้ว and **yùu** อยู่ after *specific action verbs* (Group 4)

The question can be asked, why after some verbs, **lɛ́ɛu** แล้ว refers to the actions which have been *completed* in the past? Well, after some *specific action verbs* such as **kin** กิน *to eat* and *direction verbs* such as **pai** ไป *to go* and **maa** มา *to come*, **lɛ́ɛu** แล้ว refers to *completed actions* which have been taken place *before now*.

Here, the *present time indicator* **yùu** อยู่ *state exists* changes a *completed* action into actions that happen *now* or at the *time of speaking*.

Examples

6. *kin-khâau* กิน ข้าว *to eat*

6.1 tʃán *kin-khâau lɛ́ɛu*
ฉัน กิน ข้าว แล้ว
I eat-rice already

I have already eaten.

6.2 tʃán *kin-khâau yùu*
ฉัน กิน ข้าว อยู่
I eat-rice be

I am eating.

6.3 tʃán *kin-khâau*
ฉัน กิน ข้าว
I eat-rice

I eat.

Specific action verbs
- When **lɛ́ɛu** แล้ว is used with *specific action verbs* such as **kin** กิน *to eat*, the time aspect refers to the past.

Time aspect
- These are basic sentences without *time words* or *tense markers*.

Natural time aspect
- The *natural time aspect* refers to a *completed action* since *specific action verbs* (Group 4) such as **kin-khâau** กิน ข้าว *to eat* are normally associated with *completed actions* when used with **lɛ́ɛu** แล้ว.
- **lɛ́ɛu** แล้ว connects the *present state* with the *past*. Now it is like this. Before, it was different.
- The English tense is the *Present Perfect*.

Notes
When **yùu** อยู่ *state exists* is placed after *specific action verbs*, the *time aspect* changes from the *completed action* to the action, which happens *now*. See the sentence 6.2.

- When both **lɛ́ɛu** แล้ว and **yùu** อยู่ are dropped, we cannot know whether the sentence refers to *now* or *completed action* in the past or the *future*.

e) **lɛ́ɛu** แล้ว and **yùu** อยู่ after *direction verbs* = *action verbs* (Group 5)

7. Direction verb *pai* ไป *to go*

7.1 kháu *pai tsəə* phɯ̂ɯan *lɛ́ɛu*
เขา ไป เจอ เพื่อน แล้ว
he go meet friend already

He has already gone to visit a friend.

7.2 kháu *pai tsəə* phɯ̂ɯan *yùu*
เขา ไป เจอ เพื่อน อยู่
he go meet friend be

He is visiting a friend.

7.3 kháu *pai tsəə* phɯ̂ɯan
เขา ไป เจอ เพื่อน
he go meet friend

He has gone to visit a friend.

Direction verbs
- When **lɛ́ɛu** แล้ว is used with the *direction verbs,* such as **pai** ไป *to go,* the time aspect refers to the past.

Time aspect
- These are basic sentences without *time words* or *tense markers.*

Natural time aspect
- The *natural time aspect* refers to *completed actions* when using *direction verbs,* such as **pai** ไป *to go* (Group 5) in conjunction with **lɛ́ɛu** แล้ว.
- **lɛ́ɛu** แล้ว connects the *present state* with the *past. Now it is like this. Before, it was different.*
- The English tense is the *Present Perfect.*

Notes

- When **yùu** อยู่ *state exists* is placed after a *direction verb*, the *time aspect* changes from the *completed* action to the action, which is happening *now*. See the sentence 7.2.
- When both **lɛ́ɛu** แล้ว and **yùu** อยู่ are dropped, *direction verbs* (Group 5) normally denote actions that have been *completed in the past*. Then, the sentences are blank statements without emphasis; *he has gone to visit a friend*.

Three more examples

1. *rót-tìt lɛ́ɛu*
   รถ ติด แล้ว
   car-stuck-already
   There is already a traffic jam.

2. *tham-ngaan lɛ́ɛu*
   ทำ งาน แล้ว
   do work already
   He is working now.

3. *kháu maa lɛ́ɛu*
   เขา มา แล้ว
   he come already
   He has already arrived.

Time aspect

- These are basic sentences without *time words* or *tense markers*.

Natural time aspect

- In the sentences 1 and 2, the *natural time aspect* refers to the *present time* since **tìt** ติด *to be jammed, to be stuck* is a *non-action verb* (Group 1) and **tham-ngaan** ทำ งาน *to work* is a *general action verb* (Group 3).
- **lɛ́ɛu** แล้ว connects the *present time* with the *past*. Now, there is a traffic jam, before there was not or Now he is working. Before, he was not.

- The English tenses are the *Present Simple* and *Present Continuous*.
- In the sentence 3, the *natural time aspect* refers to a *completed action* in the past since **maa** มา *to come* is a *direction verb* (Group 5).
- He has already arrived, before he was somewhere else.
- The English tense is the *Present Perfect*.

Notes

- With *non-action verbs* such as **tìt** ติด *to be jammed, to be stuck* or *general action verbs* such as **tham-ngaan** ทำ งาน *to work*, **lɛ́ɛu** แล้ว usually expresses *present time actions*.
- With *direction verbs* such as **maa** มา to come, **lɛ́ɛu** แล้ว usually expresses *completed actions* in the past.
- The direction verb **maa** มา *to come* gives an action a certain direction towards the speaker.

f) Future and **lɛ́ɛu** แล้ว

How to construct future sentences with **lɛ́ɛu** แล้ว in Thai?

The *future time* with **lɛ́ɛu** แล้ว is usually made clear by using additional indicators such as the *future time words* **phrûng-níi** พรุ่ง นี้ *tomorrow* or the *future tense marker* **tsà** จะ *will*.

The term *natural time aspect* does not apply to the future, even though **lɛ́ɛu** แล้ว is frequently used in the sentences that refer to the future. Sometimes, however, the *future* is understood from the context, and the *future tense marker* is omitted. More about the *future time* is in Secret 6.

D. Conclusion

Key: Place **lɛ́ɛu** แล้ว as a second element after any *non-action verb* (adjective/state verb) or *action verb* to describe the *temporary nature* of a condition or of an action.

When **lɛ́ɛu** แล้ว is used as a *time indicator*, it normally comes at the end of the sentence. **lɛ́ɛu** แล้ว connects the *present time* with the *past*.

Now, it is like this, before it was different. With **lɛ́ɛu** แล้ว, there is always a change in a state.

In Thai, the grammatical structure is the same in all the sentences, which belong to the verb groups 1–5 even though we may have to use different English tenses to express the correct meaning.

In this Secret, we shall introduce some terms, which may help you to understand the Thai way better.

Basic sentence

The *Basic sentence* means that there are no *time words* or *tense markers* to denote the timing of an *action* or a *state*. Then, the time aspect is understood *naturally* from the context.

Time aspect

The term *Thai time aspect* is used in the same way as the English term *"tense"*. In Thai, we rather talk about *present, past* or *future*.

Natural time aspect

The term *natural time aspect* tells how Thai people understand the meaning *naturally* from the context. The focus is on the *present time* or on *completed actions* in the past.

When the basic sentences are used, then there are not any *time words* or *tense markers*.

Verb groups

The Thai verbs have been divided into *five different groups* (Groups 1–5) in order to find out how the *Thai time aspect* is affected when **lɛ́ɛu** แล้ว is used with different verbs. This is very important since Thais often understand the meaning *naturally* from the context.

Unfamiliar language

To avoid unfamiliar language is important since it would create unnecessary confusion.

When the verb groups 4–5 are used, we have placed either **lɛ́ɛu** แล้ว *already* or **yùu** อยู่ *state exists* at the end of the statement in order to find out how the *Thai time aspect* is affected.

Examples

1. **kin-khâau** กิน ข้าว *to eat*

> 1.1 tʃán *kin-khâau*
> ฉัน กิน ข้าว
> I eat-rice
>
> *I eat.*

- This sentence is incorrect.
- The above sentence does not sound correct in Thai unless the meaning is understood from the context. There is something missing.

1.2 tʃán *kin-khâau lɛ́ɛu*
ฉัน กิน ข้าว แล้ว
I eat-rice already

I have already eaten.

- This sentence is correct.
- The *time indicator* **lɛ́ɛu** แล้ว makes the sentence to be complete.
- When the *time indicator* **lɛ́ɛu** แล้ว *already* is placed at the end of the sentence, then the sentence refers clearly to the *completed* action in the past.
- In this sentence, the main verb is an *action verb,* also called a *specific action verb* (Group 4).
- The *time aspect* refers to the *completed action* in the past.

1.3 tʃán *kin-khâau yùu*
ฉัน กิน ข้าว อยู่
I eat-rice be

I am eating.

- This sentence is correct.
- The *present time indicator* **yùu** อยู่ makes the sentence to be complete.

- When the *present time indicator* **yùu** อยู่ *state exists* is used, then the sentence refers to the action, which is taking place *now*, at the time of speaking.
- The *time aspect* refers to the *present time*.

1.4 tʃán *kamlang kin-khâau*
   ฉัน กำลัง กิน ข้าว
   I being eat-rice

   I am eating.

- This sentence is correct.
- The *present tense marker* **kamlang** กำลัง makes the sentence to be complete.
- When the *present tense marker* **kamlang** กำลัง *action in progress* is placed before the main verb, then the sentence refers to the action, which is taking place *now*, at the time of speaking.
- The *time aspect* refers to the *present time*.

2. **sòng** ส่ง *to send*

   2.1 mâi tông hùuang – tʃán *sòng* tsòt-mǎai
      ไม่ ต้อง ห่วง – ฉัน ส่ง จด หมาย
      no need worry – I send letter

      No need to worry. I am sending the letter.

- This sentence is incorrect.
- The above sentence does not sound correct in Thai. There is something missing. The sentence is not complete.

   2.2 mâi tông hùuang – tʃán *sòng* tsòt-mǎai *lɛ́ɛu*
      ไม่ ต้อง ห่วง – ฉัน ส่ง จด หมาย แล้ว
      no need worry – I send letter already

      No need to worry. I have already sent the letter.

- This sentence is correct.
- The *time indicator* **lɛ́ɛu** แล้ว makes the sentence to be complete.

- When the *time indicator* **lɛ́ɛu** แล้ว *already* is placed at the end of the sentence, then the sentence refers clearly to the *completed action* in the past.
- The main verb is an *action verb,* also called *direction verb* (Group 5).
- The *time aspect* refers to the *completed action* in the past.

2.3 mâi tôŋ hùuaŋ – tʃán sòŋ tsòt-mǎai *yùu*
 ไม่ ต้อง ห่วง – ฉัน ส่ง จด หมาย อยู่
 no need worry – I send letter be

 No need to worry. I am sending the letter.

- This sentence is correct.
- The *present time indicator* **yùu** อยู่ makes the sentence to be complete.
- When the *present time indicator* **yùu** อยู่ *state exists* is used, then the sentence refers to the action, which is taking place *now*, at the time of speaking.
- The *natural time aspect* refers to the *present time.*

2.4 mâi tôŋ hùuaŋ – tʃán *kamlaŋ sòŋ* tsòt-mǎai
 ไม่ ต้อง ห่วง – ฉัน กำลัง ส่ง จด หมาย
 no need worry – I being send letter

 No need to worry. I am sending the letter.

- This sentence is correct.
- The *present tense marker* **kamlaŋ** กำลัง makes the sentence to be complete.
- When the *present tense marker* **kamlaŋ** กำลัง *action in progress* is placed before the main verb, then the sentence refers to the action, which is taking place *now*, at the time of speaking.
- The *time aspect* refers to the *present time.*

3. **nùuai** เหนื่อย *to be tired*

3.1 *tʃán nùuai*
ฉัน เหนื่อย
I tired

I am tired.

- This sentence is correct.
- The above sentence is *perfectly fine* and sounds good in Thai. The reason is that the adjective **nùuai** เหนื่อย *to be tired* is a *non-action verb* (Group 1).
- The *natural time aspect* refers to the *present time*.

3.2 *tʃán nùuai lɛ́ɛu*
ฉัน เหนื่อย แล้ว
I tired already

I am already tired.

- This sentence is correct.
- With **lɛ́ɛu** แล้ว there is a change in the state of being tired.

3.3 *tʃán nùuai yùu*
ฉัน เหนื่อย อยู่
I tired be

I am tired.

- This sentence is correct.
- With **yùu** อยู่, there is the *state of being tired* that has been going on for some time. It has some duration.

E. Simple advice

In this Secret, we have introduced the term *natural time aspect*. That means how the Thai people understand whether the sentence refers to the *present time* or *completed actions* in the past.

The main verbs are normally either *non-action verbs* or *action verbs*. We have divided them into five groups. Together with **lɛ́ɛu** แล้ว, these verb groups play an *important role* in how Thai people understand the meaning and the *time aspect* from the context. All this becomes more clear in the following Secrets.

It is good to know that the *time indicator* **lɛ́ɛu** แล้ว can be placed after *non-action verbs* (Groups 1–2) or after *general action verbs* (Group 3) to emphasise the fact that a *certain state* or *condition* has already been *reached*. In those cases, **lɛ́ɛu** แล้ว reflects the *present state of affairs*. Now it is like this, it is already the case. Before, it was different. **lɛ́ɛu** แล้ว connects the *present state* with the *previous state*.

Since Thais often understand the meaning from the context, we need to pay attention to what type of *main verb* **lɛ́ɛu** แล้ว is used with. That reveals whether the *natural time aspect* refers to the *present time* (Groups 1–3) or to a *completed action* in the past (Groups 4–5).

lɛ́ɛu แล้ว can also be used in the sentences that refer to the *future actions*. Then, additional *time words* or *tense markers* are normally used to make sure that the *future time aspect* is clear.

One more thing

The English tense system is complicated, and it may not help you in understanding how Thai people talk about the *present*, *past* and *future time*.

So, if you ignore the names of English tenses altogether, it is fine. We have used English tenses here just to stay in the course. However, some people may find it helpful if the names of English tenses are included.

Actually, the Thai language does not have any *tenses at all*; the verbs do not change forms as they do in English. Normally, when we talk about tenses in this book, we refer to English tenses. When we are talking about the *Thai time aspect*, we refer directly to the *present, past* or *future time*.

Secret 2

Now is the only time!

Focusing on basic sentences.

แล้ว เป็น คน ที่ เก่ง มาก เกี่ยว กับ กาล ใน ภาษา ไทย – แล้ว บอก ว่า – ฉัน อยาก ทำ ให้ ทุก คน เข้า ใจ ว่า ปัจจุบัน กาล สำคัญ มาก – เพราะ ว่า ชีวิต ของ เรา กำลัง โลด แล่น อยู่ ตอน นี้ – และ เรา มี ความ สุข มาก ที่ สุด – เมื่อ ทุก อย่าง ดำ เนิน ไป ตาม พรหมลิขิต

lέεu pen khon thîi kèng mâak *kìiau-kàp* kaan nai phaasăa thai – **lέεu** bɔ̀ɔk wâa – tʃán yàak tham hâi thúk-khon khâu-tsai wâa *pàt-tsùban-na-kaan* sămkhan mâak – phrɔ́-wâa tʃiiwít khɔ̌ɔng rau kamlang *lôot-lêen* yùu tɔɔn-níi – lé rau mii-khwaam-sùk mâak thîi-sùt – mûua thúk-yàang *dam-nɔɔn* pai taam *phrom-líkhìt*

A. The present time and lέεu แล้ว

1. Group 1 – Adjectives as *non-action verbs*

1.1 dii lέεu ดี แล้ว
    khɔ̀ɔp khun khâ – an-níi *dii lέεu* khâ
    ขอบ คุณ ค่ะ – อัน นี้ ดี แล้ว ค่ะ

1.2 *rîiap-rɔ́ɔi lέεu* เรียบ ร้อย แล้ว
    mâi tông tham iik – *rîiap-rɔ́ɔi lέεu*
    ไม่ ต้อง ทำ อีก – เรียบ ร้อย แล้ว

1.3 *tʃái-dâai* lέεu ใช้ ได้ แล้ว
    tʃán khít wâa – *tʃái-dâai lέεu* khâ
    ฉัน คิด ว่า – ใช้ ได้ แล้ว ค่ะ

2. Group 2 – State verbs as *non-action verbs*

2.1 *dâai-klìn* lέεu ได้ กลิ่น แล้ว
    tʃán *dâai-klìn* baang-yàang *lέεu*
    ฉัน ได้ กลิ่น บาง อย่าง แล้ว

2.2 *mii lέεu* มี แล้ว
    kháu *mii* rót-yon *lέεu*
    เขา มี รถ ยนต์ แล้ว

2.3 *khâu-tsai lɛ́ɛu* เข้า ใจ แล้ว
mâi rúu sì – kháu khuan tông *khâu-tsai lɛ́ɛu*
ไม่ รู้ สิ – เขา ควร ต้อง เข้า ใจ แล้ว

3. Group 3 – General action verbs

3.1 *tham-ngaan lɛ́ɛu* ทำ งาน
bɔ́ɔt tʃán *tham-ngaan lɛ́ɛu*
บอส ฉัน ทำ งาน แล้ว

3.2 *yùu...lɛ́ɛu* อยู่... แล้ว
kháu *yùu* thîi lɔɔndɔɔn *lɛ́ɛu*
เขา อยู่ ที่ ลอนดอน แล้ว

3.3 *khàp...lɛ́ɛu* ขับ... แล้ว
kháu *khàp* rót kèng *lɛ́ɛu*
เขา ขับ รถ เก่ง แล้ว

B. How the language works
– lɛ́ɛu แล้ว and basic sentences

The following five exercises have been constructed for you to go deeper into the Thai language with **lɛ́ɛu** แล้ว and to understand how Thai people express the *present time* with simple *basic sentences*.

1. **lɛ́ɛu** แล้ว shares her wisdom
2. Spoken sentences and *present time*
3. **lɛ́ɛu** แล้ว and *basic sentences*
4. Overall meaning – the *Thai aspect* and *verb groups 1–3*
5. Spoken sentences translated and grammar explained

It all depends on your personal preferences and your level of the Thai language skills how to use these exercises. You may study each section in an orderly manner or skip any section and then come back later as you wish.

Sometimes, you may just wish to read Thai sentences only and skip explanations and grammar altogether. That way, you can facilitate your intuitive expression of the Thai language and learn naturally extra words and language skills.

1. léɛu แล้ว shares her wisdom

Listen to the audio many times and see if you can make the meaning clear to yourself what léɛu แล้ว says. There are not any English translations in this section. However, we shall translate some words which can be helpful to you.

This is also an excellent exercise for those who wish to practise reading the Thai script. It has been made easier for you by writing each word separately.

You may wish to skip this exercise for the time being and concentrate on the sentences section. It is up to you, however!

แล้ว เป็น คน ที่ เก่ง มาก เกี่ยว กับ กาล ใน ภาษา ไทย – แล้ว บอก ว่า – ฉัน อยาก ทำ ให้ ทุก คน เข้า ใจ ว่า ปัจจุบัน กาล สำคัญ มาก – เพราะ ว่า ชีวิต ของ เรา กำลัง โลด แล่น อยู่ ตอน นี้ – และ เรา มี ความ สุข มาก ที่ สุด – เมื่อ ทุก อย่าง ดำ เนิน ไป ตาม พรหมลิขิต

léɛu pen khon thîi kèng mâak *kìiau-kàp* kaan nai phaasăa thai – léɛu bɔ̀ɔk wâa – tʃán yàak tham hâi thúk-khon khâu-tsai wâa *pàt-tsùban-na-kaan* sămkhan mâak – phrɔ́-wâa tʃiiwít khɔ̌ɔng rau kamlang *lôot-lêen* yùu tɔɔn-níi – lé rau mii-khwaam-sùk mâak thîi-sùt – mûɯa thúk-yàang *dam-nɔən* pai taam *phrom-líkhìt*

Words:

kìiau-kàp	เกี่ยว กับ	*about, regarding, concerning*
kaan	กาล	*tense, time, period, era**
pàt-tsùbanna-kaan	ปัจจุบัน กาล	*present time, now* or *nowadays*
lôot-lêen	โลด แล่น	*to move, to rush, to run*
dam-nɔən	ดำ เนิน	*to proceed, to walk*
phrom-líkhìt	พรหม ลิขิต	*destiny, fate*

* **kaan** กาล *tense* is pronounced the same as a prefix **kaan** การ *job, work, task*, but is written differently in Thai script. The grammatical function of the prefix **kaan** การ is totally different.

2. Spoken sentences and *present time*

Listen to the audio several times. See if you understand all the spoken sentences, and how Thai people express themselves when using the *present time* and the *natural time aspect*.

Here are some grammatical words and expressions which can be helpful to you.

lɛ́ɛu แล้ว as a *time indicator* with the verb groups 1–3

1. Group 1 – Adjectives as non-action verbs

dii	ดี	*to be good*
rîiap-rɔ́ɔi	เรียบ ร้อย	*to be ready, to be fine, to be smooth*
tʃái-dâai	ใช้ ได้	*to be usable, can be used, can be done*

2. Group 2 – State verbs as non-action verbs

dâai-klìn	ได้ กลิ่น	*to smell*
mii	มี	*to have*
khâu-tsai	เข้า ใจ	*to understand*

3. Group 3 – General action verbs

tham-ngaan	ทำ งาน	*to work*
yùu	อยู่	*to live, to stay*
khàp	ขับ	*to drive*

3. lɛ́ɛu แล้ว and *basic sentences*

In this Secret, we are focusing on *basic sentences* and on the *present time*. Normally, **lɛ́ɛu** แล้ว emphasises the *present state* in relation to the *previous state*. The time indicator **lɛ́ɛu** แล้ว is used to tell that a certain state, condition or action *has been reached* or *obtained*.

In the basic sentences, when **lɛ́ɛu** แล้ว is used as a time indicator, the *natural time aspect* refers to the *present time, now* or *nowadays*. It is understood from the context and from the main verbs (Groups 1–3).

When **lɛ́ɛu** แล้ว is used with adjectives (Group 1) also called *non-action verbs* or *state verbs*, sentences normally express the *present state of affairs*.

Non-action verbs (Group 2) also called *state verbs* express facts, thoughts, possessions, opinions and feelings, etc. With *non-action verbs*, **lɛ́ɛu** แล้ว normally expresses the *present state of affairs*.

General action verbs (Group 3) describe an *action* rather than a *state*. They are things we can do. When **lɛ́ɛu** แล้ว is used with *general action verbs*, the emphasis is on the *now*, at the *time of speaking* or *nowadays*.

It is often said that **lɛ́ɛu** แล้ว refers to *completed actions* in the past. In this Secret, we wish to prove that the focus of **lɛ́ɛu** แล้ว is more on the *present state of time* rather than on the *completed* actions in the past. Therefore, and depending on the context, **lɛ́ɛu** แล้ว can sometimes be translated into English as *now*.

Word order

When **lɛ́ɛu** แล้ว is used as a *time indicator* it normally comes at the *end of the sentence*.

Thai time aspects

The English tense system is rather complicated. In Thai, we normally talk about the three main time aspects as follows.

pàt-tsùbanna-kaan	ปัจจุบัน กาล	*present time, now* or *nowadays*
adìitta-kaan	อดีต กาล	*past time, completed actions*
anaakhótta-kaan	อนาคต กาล	*future time, future planning* or *prediction*

Present time aspect

In this Secret, the focus is on the *present time of affairs* – **pàt-tsùbanna-kaan** ปัจจุบัน กาล *present time, now* or *nowadays*.

Natural time aspect

Without any *time words* or *tense markers,* the Thai *time aspect* is understood from the context; then, it is a *basic sentence.* In this book, this *time aspect* is called the *natural time aspect.* The *basic sentences* are normally translated into *English in italics.*

When **lɛ́ɛu แล้ว** is used as a *time indicator,* the *natural time aspect* is clear. That is to say that the sentences refer to the *present time* when the verb groups 1–3 are used.

English tenses

In this Secret, the English tenses are the *Present Simple* or the *Present Continuous.*

You may ignore the names of the English tenses since they do not directly help you in understanding the Thai way.

4. Overall meaning – *the Thai time aspect* and *verb groups 1-5*

Try to make clear to yourself what overall meaning **lɛ́ɛu แล้ว** plays in this Secret as far as the *Thai time aspect* is concerned.

Since we are using *basic sentences* and the main verbs that belong to the verb groups 1–3 without *other time words* or *tense markers,* the *natural time aspect* refers to the *present time.*

There are two types of verbs, *action verbs* and *non-action verbs.* In this Secret, we have divided the Thai verbs into three groups (Groups 1–3).

The point is to show that when *basic sentences* are used with the verb groups 1–3, the sentences refer to the *present time.* This is very important since the *Thai time aspect* is often understood from the context. **lɛ́ɛu แล้ว** connects the *present state* with the *past.*

Examples

1. Group 1 – *Adjectives* as *non-action verbs*

Adjectives in Thai can also be called *state verbs.* When *non-action verbs* are used, the focus falls *naturally* on the *present time.*

See the list of *adjectives* (Group 1) at the Grammar section, page 258 at the end of the book.

Example

kháu *kròot lɛ́ɛu*
เขา โกรธ แล้ว
he angry already

He is already angry. / He is angry now.

Time aspect
- In the above sentence, there are not any *time words* or *tense markers*. Therefore, the time aspect is understood from the context. It is called the *natural time aspect*.

Natural time aspect
- Here, the adjective **kròot** โกรธ to be angry refers to *present time* since it is a non-action verb (Group 1).
- The *natural time aspect* refers to *now* or *nowadays*.
- The English tense is the *Present Simple*.

Notes
- In Thai, adjectives can also play the role of a verb.
- **lɛ́ɛu** แล้ว connects the *present state* with the *previous state*. *He is angry now. Before, he was not.*

2. Group 2 – *State verbs* as *non-action verbs*.

   State verbs describe a *state* or *condition*. Good examples of state verbs (non-action verbs) in English are: *to like, to love, to hate, to want, to need, to hear, to see,* etc.

   When *non-action verbs* are used, the focus falls *naturally* on the *present time*.

   See the list of *state verbs* (Group 2) at the Grammar section, page 259 at the end of the book.

Example

tʃán *klìiat* nɯ́ɯa-sàt *lɛ́ɛu*
ฉัน เกลียด เนื้อ สัตว์ แล้ว
I hate meat-animal already

I already hate to eat meat. / I hate to eat meat now.

Time aspect

- In the above sentence, there are not any *time words* or *tense markers*. Therefore, the time aspect is understood from the context. It is called the *natural time aspect.*

Natural time aspect

- The *state verb* **klìiat** โกรธ *to hate* (Group 2) is a *non-action verb* and *denotes* the *present time.*
- The *natural time aspect* refers to *now* or *nowadays*.
- The English tense is the *Present Simple.*

Notes

- **lɛ́ɛu** แล้ว connects the *present state* with the *previous state. He hates to eat meat now. Before, he did not.*

3. Group 3 – *General action verbs*

General action verbs may be conveniently used together with **lɛ́ɛu** แล้ว. Action verbs are used when something happens or when somebody is performing an action.

The *action verbs* are more dynamic; they usually express a movement. *State verbs* express a quality or condition of something or somebody.

When **lɛ́ɛu** แล้ว is used with *general action verbs*, the situation is usually expressed in English by the *Present Continuous.*

See the list of *general action verbs* (Group 3) at the Grammar section, page 260 at the end of the book.

Example

rau *yùu* thîi ɔ̌ɔpfít *lɛ́ɛu*
เรา อยู่ ที่ ออฟฟิศ แล้ว
we stay in the office already

We are already staying in the office.
We are staying in the office now.

Time aspect

- In the above sentence, there are not any *time words* or *tense markers*. Therefore, the time aspect is understood from the context. It is called the *natural time aspect*.

Natural time aspect

- When the *general action* verb **yùu** อยู่ *to stay, to live* (Group 3) is used together with **lɛ́ɛu** แล้ว, it reflects the *present time*.
- The *natural time aspect* refers to *now* or *nowadays*.
- The English tense is the *Present Continuous*.

Notes

- **lɛ́ɛu** แล้ว connects the *present state* with the *previous state*. We are in the office now. Before, we were somewhere else.

4. Group 4 – *Specific action verbs*

   Compare the groups 4–5 with groups 1–3. When *specific action verbs* are used, the focus falls *naturally* on the *completed action* in the past.

   See the list of *specific action verbs* (Group 4) at the Grammar section, page 261 at the end of the book.

Example

phǒm *tham* man sèt *lɛ́ɛu*
ผม ทำ มัน เสร็จ แล้ว
I do it finish already

I have done it already.

Time aspect
- In the above sentence, there are not any *time words* or *tense markers*. Therefore, the time aspect is understood from the context. It is called the *natural time aspect*.

Natural time aspect
- Here the *specific action* verb **tham** ทำ to do (Group 4) is used together with **lɛ́ɛu** แล้ว. It refers to the *past*.
- The *natural time aspect* reflects a *completed action* in the past.
- The English tense is the *Present Perfect*.

Notes
- **lɛ́ɛu** แล้ว connects the *present state* with the *previous state*. It has been done now. Before, it was not.

5. Group 5 – *direction verbs*

When *direction verbs* are used, the focus falls *naturally* on the *completed action* in the past.

See the list of *direction verbs* (Group 5) at the Grammar section, page 262 at the end of the book.

kháu *hâi* khɔ̌ɔng-khwǎn tʃán *lɛ́ɛu*
เขา ให้ ของ ขวัญ ฉัน แล้ว
he give thing-spirit I already

He has already given me a present.

Time aspect
- In the above sentence, there are not any *time words* or *tense markers*. Therefore, the time aspect is understood from the context. That is called the *natural time aspect*.

Natural time aspect
- The *direction verb* **hâi** ให้ *to give* (Group 5) is used together with **lɛ́ɛu** แล้ว. It refers to the *past*.
- The *natural time aspect* reflects a *completed action* in the past.
- The English tense is the *Present Perfect*.

Notes

- **lέɛu แล้ว** connects the *present state* with the *previous state. It has been done now. Before, it was not.*

5. Spoken sentences translated and grammar explained

Study the details of each sentence in this Secret and make sure that you understand all the words and how Thai people express the *present time aspect* with *basic sentences* and **lέɛu แล้ว**.

Grammatical explanations are given when appropriate. Every sentence is translated into English. In addition, "word-for-word" translation is included so that the reader can easily follow the structure of the Thai language and learn extra words.

All sentences are also written with transliterated text. It helps you to get the pronunciation and tones right. Transliterations, which represent how words are pronounced in Thai, can be used alongside the spoken audio file.

Consider the following spoken sentences:

A. The present time and with **lέɛu แล้ว**

1. Group 1 – adjectives as *non-action verbs*

   With *non-action verbs*, **lέɛu แล้ว** is frequently used to express a *present state of affairs. Non-action verbs* are often also called *state verbs* or *stative verbs*.

1.1 khɔ̀ɔp-khun khâ – an-níi *dii-lέɛu* khâ
ขอบ คุณ ค่ะ – อัน นี้ ดี แล้ว ค่ะ
thank-you khâ – piece-this good-already khâ

Thank you! This is already good.

1.2 mâi tông tham ìik – *rîiap-rɔ́ɔi-lέɛu*
ไม่ ต้อง ทำ อีก – เรียบ ร้อย แล้ว
no must do more – smooth-together-already

There is no need to do it anymore. That's fine now.

1.3 tʃán khít wâa – *tʃái-dâai léɛu* khâ
ฉัน คิด ว่า – ใช้ ได้ แล้ว ค่ะ
I think that – use-can already khâ
I think it should be OK now.

Time aspect
- In the above sentences, there are not any *time words* or *tense markers*. Therefore, the time aspect is understood from the context. It is called the *natural time aspect*.

Natural time aspect
- Adjectives such as **dii** ดี *to be good,* **rîiap-rɔ́ɔi** เรียบ ร้อย *when ready* and **tʃái-dâai** ใช้ ได้ *can be done* refer to the *present time* since they are *non-action verbs* (Group 1).
- The *natural time aspect* refers to *now* or *nowadays*. The state or condition has been *reached, it is already the case.*
- The English tense is *Present Simple.*

Notes
- **léɛu** แล้ว connects the *present state* with the *previous state*. In Thai, adjectives can also play the role of a *verb*.

2. Group 2 – State verbs as *non-action verbs*
   With *non-action verbs,* **léɛu** แล้ว is frequently used to express a *present state of affairs. Non-action verbs* are often also called *state verbs* or *stative verbs.*

2.1 tʃán *dâai-klìn* baang-yàang *léɛu*
ฉัน ได้ กลิ่น บาง อย่าง แล้ว
I get-smell some-sort already
I already smell something. / I smell something now.

2.2 kháu *mii* rót-yon *léɛu*
เขา มี รถ ยนต์ แล้ว
he have car-motor already
He has already a car. / He has a car now.

2.3 mâi rúu sì – kháu khuan tông *khâu-tsai-lɛ́ɛu*
ไม่ รู้ สิ – เขา ควร ต้อง เข้า ใจ แล้ว
no know sì – he should must enter-heart already

I do not really know! He should understand it by now.

Time aspect

- In the above sentences, there are not any *time words* or *tense markers*. Therefore, the time aspect is understood from the context. It is called the *natural time aspect*.

Natural time aspect

- State verbs such as **dâai-klìn** ได้ กลิ่น *to smell*, **mii** มี *to have* and **khâu-tsai** เข้า ใจ *to understand* reflect the *present time* since they are *non-action verbs* (Group 2).
- The *natural time aspect* refers to *now* or *nowadays*.
- The English tense is *Present Simple*.

Notes

- **lɛ́ɛu** แล้ว connects the *present state* with the *previous state*. The state or condition has been *reached; that is already the case.*
- **lɛ́ɛu** แล้ว *already* can often be translated into English as *now*.

3. Group 3 – General action verbs

With many *general action verbs*, **lɛ́ɛu** แล้ว is frequently used to express the *present state of affairs*.

3.1 bɔ́ɔt tʃán *tham-ngaan lɛ́ɛu*
บอส ฉัน ทำ งาน แล้ว
boss I do-work already

My boss is already working. / My boss is working now.

3.2 kháu *yùu* thîi lɔɔndɔɔn *lɛ́ɛu*
เขา อยู่ ที่ ลอนดอน แล้ว
he live at London already

He is already living in London. / He lives in London now.

3.3 kháu *khàp* rót *kèng-lɛ́ɛu*
เขา ขับ รถ เก่ง แล้ว
he drive car skilful-already

He is already driving well. / He drives well now.

Time aspect
- In the above sentences, there are not any *time words* or *tense markers*. Therefore, the time aspect is understood from the context. It is called the *natural time aspect*.

Natural time aspect
- *General action verbs* (Group 3) such as **tham-ngaan** ทำ งาน *to work,* **yùu** อยู่ *to live* and **khàp** ขับ *to drive* normally reflect the *present time*.
- The *natural time aspect* refers to *now* or *nowadays*.
- The English tense is the *Present Continuous* or *Present Simple*.

Notes
- **lɛ́ɛu** แล้ว connects the *present state* with the *previous state*. The state or condition has been *reached, that is already the case*.
- Even though **tham-ngaan** ทำ งาน *to work* is an action verb, with **lɛ́ɛu** แล้ว, it refers to the *state of working* that happens now.

C. Language hints

In this Secret, we have placed more emphasis on the *present time* rather than on the *past* or *future time*. We have also used basic sentences without *time words* or *tense markers*. In the following Secrets 3–6, we shall introduce *time words* and *tense markers*.

Basically, **lɛ́ɛu** แล้ว *already* can be used in the sentences that refer to the *present, past* and *future*.

Consider the following sentences:
a) Present
Depending on the context, **lɛ́ɛu** แล้ว *already* can also be translated into English as *now*. The meaning is understood from the context and from the *type of verbs* (Groups 1–3) **lɛ́ɛu** แล้ว is used with.

Examples

1. tʃán *khrîiat lɛ́ɛu*
   ฉัน เครียด แล้ว
   I stressed-already

   I am already worried. / I am worried now.

2. tʃán *tham-ngaan* thîi ráan khăai năngsɯ̌ɯ *lɛ́ɛu*
   ฉัน ทำ งาน ที่ ร้าน ขาย หนังสือ แล้ว
   I do-work at shop sell book already

   I am working in the bookshop now.

3. kháu *sɔ̌ɔn* phaasăa angkrìt *lɛ́ɛu*
   เขา สอน ภาษา อังกฤษ แล้ว
   she teach language English already

   She is already teaching English.

Time aspect

- In the above sentences, there are not any *time words* or *tense markers*. Therefore, the time aspect is understood from the context. It is called the *natural time aspect*.

Natural time aspect

- The *natural time aspect* refers to the *now* or *nowadays* since **khrîiat** เครียด is a *non-action verb* (Group1) and **tham-ngaan** ทำ งาน and **sɔ̌ɔn** สอน are *general action verbs* (Group 3).
- The English tenses are the *Present Simple* and *Present Continuous*.

Notes

- Sometimes it sounds better to translate **lɛ́ɛu** แล้ว into English as *now* instead of *already*.
- More about the *present time* with **lɛ́ɛu** แล้ว is found in the next Secret 3.

b) Completed actions

lɛ́ɛu แล้ว *already* can also be conveniently used to express actions that have been *completed* in the past. The structure in Thai is the same as in the previous section. The meaning is understood from the context and from the *type of verbs* (Groups 4–5) **lɛ́ɛu** แล้ว is used with.

Examples

1. tʃán *kin-lɛ́ɛu*
   ฉัน กิน แล้ว
   I eat-already

   I have already eaten.

2. kháu *pai-hăa* mɔ̌ɔ *lɛ́ɛu*
   เขา ไป หา หมอ แล้ว
   he go-search doctor already

   He has already gone to see the doctor.

3. kháu *pai-lɛ́ɛu* khâ
   เขา ไป แล้ว ค่ะ
   he go-already khâ

   He has already left.

Time aspect
- In the above sentences, there are not any *time words* or *tense markers*. Therefore, the time aspect is understood from the context. It is called the *natural time aspect*.

Natural time aspect
- **lɛ́ɛu** แล้ว is positioned after the *specific action verb* **kin** กิน *to eat* (Group 4) and *direction verbs* **pai-hăa** ไป หา *to go, to visit* and **pai** ไป *to go* (Group 5).
- The *natural time aspect* refers to *completed actions* in the past. *It is done! It is already the case.*
- The English tense is the *Present Perfect*.

Notes
- **lɛ́ɛu** แล้ว connects the *completed action* with *now* or *nowadays.*
- Even though the action has been completed in the past, **lɛ́ɛu** แล้ว tells how things are *now. Before, it was different.*

- More about the completed actions with **lɛ́ɛu** แล้ว is found in Secret 5.

c) Future

How to form future sentences with **lɛ́ɛu** แล้ว?

lɛ́ɛu แล้ว *already* can be conveniently used with *anticipated future actions*.

Normally, when expressing *future* actions, Thais like to place the future tense marker **tsà** จะ *will* before the main verb to mark that the action refers to the *future*.

Hence, the term *natural time aspect* does not apply to the *future actions* unless the *future time aspect* is understood from the *context*.

Examples

1. tʃán *tsà* pai *lɛ́ɛu* ná
   ฉัน จะ ไป แล้ว นะ
   I will go already ná

   I am going now.

2. ìik-hâa-naa-thii tʃán *tsà* dʉ̀ʉm kaafɛɛ *lɛ́ɛu*
   อีก ห้า นาที ฉัน จะ ดื่ม กาแฟ แล้ว
   more-five-minute I will drink coffee *already*

   In five minutes, I will be drinking coffee.

Future time aspect
- The Thai time aspect, which refers to the future, is made clear here by the *future time words* such as **ìik-hâa-naa-thii** อีก ห้า นาที *in five minutes* and by the *future tense marker* **tsà** จะ *will*.
- The English tense is the *Present Continuous*.

Notes
- In order to make the *future time aspect clear*, Thais often like to use the *future tense marker* **tsà** จะ *will* when talking about the *future*.

- More about the *anticipated future actions* with **lɛ́ɛu แล้ว** is found in Secret 6.

D. Conclusion

Key: Place **lɛ́ɛu แล้ว** *already* at the end of the sentence to express the fact that the certain state *has been reached, obtained* or *attained*. The meaning is similar to the phrase; *it is already the case*. **lɛ́ɛu แล้ว** connects the *present* with the *past*.

One way to understand **lɛ́ɛu แล้ว** is to compare it with the English word *already*. They are used in a similar way. However, **lɛ́ɛu แล้ว** is a far more important word in Thai than *already* is in English. Depending on the context, **lɛ́ɛu แล้ว** can also often be translated into English as *now*.

lɛ́ɛu แล้ว can be conveniently used in the sentences that express the *present state of affairs* with *adjectives* (Group 1), *state verbs* (Group 2) and *general actions verbs* (Group 3).

However, when **lɛ́ɛu แล้ว** is used with *specific action verbs* or *direction verbs* (Groups 4–5), it normally refers to *completed actions* in the past.

The meaning is very much understood from the context and the type of main verbs **lɛ́ɛu แล้ว** is used with.

In order to understand the *time indicator* **lɛ́ɛu แล้ว**, just think in terms that it always has some connection to the *present state*. We are here looking into the *present* (now) in relation to the *past* (previous state) or even the *future* (next state).

It can be concluded that **lɛ́ɛu แล้ว** is dynamic by its nature. It always describes a change in a *state* or *condition*.

Unfamiliar expressions
Try to avoid unfamiliar language since it would create unnecessary confusion.

Spoken Thai language develops and changes continuously. The sentence can be grammatically correct, but it may sound unnatural to the Thai ear. Thais may say: *you are correct, but I have never heard anybody saying it like that.*

The thinking goes that if many people use the expression, it must be correct. If you use unfamiliar language, you may not be understood however correct your sentence is grammatically. Also, younger generation may use words or expressions that older generations do not understand.

Examples

> 1. khɔ̌ɔ **népkîn** dûuai
> ขอ แนปกิน ด้วย
> ask napkin also
>
> *Could I get a napkin?*

- This sentence is grammatically correct, but...
- Thai people use a lot of borrowed English words. However, the English word **népkîn** แนปกิน is not used in Thailand, and most likely is not understood.

1.2 khɔ̌ɔ **thít-tʃuu** dûuai
ขอ ทิชชู ด้วย
ask tissue also

Could I get a tissue?

1.3 khɔ̌ɔ **kràdàat-tʃét-pàak** dûuai
ขอ กระดาษ เช็ด ปาก ด้วย
ask paper-clean-mouth also

Could I get a tissue?

- These sentences 1.2 and 1.3 are correct.
- When *napkin* in English is used, Thais normally say **kràdàat-thít-tʃûu** กระดาษ ทิชชู *paper tissue.*

- **kràdàat-tʃét-pàak** กระดาษ เช็ด ปาก is the original Thai expression for *tissue*, literally translated into English as *paper-clean-mouth*.
- If you wish to be easily understood, use **thít-tʃûu** ทิชชู *tissue* or the *original Thai expression* instead of **népkîn** แนปกิน in Thailand.

> 2. tʃán **wɔ́ɔk** *lɛ́ɛu*
> ฉัน เวิร์ก แล้ว
> I work already
>
> *I am already working.*

- This sentence is incorrect.
- The borrowed English word *work* is used frequently in Thai. However, to use this word with people is incorrect.
- Thais never make a sentence like this; they would be puzzled if they hear it.

2.1 tʃán **tham-ngaan** *lɛ́ɛu*
ฉัน ทำ งาน แล้ว
I do-work already

I am already working.

- This sentence is correct.
- **wɔ́ɔk** เวิร์ก *to work* is not used as a *verb* with *people* in Thai. You must say **kháu tham-ngaan** เขา ทำงาน *he works*.

2.2 man **wɔ́ɔk** *lɛ́ɛu*
มัน เวิร์ก แล้ว
it work already

It already works.

- This sentence is correct.
- It is perfectly fine to use it with *things* such as **man wɔ́ɔk** มัน เวิร์ก *it works*.
- The original Thai expression for the same would be **tham-dâai** ทำ ได้ or **tʃái-dâai** ใช้ ได้ *it works, it is possible, can be done*.

2.3 **wɜ́ɜk** เวิร์ก *work* is used as a *noun* in several ways in Thai
Examples

nét-wɜ̀ɜk	เน็ตเวิร์ก	*network*
áat-wɜ̀ɜk	อาร์ต เวิร์ก	*artwork*
thiim-wɜ̀ɜk	ทีม เวิร์ก	*teamwork*
wɜ́ɜk-krúp	เวิร์ก กรุ๊ป	*workgroup*
wɜ́ɜk-tʃiit	เวิร์ก ชีต	*worksheet*
wɜ́ɜk-búk	เวิร์ก บุ๊ก	*workbook*
wɜ́ɜk-lòot	เวิร์ก โหลด	*workload*
wɜ́ɜk-phɜɜmìt	เวิร์ค เพอร์มิท	*work permit*

- The borrowed English word **wɜ́ɜk** เวิร์ค *work* is not normally used alone as a noun.
- It is used in combined constructions as above.

Sometimes, there are no similar Thai expressions, and only the English expression is used. Sometimes, the English expression is preferred to the Thai expression, and sometimes the Thai expression is preferred.

It is an art to use borrowed English words in Thai. There also is a question of how to pronounce them. The subject is vast.

Do not worry, there will be a book coming soon on how to use *borrowed English* words in Thai.

The book will contain more than one thousand commonly used English words. It includes pronunciation tips, grammar rules, meanings and a lot of vocabulary. That is a must for anyone studying or wanting to learn Thai fluently.

More information can be found on the website **www.thaibooks.net**

E. Simple advice

The Thai lifestyle is very much focused on the *present time*, and that is reflected how words and sentences are understood. Therefore, **lɛ́ɛu** แล้ว as a *time indicator* can often be translated into English as *now*.

lɛ́ɛu แล้ว connects the *present state* with the *past,* the *previous state* in the past.

In this Secret, **lɛ́ɛu** แล้ว is used without *time words* or *tense markers;* we have placed much emphasis on the *present time conditions* rather than on the *completed actions* in the past. That way, it is easier to understand the true nature of **lɛ́ɛu** แล้ว. It is important to note that Thais often understand the meaning *naturally* from the *context* – from the *type of verbs* (Groups 1– 5) **lɛ́ɛu** แล้ว is used with.

The time indicator **lɛ́ɛu** แล้ว tells that a certain *state* or *condition* has already been *reached, attained* or *obtained.* Omitting **lɛ́ɛu** แล้ว may change the *focus* or the *time aspect* of the sentence. Sometimes, the sentence is not complete if **lɛ́ɛu** แล้ว is left out. In *basic sentences* (Groups 1– 5), **lɛ́ɛu** แล้ว makes the *time aspect clear;* it is understood *naturally* from the context. It connects the *present state* (now) with the *previous state* (before).

One more thing

Do not underestimate **lɛ́ɛu** แล้ว. It is a much more important word in Thai than the English translation *already* implies. It can be used several ways: as a *time indicator,* as a *conjunction word* or in *combination* with other words. **lɛ́ɛu** แล้ว plays various *grammatical functions.*

Get to know it well, and your Thai language skills will improve tremendously.

Secret 3

At the time of speaking!

Focusing on actions that happen now.

แล้ว มี เพื่อน หลาย คน ที่ ช่วย ให้ เขา จำ ได้ ว่า ปัจจุบันกาล คือ ที่ นี่ เดี๋ยว นี้ – ไม่ ใช่ พรุ่ง นี้ – แล้ว บอก ว่า – ส่วน ใหญ่ ฉัน ชอบ เล่น กับ กำลัง และ อยู่ – เพราะ ว่า พวก เขา อยู่ กับ ปัจจุบันกาล เสมอ – ไม่ ไป ไหน เลย

lɛ́ɛu mii phûuan lăai khon thîi tʃûuai-hâi kháu *tsam-dâai-wâa pàt-tsùban-na-kaan* khɯɯ thîi-nîi dĭiau-níi – mâi tʃâi phrûng-níi – **lɛ́ɛu** bɔ̀ɔk wâa – sùuan-yài tʃán tʃɔ̂ɔp lên kàp **kamlang** lé **yùu** – phrɔ́-wâa phûuak-kháu yùu kàp *pàt-tsùban-na-kaan sàmɘ̌ɘ* – *mâi* pai năi lɘɘi

A. lɛ́ɛu แล้ว and the present time words and tense markers

1. Using *present time* words

1.1 *dĭiau-níi* เดี๋ยว นี้
   dĭiau-nii tʃán duu fútbɔɔn *lɛ́ɛu*
   เดี๋ยว นี้ ฉัน ดู ฟุตบอล แล้ว

1.2 *tɔɔn-níi* ตอน นี้
   tɔɔn-níi kháu tʃái khɔɔmphiutɘ̂ɘ thîi-nân *lɛ́ɛu*
   ตอน นี้ เขา ใช้ คอมพิวเตอร์ ที่ นั่น แล้ว

1.3 *pàt-tsùban-níi* ปัจจุบัน นี้
   pàt-tsùban-níi tʃán tham-ngaan *lɛ́ɛu*
   ปัจจุบัน นี้ ฉัน ทำ งาน แล้ว

2. Using the present tense marker *kamlang* กำลัง

2.1 fáa *kamlang* rɔ́ɔng *lɛ́ɛu*
   ฟ้า กำลัง ร้อง แล้ว

2.2 tʃán *kamlang* tham aahăan *lɛ́ɛu*
   ฉัน กำลัง ทำ อาหาร แล้ว

2.3 kháu *kamlang* riian-năngsɯ̌ɯ *lɛ́ɛu*
   เขา กำลัง เรียน หนังสือ แล้ว

3. Using the present time indicator *yùu* อยู่ instead of *kamlang* กำลัง

3.1 kháu pai thánaakhaan *yùu*
เขา ไป ธนาคาร อยู่

3.2 tʃán duu-lɛɛ man *yùu*
ฉัน ดู แล มัน อยู่

3.3 nák-riian tham-tuua dii *yùu*
นัก เรียน ทำ ตัว ดี อยู่

4. Present point of time with *tâng-tèe* ตั้ง แต่ and *lăng-tsàak* หลัง จาก

4.1 *tâng-tèe níi pen-tôn-pai* – tʃán tsà mâi tham phìt *ìik-lɛ́ɛu*
ตั้ง แต่ นี้ เป็น ต้น ไป – ฉัน จะ ไม่ ทำ ผิด อีก แล้ว

4.2 *tâng-tèe wan-níi pen-tôn-pai* – khun tsà pen hŭua-nâa *lɛ́ɛu*
ตั้ง แต่ วัน นี้ เป็น ต้น ไป – คุณ จะ เป็น หัว หน้า แล้ว

4.3 tʃán wăng wâa – *lăng-tsàak tɔɔn-níi* – thúk-sìng thúk-yàang tsà dii khûn *lɛ́ɛu*
ฉัน หวัง ว่า – หลัง จาก ตอน นี้ – ทุก สิ่ง ทุก อย่าง จะ ดี ขึ้น แล้ว

B. How the language works
– tɔɔn-níi ตอน นี้, yùu อยู่, kamlang กำลัง

The following five exercises have been constructed for you to go deeper into the Thai language with **lɛ́ɛu** แล้ว and to understand how Thai people express the *present time* with *present time words* such as **tɔɔn-níi** ตอน นี้ *now* or *nowadays, present time indicator* **yùu** อยู่ *state or action exists* and the *present tense marker* **kamlang** กำลัง *action in progress.*

1. **lɛ́ɛu** แล้ว shares her wisdom
2. Spoken sentences and the *present time*
3. **lɛ́ɛu** แล้ว and *present time words* and *present tense markers*
4. Overall meaning – the *present time aspect* and *verb groups 1–5*
5. Spoken sentences translated and grammar explained

It all depends on your personal preferences and your level of the Thai language skills how to use these exercises. You may study each section in an orderly manner or skip any section and then come back later as you wish.

Sometimes, you may just wish to read Thai sentences only and skip explanations and grammar notes altogether. That way, you can facilitate your intuitive expression. You learn naturally unfamiliar words and improve your language skills.

1. lɛ́ɛu แล้ว shares her wisdom

Listen to the audio many times and see if you can make the meaning clear to yourself what lɛ́ɛu แล้ว says. There are not any English translations in this section. However, we shall translate some words, which may prove to be helpful to you.

This is also an excellent exercise for those who wish to practise reading the Thai script. It has been made easier for you by writing each word separately.

You may wish to skip this exercise for the time being and concentrate on the sentences section. It is up to you, however!

แล้ว มี เพื่อน หลาย คน ที่ ช่วย ให้ เขา จำ ได้ ว่า ปัจจุบันกาล คือ ที่ นี่ เดียว นี้ – ไม่ ใช่ พรุ่ง นี้ – แล้ว บอก ว่า – ส่วน ใหญ่ ฉัน ชอบ เล่น กับ กำลัง และ อยู่ – เพราะ ว่า พวก เขา อยู่ กับ ปัจจุบันกาล เสมอ – ไม่ ไป ไหน เลย

lɛ́ɛu mii phʉ̂ʉan lăai khon thîi tʃûuai-hâi kháu *tsam-dâai-wâa pàt-tsùban-na-kaan* khʉʉ thîi-nîi dĭiau-níi – mâi tʃâi phrûng-níi – **lɛ́ɛu** bɔ̀ɔk wâa – sùuan-yài tʃǎn tʃɔ̂ɔp lên kàp **kamlang** lɛ́ **yùu** – phrɔ́-wâa phûuak-kháu yùu kàp *pàt-tsùban-na-kaan sàmə̌ə* – *mâi* pai nǎi lə ̌əi

Words:

pàt-tsùbanna-kaan	ปัจจุบัน กาล	*present time, now* or *nowadays*
kamlang	กำลัง	*action in progress (used as a tense marker)**

yùu	อยู่	*state or action exists (used as a time indicator)**
tʃûuai-hâi	ช่วย ให้	*to help someone*
tsam-dâai-wâa	จำ ได้ ว่า	*to remember that*
sàmɔ̌ɔ	เสมอ	*always*
mâi...ləəi	ไม่...เลย	*not at all*

* **yùu** อยู่ can also be used as a main verb. Then, the meaning is *to stay* or *to live*.
* **kamlang** กำลัง can also be used as a noun, meaning *power, energy, strength*.

2. Spoken sentences and the present time

Listen to the audio several times and see if you understand the above sentences and how Thai people use *present time words* and *present tense markers*.

Here are some grammatical words and expressions which can be helpful.

lέεu แล้ว as a *time indicator*

Present time words

dǐiau-níi	เดี๋ยว นี้	*now, at the moment*
tɔɔn-níi	ตอน นี้	*now*
pàttsùban-níi	ปัจจุบัน นี้	*nowadays*

Present tense marker

kamlang	กำลัง	*action in progress*

Present time indicator

yùu	อยู่	*state or action exists*

Point of time/present time

tâng-tὲε	ตั้ง แต่	*from, from now onwards, after*
lǎng-tsàak	หลัง จาก	*after*

3. léɛu แล้ว and *present time words* and *present tense markers*

In this Secret, we are focusing on the *present time* with *present time words* such as **tɔɔn-níi** ตอน นี้ *now* and with the *present tense marker* **kamlang** กำลัง *action in progress* and with the *present time indicator* **yùu** อยู่ *state exists*.

Now, we can express nuances, place some additional emphasis on the *present time* or make the *present time* clear. The focus is on *now, at the time of speaking* or *nowadays*. **léɛu** แล้ว is used to emphasise meanings like the *state* or *condition reached* or *obtained*.

With **léɛu** แล้ว, there is always a *change in a state*. It expresses the *present state, how things are now* in relation to the *previous state*. **léɛu** แล้ว functions as a *bridge* between the *two states, present* and *past*.

In order to understand the time indicator **léɛu** แล้ว *already*, just think in terms that it always has some connection to the *present state*, a certain state has been *reached* or *attained, it is already the case*.

For the actions, which are happening at the *time of speaking* or *nowadays,* different indicators such as the *time word* **dĭiau-níi** เดี๋ยว นี้ *now* or the *present tense marker* **kamlang** กำลัง *action in progress* can be used in order to emphasise the *present state of affairs*. We may also use the *present time indicator* **yùu** อยู่ *state exists*, which has a similar meaning to **kamlang** กำลัง *action in progress*.

Word order

When **léɛu** แล้ว is used as a *time indicator* it normally comes at the end of the sentence.

The *time words* such as **dĭiau-níi** เดี๋ยว นี้ *now* are often placed at the beginning of the sentence. All the *tense markers* such as **kamlang** กำลัง are always placed before the main verb.

Even thought **yùu** อยู่ *state exists* has a similar meaning as **kamlang** กำลัง, it is considered to be the *present time indicator* similar to **léɛu** แล้ว. Hence, it is placed at the end of the sentence.

Thai time aspects

In Thai, we normally talk about the three main time aspects as follows:

pàt-tsùbanna-kaan	ปัจจุบัน กาล	*present time, now* or *nowadays*
adìitta-kaan	อดีต กาล	*past time, completed actions*
anaakhótta-kaan	อนาคต กาล	*future time, future planning* or *prediction*

Present time aspect

In this Secret, the focus is on the *present time of affairs* – **pàt-tsùbanna-kaan** ปัจจุบัน กาล *present time, now* or *nowadays*.

With *present time words* and the *present tense markers*, the *present time aspect* can be made clear. Also, if we wish to give the *exact timing* of an action, the *present time words* can be used.

The *present tense markers* are used to place extra *focus* on the *present time* to tell that the action happens *now* or at the *time of speaking*.

Natural time aspect

The *basic sentences,* which denote the *natural time aspect,* are normally translated into *English in italics*.

When the *present time words* and the *present tense markers* are omitted, the *time aspect* is understood *naturally* from the context.

Non-action verbs (Groups 1–2) and *general action verbs* (Group 3) normally denote the *present time* with **lέεu** แล้ว.

English tenses

When **lέεu** แล้ว is used in the sentences that happen at the *time of speaking* or *nowadays*, the English tense is normally the *Present Continuous.*

When the exact timing of an action is given with *present time words,* the English tense is normally *Present Simple.*

English translations

Often there is more than one translation into English – one with *time words* or *tense markers* and one without them.

The *basic sentences* denote the *natural time aspect* and are translated into *English in italics*.

4. Overall meaning – *natural time aspect* and *verb groups 1-5*

Try to understand the overall meaning, how the *time indicator* **lɛ́ɛu แล้ว** is used with *present time words* and *present tense markers*.

In the previous Secrets 1 and 2, *basic sentences* are used. It means that there are not any additional *time words* or *tense markers*.

In this Secret, *time words* and *tense markers* are used to make the *time aspect* clear. If they are omitted, the meaning must be understood from the context and from the main verbs (Groups 1–5) **lɛ́ɛu แล้ว** is used with.

lɛ́ɛu แล้ว functions as a bridge between the *present time* and the *past*. **lɛ́ɛu แล้ว** connects the *present time* with the *previous state*.

Compared to *basic sentences*, the difference here is that now the *present time* can be expressed with all kinds of verbs (Groups 1–5).

Examples

a) Non-action verbs (Groups 1–2)

In this section, the time aspect is made clear by *time words* such as **dǐiau-níi** เดี๋ยว นี้ *now,* **tɔɔn-níi** ตอน นี้ *now*.

When the *time words* and *tense markers* are omitted in groups 1–2, the *Thai time aspect* does not normally change.

The *basic sentences* denote the *natural time aspect,* which are translated into *English in italics*.

1. Group 1 – *Adjectives* are *non-action verbs*, also called *state verbs*

Examples

dĭiau-níi kháu *kèng-lɛ́ɛu*
เดี๋ยว นี้ เขา เก่ง แล้ว
moment-this he good already

Now, he is already efficient/smart.
He is already efficient/smart.

Present time aspect
- The *present time word* **dĭiau-níi** เดี๋ยว นี้ *now* is used to place some extra emphasis on the *present time*.
- The English tense is the *Present Simple*.

Natural time aspect
- If we omit **dĭiau-níi** เดี๋ยว นี้ *now*, the sentence would still denote the *present time* since the adjective **kèng** เก่ง *to be efficient* is a *non-action verb* (Group 1).
- The English tense is the *Present Simple*.

Notes
- The adjective **kèng** เก่ง *to be efficient, to be smart* (Group 1) also plays the role of a verb here.
- **lɛ́ɛu** แล้ว connects the *present state* with the *past*. *Now, he is efficient. Before, he was not.*

2. Group 2 – *State verbs* are *non-action verbs*
   They describe a *state* or *condition*.

   The time indicator **lɛ́ɛu** แล้ว can be used together with *non-action verbs / state verbs* to express the *present time* condition that has been *attained, reached* or *obtained; it is already the case!*

Examples

tɔɔn-níi tʃán *tʃɔ̂ɔp* kháu *lɛ́ɛu*
ตอน นี้ ฉัน ชอบ เขา แล้ว
at-this I like he already

Now, I already like him.
I already like him.

Present time aspect
- The *present time word* **tɔɔn-níi** ตอน นี้ *now* is used to place some extra emphasis on the *present time*. The present time aspect refers to *now*.
- The English tense is the *Present Simple*.

Natural time aspect
- If we omit **tɔɔn-níi** ตอน นี้ *now*, the sentence would still denote the *present time* since the *state verb* **tʃɔ̂ɔp** ชอบ *to like* is a *non-action verb* (Group 2).
- The English tense is the *Present Simple*.

Notes
- **lɛ́ɛu** แล้ว connects the *present state* with the *past*. *She already likes him. Before, she did not like him.*

b) Action verbs

Action verbs are used when something happens or when somebody is performing an action.

Action verbs are more dynamic; they usually express a movement. *State verbs*, on the other hand, express a quality or condition of something or somebody.

In this section, the time aspect is made clear by the *present tense marker* **kamlang** กำลัง *action in progress*.

When the *time words* and *tense markers* are omitted, the *Thai time aspect* normally changes. However, when *general action verbs* (Group 3) are used, the *time aspect* remains the same.

The *basic sentences* denote the *natural time aspect*, which are translated into *English in italics*.

3. Group 3 – *General action verbs*

General action verbs denote the *present time*, which is expressed in English as verb + **ing**.

Examples

phǒm **kamlang** *riian* phaasǎa thai *lɛ́ɛu*
ผม กำลัง เรียน ภาษาไทย แล้ว
I being study language Thai already

I am already study**ing** Thai.
I am already studying Thai.

Present time aspect
- The *present tense marker* **kamlang** กำลัง *action in progress* is used to place some *extra emphasis* on the *present time.* **kamlang** กำลัง is always placed before the main verb, here **riian** เรียน *to study.*
- The English tense is the *Present Continuous.*

Natural time aspect
- If we omit **kamlang** กำลัง, the sentence would still denote the *present time* since **riian** เรียน *to study* is a *general action verb* (Group 3).
- The English tense is the *Present Continuous Tense.*

Notes
- **lɛ́ɛu** แล้ว connects the *present state* with the *past. I am already studying Thai. Before, I was not studying Thai.*

4. Group 4 – *Specific action verbs*

Without tense markers, and when **lɛ́ɛu** แล้ว is used with *specific action verbs,* the sentence usually refers to a *completed action* in the past.

Examples

4.1 **kamlang** *dùum* kaafɛɛ *lɛ́ɛu*
ผม กำลัง ดื่ม กาแฟ แล้ว
I being drink coffee already

I am already drink**ing** coffee.
I have already been drinking coffee.

Present time aspect
- The *present tense marker* **kamlang** กำลัง *action in progress* is placed before the main verb to tell that the action is happening *now*.
- The English tense is the *Present Continuous*.

Natural time aspect
- If we omit **kamlang** กำลัง, the *time aspect* changes to denote a *completed action* in the past since **dùum** ดื่ม *to drink* is a *specific action verb* (Group 4).
- The English tense is the *Present Perfect Continuous*.

Notes
- **lέεu** แล้ว connects the *present state* with the *past*.

5. Group 5 – *Direction verbs*

   lέεu แล้ว can also be used with *direction verbs* such as **maa** มา *to come* and **pai** ไป *to go*.

   Without additional indicators, and when **lέεu** แล้ว is used with *direction verbs*, the sentence usually refers to *completed actions* in the past.

Examples

   kháu **kamlang** klàp-maa lέεu
   เขา กำลัง กลับ มา แล้ว
   he being return-come already

   He is already on **his way back.** / He is already coming back.
   He has already returned. / He has already come back.

Present time aspect
- The *present tense marker* **kamlang** กำลัง *action in progress* is placed before the main verb to tell that the action is happening now.
- The English tense is the *Present Continuous*.

Natural time aspect

- If we omit **kamlang** กำลัง, the sentence reflects a *completed action* in the past since **klàp-maa** กลับ มา *to return* is a *direction verb* (Group 5).
- The English tense is the *Present Perfect.*

Notes

- **lέεu** แล้ว connects the *present state* with the *past*.

5. Spoken sentences translated and grammar explained

Study the details of each sentence in this Secret and make sure that you understand all the words, and how Thai people express the *present time aspect* with **lέεu** แล้ว.

Grammatical explanations are given when appropriate. Every sentence is translated into English. In addition, "word-for-word" translation is included. That helps the reader follow the structure of the Thai language and learn unfamiliar words.

All sentences are written with *transliterated text* with *tone marks*. It helps you to get the pronunciation and tones right. Transliterations, which represent how words are pronounced in Thai, can be used alongside the spoken audio file.

In the following sentences, the *present time* is emphasised by using *present time words* and *present tense markers*.

1. Using present time words

    In this section, the time aspect is made clear by the *time words* such as **dǐiau-nii** เดี๋ยว นี้ *now,* **tɔɔn-níi** ตอน นี้ *now* and **pàttsùban-nii** ปัจจุบัน นี้ *nowadays.*

    When the *time words* are omitted, the *Thai time aspect* normally changes. However, *general actions verbs* (Group 3) are an exception.

    The *basic sentences* denote the *natural time aspect,* which are translated into *English in italics.*

Examples

1.1 **dǐiau-níi** เดี๋ยว นี้ *now, at this moment*
dǐiau-níi tʃán duu fútbɔɔn *lɛ́ɛu*
เดี๋ยว นี้ ฉัน ดู ฟุตบอล แล้ว
moment-this I see football already

Now, I am already watching football.
I am already watching football.

1.2 **tɔɔn-níi** ตอน นี้ *now*
tɔɔn-níi kháu tʃái khɔɔmphiutəə thîi-nân *lɛ́ɛu*
ตอน นี้ เขา ใช้ คอมพิวเตอร์ ที่ นั่น แล้ว
at-this he use computer at-there already

Now, he is already using a computer over there.
He is already using a computer over there.

1.3 **pàttsùban-níi** ปัจจุบัน นี้ *nowadays*
pàttsùban-níi tʃán tham-ngaan *lɛ́ɛu*
ปัจจุบัน นี้ ฉัน ทำ งาน แล้ว
nowadays I do-work already

Nowadays, I am already working.
I am already working.

Present time aspect
- Some extra information has been given by the *present time words* such as **dǐiau-níi** เดี๋ยว นี้ *now*, **tɔɔn-níi** ตอน นี้ *now*, **pàttsùban-níi** ปัจจุบัน นี้ *nowadays*.
- They are placed here at the beginning of the sentence in order to give the specific timing of an action.
- The English tense is the *Present Continuous*.

Natural time aspect
- When the *time words* are omitted, the focus would still fall *naturally* on the *present time* since the main verbs **duu** ดู *to watch*, **tʃái** ใช้ *to use* and **tham-ngaan** ทำ งาน *to work* are *general action verbs* (Group 3).
- The English tense is the *Present Continuous*.

Notes
- The action happens *now, nowadays* or *at the time of speaking.*
- **lɛ́ɛu** แล้ว connects the *present state* with the *previous state. Now it is like this. Before, it was different.*

2. Using the present tense marker **kamlang** กำลัง

In this section, the time aspect is made clear with the *present tense marker* **kamlang** กำลัง *action in progress.* **kamlang** กำลัง *action in progress* is normally used for actions, which happen at the *time of speaking.*

When the *tense marker* is omitted, the *Thai time aspect* normally changes. However, *general actions verbs* (Group 3) are an exception.

The *basic sentences* denote the *natural time aspect,* which are translated into *English in italics.*

Examples

2.1 fáa **kamlang** rɔ́ɔng *lɛ́ɛu*
ฟ้า กำลัง ร้อง แล้ว.
sky being cry already

It is already thunder**ing**.
It is already thundering.

2.2 tʃán **kamlang** tham aahǎan *lɛ́ɛu*
ฉัน กำลัง ทำ อาหาร แล้ว
I being make food already

I am already mak**ing** food.
I have already made some food.

2.3 kháu **kamlang** riian-nǎngsǔɯ *lɛ́ɛu*
เขา กำลัง เรียน หนังสือ แล้ว
he being study books already

He is already study**ing**.
He is already studying.

Present time aspect

- The *present tense marker* **kamlang** กำลัง *action in progress* is always placed before the main verb.
- The action happens at the *time of speaking*.
- **kamlang** กำลัง *action in progress* is used here to place some more emphasis on the action, which happens *now*.
- The English tense is the *Present Continuous*.

Natural time aspect

- Without the *present tense marker* **kamlang** กำลัง *action in progress*, the *focus* would still fall *naturally* on the *present time* in the sentences 2.1 and 2.3 since the main verbs **rɔ́ɔng** ร้อง *to cry* and **riian-nǎngsʉ̌ʉ** เรียน หนังสือ *to study* are *general action verbs* (Group 3).
- The English tense is the *Present Continuous*.
- However, in the sentence 2.2 the *natural time aspect* denotes a *completed action* in the past since the main verb **tham** ทำ *to do* is a *specific action verb* (Group 4).
- The English tense is the *Present Perfect*.

Notes

- **lɛ́ɛu** แล้ว makes the bridge between the *present time* and the *past*.

3. Using the present time indicator **yùu** อยู่ instead of **kamlang** กำลัง

   In this section, the *time aspect* is made clear by the *present time indicator* **yùu** อยู่ *state exists*.

   yùu อยู่ *state exists* is frequently used instead of **kamlang** กำลัง *action in progress*.

   Sometimes, **yùu** อยู่ is used even instead of **lɛ́ɛu** แล้ว. **yùu** อยู่ gives the action *some duration*.

   When the *present time indicator* is omitted, the *Thai time aspect* normally changes. However, *general actions verbs* (Group 3) are an exception.

The *basic sentences* denote the *natural time aspect,* which are translated into *English in italics*.

Examples

3.1 kháu pai thánaakhaan **yùu**
เขา ไป ธนาคาร อยู่
he go bank be

He is on his **way to** the bank.
He has gone to the bank.

3.2 tʃán duu-lɛɛ man **yùu**
ฉัน ดู แล มัน อยู่
I see-look it be

I am look**ing** after it.
I am looking after it.

3.3 nák-riian tham-tuua dii **yùu**
นัก เรียน ทำ ตัว ดี อยู่
person-study do-body good be

Students are behav**ing** well.
Students are behaving well.

Present time aspect
- The *present time indicator* **yùu** อยู่ is normally translated into English as *state* or *condition exists*. Often, it is used instead of **kamlang** กำลัง *action in progress,* particularly in speaking.
- **yùu** อยู่ emphasises the fact that the action has some *duration*.
- The English tense is the *Present Continuous*.

Natural time aspect
- In the sentence 3.1, when **yùu** อยู่ is dropped, the focus falls on a *completed action* in the past since the main verb **pai** ไป *to go* is a *direction verb* (Group 5).
- The English tense is the *Present Perfect*.
- However, the sentences 3.2 and 3.3 refer to the *present time* since **duu-lɛɛ** ดู แล *to look after* and **tham-thua** ทำ ตัว *to behave* are *general action verbs* (Group 3).

- When the *general action verbs* (Group 3) are used, the translation is the same or very similar even if the *present time indicator* **yùu** อยู่ is omitted.
- The English tense is the *Present Continuous*.

Notes
- In this context, **yùu** อยู่ cannot be followed by **léɛu** แล้ว. The meaning would change. **yùu-léɛu** อยู่ แล้ว is translated into English as *of course*.
- Grammatically, the *present time indicator* **yùu** อยู่ is used in the same way as **léɛu** แล้ว. Both are placed at the end of the sentence.
- Sometimes, **yùu** อยู่ *state exists* is used instead of **léɛu** แล้ว *already, now*.
- However, depending on the context, **yùu** อยู่ can have a similar meaning as **kamlang** กำลัง *action in progress*, which is always placed before the main verb.
- All this becomes clear in the following Secrets.

4. The present point of time with **tâng-tɛ̀ɛ** ตั้ง แต่ and **lăng-tsàak** หลัง จาก

   When the action refers to a certain point of time, which is *now*, **tâng-tɛ̀ɛ** ตั้ง แต่ is normally translated into English as *from now onwards*.

   To translate **tâng-tɛ̀ɛ** ตั้ง แต่ as *since* would not be correct here in English, because *since* refers to a certain point of time in the past. In Thai, we may place the phrase **pen-tôn-pai** เป็น ต้น ไป *onwards* after the point of time to emphasise the continuation of the action.

   The following sentences are *complex*. Thai speakers understand these sentences by considering the *context* and the other words used to convey the meaning. It is always possible to translate these Thai sentences into English and use the appropriate English tense.

   The point of time is made clear by the *present time words* **wan-níi** วัน นี้ *today* and **tɔɔn-níi** *now*.

   The *future tense marker* **tsà** จะ *will* is used to emphasise the *future time aspect in the second clause*.

When the **tâng-tɛ̀ɛ** ตั้ง แต่ *time phrases* and *tense markers* are omitted, the *Thai time aspect* normally changes.

The *basic sentences* denote the *natural time aspect,* which are translated into *English in italics.*

Examples

4.1 **tâng-tɛ̀ɛ kráng-níi pen-tôn-pai** – tʃǎn **tsà** mâi tham phìt ìik-*lɛ́ɛu*
ตั้ง แต่ ครั้ง นี้ เป็น ต้น ไป – ฉัน จะ ไม่ ทำ ผิด อีก แล้ว
set-from time-this be-start-go I will no do wrong more-already

From now on, I **will** not make mistakes anymore.
I have not made mistakes anymore.

4.2 **tâng-tɛ̀ɛ wan-níi pen-tôn-pai** – khun **tsà** pen hǔua-nâa *lɛ́ɛu*
ตั้ง แต่ วัน นี้ เป็น ต้น ไป – คุณ จะ เป็น หัว หน้า แล้ว
set-from today be-start-go – you will be head-front already

From today onwards, you **will** already be the boss.
You are the boss now.

4.3 tʃǎn wǎng wâa – **tâng-tɛ̀ɛ tɔɔn-níi** – thúk-sìng thúk-yàang **tsà** dii khûn *lɛ́ɛu*
ฉัน หวัง ว่า – ตั้ง แต่ ตอน นี้ – ทุกสิ่ง ทุก อย่าง จะ ดี ขึ้น แล้ว
I hope that – set-from at-this – every-thing every-kind will good increase already

I hope that **from now on**, everything **will** be better.
I hope everything is better now.

Point of time
- The point of time is *now*, but action is in the future.
- **tâng-tɛ̀ɛ** ตั้ง แต่ is placed before the *point of time*.
- *Time words* such as **wan-níi** วัน นี้ *today* or **tɔɔn-níi** ตอน นี้ *now* are used to tell that *from now onwards* it will be like that.

Time aspect
- When the starting point of time is *now*, the sentence refers to the *future*.
- The *future tense marker* **tsà** จะ is often used to emphasise the *future time aspect*.
- The English tense is the *Future Simple*.

Natural time aspect
- Without the **tâng-tɛ̀ɛ** ตั้ง แต่ *time phrase* and *future tense marker* **tsà** จะ, the *natural time aspect* is as follows.
- The sentence 4.1 refers to the *completed action* in the past since **tham** ทำ *to do* is a *specific action verb* (Group 4).
- The English tense is the *Present Perfect*.
- The sentences 4.2 and 4.3 reflect the *present time* since **pen** เป็น *to be* and **dii** ดี *to be good* are *non-action verbs* (Groups 1–2).
- The English tense is the *Present Simple*.

Notes
- The Thai word **lăng-tsàak** หลัง จาก *after* could be used instead of **tâng-tɛ̀ɛ** ตั้ง แต่, and the meaning would be the same or very similar.
- **pen-tôn-pai** เป็น ต้น ไป is optional here.
- However, **pen-tôn-pai** เป็น ต้น ไป can also be used alone instead of **tâng-tɛ̀ɛ** ตั้ง แต่, and the meaning is the same or very similar. It is placed after the point of time, however.

C. Language hints

The time indicator **lɛ́ɛu** แล้ว can be omitted or replaced with **yùu** อยู่ *state* or *action exists* or **kamlang** กำลัง *action in progress* and the meaning is very similar. The exact meaning into English is not always easy to translate.

We have the following words to play with:

lɛ́ɛu	แล้ว	*already, state reached*
yùu	อยู่	*state or action exists*
tɔɔn-níi	ตอน นี้	*now*

kamlang	กำลัง	*action in progress*
tâng-tὲɛ-níi	ตั้ง แต่ นี้	*from now, starting from now onwards*

1. Time words, time indicators and tense markers

In this section, the time aspect is made clear by *time words* such as **tɔɔn-níi** ตอน นี้ *now,* the *present time indicator* **yùu** อยู่ *state exists* and the *present tense marker* **kamlang** กำลัง *action in progress.*

When the *time words* and *tense markers* are omitted, the *Thai time aspect* normally changes.

The *basic sentences* denote the *natural time aspect,* which are translated into *English in italics.*

Examples

1.1 **tɔɔn-níi** tʃán sàbaai-dii *lέɛu*
ตอน นี้ ฉัน สบาย ดี แล้ว
at-this I fine-good already

Now, I am already fine.
I am already fine. / I am fine now.

1.2 tʃán sàbaai-dii **yùu**
ฉัน สบาย ดี อยู่
I fine-good be

I am feel**ing** fine.
I am fine.

1.3 tʃán **kamlang** sàbaai-dii
ฉัน กำลัง สบาย ดี
I being fine-good

I am feel**ing** fine.
I am fine.

1.4 **tɔɔn-níi** tʃán **kamlang** sàbaai-dii **yùu**
ตอน นี้ ฉัน กำลัง สบาย ดี อยู่
at-this I being well-good be

Now, I am feel**ing** fine.
I am fine.

Present time aspect
- In the sentences 1.1–1.3, the *present time word* **tɔɔn-níi** ตอน นี้, the *present tense marker* **kamlang** กำลัง *action in progress* and the *present time indicator* **yùu** อยู่ *state exists* are used to emphasise the fact that the action happens at the *time of speaking*.
- The English tenses are the *Present Simple* and *Present Continuous*.
- In the last sentence 1.4, all of the above *present time indicators* are used in the same sentence to emphasise the *present time*.
- The English tense is the *Present Continuous*.

Natural time aspect
- Without the *time words* and *tense markers*, the *natural time aspect* refers to the *present time* since the adjective **sàbaai-dii** สบาย ดี *to be fine* is a *non-action verb* (Group 1).
- The English tense is the *Present Simple*.

Notes
- It is not possible to translate all the *nuances* accurately into English.
- In this context, **yùu** อยู่ cannot be followed by **lɛ́ɛu** แล้ว. The meaning would change. **yùu-lɛ́ɛu** อยู่แล้ว is translated into English as *of course*.

2. **tâng-tɛ̀ɛ-níi** ตั้ง แต่ นี้ *from now, starting from now, from now onwards*

   The following sentences are *complex*. Thai people understand these kinds of sentences from the *context* and *other words* used. However, it is always possible to translate the Thai sentences into English and use the correct English tense.

The point of time is made clear by the *present time words* **kráng-níi** ครั้ง นี้ *this time* or just **níi** นี้ *this*. The *future tense marker* **tsà** จะ *will* is used to emphasise the *future time aspect of the sentence*.

When the **tâng-tɛ̀ɛ** ตั้ง แต่ *time phrases* and *tense markers* are omitted, the *Thai time aspect* normally changes.

The *basic sentences* denote the *natural time aspect,* which are translated into *English in italics*.

2.1 **tâng-tɛ̀ɛ kráng-níi pen-tôn-pai** – phŏm **tsà** nùuai mâak
ตั้ง แต่ ครั้ง นี้ เป็น ต้น ไป – ผม จะ เหนื่อย มาก
set-from time-this be-start-go – I will tired very

After this, I **will** be dead tired.
I am dead tired.

2.2 **tâng-tɛ̀ɛ níi pen-tôn-pai** – phŏm **tsà** nùuai mâak
ตั้ง แต่ นี้ เป็น ต้น ไป – ผม จะ เหนื่อย มาก
set-from this be-start-go – I will tired very

After this, I **will** be dead tired.
I am dead tired.

Point of time
- The starting point of time is *now*, but the action refers to the *future*.
- We can drop the *time word* **kráng** ครั้ง *time* and use only **níi** นี้ *this* with **tâng-tɛ̀ɛ** ตั้ง แต่ simply like this: **tâng-tɛ̀ɛ-níi** ตั้ง แต่ นี้ *from now onwards* (sentence 2).

Time aspect
- The *future tense marker* **tsà** จะ is placed before the main verb **nùuai** เหนื่อย *to be tired*.
- The English tense is the *Future Simple*.
- When the starting point is in the *present*, we need to have a *time word* to tell that *"from now onwards"* it will be like that. The following time words are commonly used with **tâng-tɛ̀ɛ** ตั้ง แต่ to indicate the *present point of time*.

níi	นี้	*this*
tɔɔn-níi	ตอน นี้	*now*
weelaa-níi	เวลา นี้	*at the moment, now*
kráng-níi	ครั้ง นี้	*this time*
aathít-níi	อาทิตย์ นี้	*this week*
dʉʉan-níi	เดือน นี้	*this month*
pii-níi	ปี นี้	*this year*
pen-tôn-pai	เป็น ต้น ไป	*onwards*

Natural time aspect

- When the **tâng-tɛ̀ɛ** ตั้ง แต่ *time phrases* and the *future tense marker* **tsà** จะ are omitted, then the *natural time aspect* refers to the *present time* since **nʉ̀ʉai** เหนื่อย *to be tired* is a *non-action verb* (Group 1).
- The English tense is the *Present Simple*.

Notes

- Often, with **tâng-tɛ̀ɛ** ตั้ง แต่, **lɛ́ɛu** แล้ว is omitted.
- The overall meaning refers to the *future*, but the *starting point* is *now*.
- **pen-tôn-pai** เป็น ต้น ไป is often used to emphasise the fact that after a certain point of time something follows. It could also give the statement more flavour and flow.
- **pen-tôn-pai** เป็น ต้น ไป *onwards* is optional after **tâng-tɛ̀ɛ** ตั้ง แต่, however.

D. Conclusion

Key: Place **lɛ́ɛu** แล้ว *already* at the end of the sentence to express the fact that a certain state *has been reached, obtained* or *attained*. The meaning is similar to the phrase *it is already the case*.

lɛ́ɛu แล้ว is often used in sentences which express the *present state of affairs*, actions happening *now* or at the *time of speaking*. **lɛ́ɛu** แล้ว connects the *present time* with the *past* – with the *previous state*.

Time words such as **tɔɔn-níi** ตอน นี้ *now* are usually placed at the beginning of the sentence, and **lɛ́ɛu** แล้ว is placed at the end of the sentence to *emphasise* the fact that the action is happening *now* or *nowadays*.

Place the *present tense marker* **kamlang** กำลัง *action in progress* before the main verb and **léɛu** แล้ว at the end of the sentence to *emphasise* the fact that the action is happening at the *time of speaking*.

Place the *present time indicator* **yùu** อยู่ *state exists* at the end of the sentence to *emphasise* the fact that the action is happening at the *time of speaking* and has some duration. It has a similar meaning as **kamlang** กำลัง *action in progress* and is often preferred in speaking.

Moreover, **yùu** อยู่ *state exists* can often be used instead of **léɛu** แล้ว to give an *action* or *condition* some *duration*. **léɛu** แล้ว is used to denote a change in a *state* or *condition*.

Place **tâng-tɛ̀ɛ** ตั้งแต่ before the *point of time* to express meanings like *after this, from now onwards, starting from now* etc.

Sometimes, **léɛu** แล้ว is referred to as a kind of past tense marker, *action completed*. More accurate meaning would be to describe it as a time indicator, *state reached* or *attained, now it is like this, it is already the case*.

One way to understand **léɛu** แล้ว is to compare it with the English word *already*. They are used in a similar way. However, **léɛu** แล้ว is a far more important word in Thai than *already* is in English. There are several grammatical reasons for this.

The focus of **léɛu** แล้ว is more on the *present state*, how things are *now* rather than on *completed actions*. It connects the *past* with the *present*, emphasising the *present state*.

Unfamiliar expressions

All the sentences in this book reflect the spoken Thai language. Sometimes, when we are illustrating a particular grammar point, the sentence may sound unfamiliar to the Thai ear, even though it would be grammatically correct. In those cases, we point it out.

Examples

a) **tɔɔn-níi** ตอน นี้ *now,* **kamlang** กำลัง *action in progress* and **yùu** อยู่ *state exists*

> 1. **tɔɔn-níi** tʃán **kamlang** khâu-tsai **yùu**
> ตอน นี้ ฉัน กำลัง เข้าใจ อยู่
> at-this I being enter-heart be
>
> *Now, I understand.*

- This sentence is grammatically correct but...
- It sounds odd since **khâu-tsai** เข้าใจ *to understand* is a *non-action verb*.
- The sentence has too many words, which refer to the *present time*. Thais would not make a sentence like this.

2. khâu-tsai **yùu**
เข้า ใจ อยู่
enter-heart be

I understand.

- This sentence is correct.
- The simple reply sounds more natural. **yùu** อยู่ *state exists* expresses a *continuous* nature of the state of *understanding*.

3. khâu-tsai **lɛ́ɛu**
เข้าใจ แล้ว
enter-heart already

I understand now / already.

- This sentence is correct.
- The simple reply sounds natural. **lɛ́ɛu** แล้ว *already* emphasises the state of *understanding* being *reached* or *obtained*.

4. khâu-tsai **khâ**
เข้า ใจ ค่ะ
enter-heart khâ

I understand.

- This sentence is correct.
- This simple reply is a polite way to express the same meaning. **khâ** ค่ะ at the end of the state is used frequently by Thais to show the *positive attitude*.

5. **tɔɔn-níi** tʃán **kamlang** riian phaasăa-thai **yùu**
ตอน นี้ ฉัน กำลัง เรียน ภาษา ไทย อยู่
at-this I being study language-thai be

Now, I am studying Thai.

- This sentence is correct.
- This sentence sounds good since **riian** เรียน *to study* is an *action verb*. Here, the *continuous nature of studying* is being emphasised. Compare this sentence to the sentence 1.

b) **pen-tôn-maa** เป็น ต้น มา and **pen-tôn-pai** เป็น ต้น ไป

> 1. tâng-tɛ̀ɛ níi **pen-tôn-maa** – tʃán **tsà** mâi tham phìt ìik-lɛ́ɛu
> ตั้ง แต่ นี้ เป็น ต้น มา – ฉัน จะ ไม่ ทำ ผิด อีก แล้ว
> set-from this be-start-come – I will no do wrong more-already
>
> *From now on, I will not make mistakes anymore.*

- This sentence is incorrect.
- **pen-tôn-maa** เป็น ต้น มา is translated into English as *until now*. It refers to the point of time, which is in the past. So, it would be wrong to use it in the future type of context.

2. tâng-tɛ̀ɛ níi **pen-tôn-pai** – tʃán **tsà** mâi tham phìt ìik-lɛ́ɛu
ตั้ง แต่ นี้ เป็น ต้น ไป – ฉัน จะ ไม่ ทำ ผิด อีก แล้ว
set-from this be-start-go I will no do wrong more-already

From now on, I will not make anymore mistakes.

- This sentence is correct.
- **pen-tôn-pai** เป็น ต้น ไป is translated into English as *from now on*. It is correct in this context and sounds fine since it is used in the future context.

- More about **pen-tôn-maa** เป็น ต้น มา *until now* and **pen-tôn-pai** เป็น ต้น ไป *from now on* in Secrets 4 and 6.

E. Simple advice

In this Secret, we have concentrated on actions, which happen *now*, *nowadays* or *at the time of speaking*. The function of **lɛ́ɛu** แล้ว is to connect the *present time* with the *past*.

In order to place more emphasis on the *present time*, we may use different indicators such as *present time words* and *present tense markers*.

For the actions which are happening *now* or *nowadays*, we may use *time words* such as **dǐiaŭ-níi** เดี๋ยว นี้ *now*, **tɔɔn-níi** ตอน นี้ *now* or **pàttsùban-níi** ปัจจุบัน นี้ *nowadays*.

For the actions which are happening at the *time of speaking* or *nowadays*, we may use the *present tense marker* **kamlang** กำลัง *action in progress* or the *present time indicator* **yùu** อยู่ *state exists* to emphasise the *continuous nature* of the action in question. **yùu** อยู่ *state exists* is more often used in speaking while **kamlang** กำลัง *action in progress* is used in writing, speaking and official situations.

Even though, when the *present time words* or *present tense markers* are used, there must have been another state *before now*. **lɛ́ɛu** แล้ว functions as the *bridge* between the *two states*, the *present* and the *past*. With **lɛ́ɛu** แล้ว, there is always a change in a state.

When *basic sentences* are used, the *natural time aspect* is determined by the context and by the *type of verbs* (Groups 1– 5) **lɛ́ɛu** แล้ว is used with. When **lɛ́ɛu** แล้ว is used this way as a *time indicator*, it normally comes at the end of the sentence.

In fact, **lɛ́ɛu** แล้ว can be conveniently used in the *present* and *past* time sentences or even in the sentences that refer to the *future*, which we will review in Secret 6.

One more thing

The term *natural time aspect* refers to the simple *basic sentences* only. When Thais reply to questions, they often use *simple basic sentences*.

Then, the meaning and the *time aspect* are understood from the *context* – the *question* asked and from the *verb groups* 1–5.

Secret 4

Things keep rolling!

Focusing on ongoing actions.

แล้ว ชอบ เล่น กับ เพื่อน มากๆ – **แล้ว** บอก ว่า – ฉัน กับ **มา** – **ได้** และ **ไป** อยาก ทำ ให้ ทุก คน เข้า ใจ ว่า – บาง ครั้ง การ กระทำ ที่ ยัง ไม่ เสร็จ สิ้น จะ ต้อง ดำ เนิน ต่อ ไป – ฉัน จะ อธิบาย ให้ คุณ เข้า ใจ เอง

lέεu tʃɔ̂ɔp lên *kàp* phûɯan mâak-mâak – lέεu bɔ̀ɔk wâa – tʃán kàp maa – dâai lé pai yàak tham hâi thúk-khon khâu-tsai wâa – baang khráng *kaan-kràtham* thîi yang mâi *sèt-sîn* tsà tôŋ *dam-nəən* tɔ̀ɔ pai – tʃán tsà athíbaai hâi khun khâu-tsai *eeŋ*

A. lέεu แล้ว and the duration of time

1. Using *lέεu* แล้ว

1.1 kháu khàp rót-théksîi *naan lέεu*
    เขา ขับ รถ แท็กซี่ นาน แล้ว

1.2 tʃán yùu thîi-nîi *tsèt wan lέεu*
    ฉัน อยู่ ที่ นี่ เจ็ด วัน แล้ว

1.3 tʃán tʃái prookrɛɛm níi *nùŋ pii lέεu*
    ฉัน ใช้ โปรแกรม นี้ หนึ่ง ปี แล้ว

2. Using *maa...lέεu* มา แล้ว

2.1 *tɔɔn-níi* tʃán pen khruu *maa sìi pii lέεu*
    ตอน นี้ ฉัน เป็น ครู มา สี่ ปี แล้ว

2.2 kháu pen nák-sùksăa *maa pràmaan sìp dɯɯan lέεu*
    เขา เป็น นัก ศึกษา มา ประมาณ สิบ เดือน แล้ว

2.3 tʃán pháyaayaam tham man *maa naan lέεu*
    ฉัน พยายาม ทำ มัน มา นาน แล้ว

3. Using *dâai* ได้ and *maa-dâai* มา ได้

3.1 tʃán yùu udɔɔn-thaanii *dâai hòk pii lέεu*
    ฉัน อยู่ อุดรธานี ได้ หก ปี แล้ว

3.2 tʃán riian phaasăa-thai *maa-dâai klâi-tsà-khrɔ́p sìi pii lέεu*
    ฉัน เรียน ภาษา ไทย มา ได้ ใกล้ จะ ครบ สี่ ปี แล้ว

3.3 kháu mâi sàbaai *maa-dâai sɔ̌ɔng wan lɛ́ɛu*
เขา ไม่ สบาย มา ได้ สอง วัน แล้ว

4. Using *pai...lɛ́ɛu* ไป แล้ว

4.1 nùuai tsang – tʃǎn tham-ngaan *pai sǎam tʃûua moong lɛ́ɛu*
เหนื่อย จัง – ฉัน ทำ งาน ไป สาม ชั่ว โมง แล้ว

4.2 tʃǎn rɔɔ kháu *pai yîi-sìp naa-thii lɛ́ɛu*
ฉัน รอ เขา ไป ยี่สิบ นาที แล้ว

4.3 *pàan-pai sìp naa-thii lɛ́ɛu* – man yang mâi kɔ̀ət-khûn
ผ่าน ไป สิบ นาที แล้ว – มัน ยัง ไม่ เกิด ขึ้น

5. Point of time in the past – using *tâng-tɛ̀ɛ* ตั้ง แต่ and *lǎng-tsàak* หลัง จาก

5.1 khun yùu thîi-nîi – *tâng-tɛ̀ɛ mûua-rài lɛ́ɛu*
คุณ อยู่ ที่ นี่ ตั้ง แต่ เมื่อไหร่ แล้ว

5.2 kháu tham-ngaan thîi lɔɔndɔɔn – *tâng-tɛ̀ɛ pii thîi-lɛ́ɛu*
เขา ทำ งาน ที่ ลอนดอน – ตั้ง แต่ ปี ที่ แล้ว

5.3 *lǎng-tsàak duuan-thanwaa-khom pen-tôn-maa* – aakàat thîi krungthêep nǎau
หลัง จาก เดือน ธันวาคม เป็น ต้น มา – อากาศ ที่ กรุงเทพ หนาว

B. How the language works – naan-lɛ́ɛu นาน แล้ว, tsèt-wan-lɛ́ɛu เจ็ด วัน แล้ว

The following five exercises have been constructed for you to go deeper into the Thai language with **lɛ́ɛu** แล้ว and to understand how Thais express the *duration* of *time*.

1. **lɛ́ɛu** แล้ว shares her wisdom
2. Spoken sentences and the *duration of time*
3. **lɛ́ɛu** แล้ว and *ongoing actions*, the *duration of time* "up to now"
4. Overall meaning–the *time aspect* and *verb groups 1–5*
5. Spoken sentences translated and grammar explained

How you use these exercises depends on your personal preferences and your level of Thai language skills. You may study each section in an orderly manner or skip any section and then come back later as you wish.

Sometimes, you may just wish to read Thai sentences only and skip the grammar explanations altogether. That way, you can facilitate your intuitive language expression, learn naturally additional Thai words and improve your language skills.

1. lɛ́ɛu แล้ว shares her wisdom

Listen to the audio several times and see if you can make the meaning clear to yourself what lɛ́ɛu แล้ว says. There are not any English translations in this section. However, we shall translate some keywords.

This is also an excellent exercise for those who wish to practise reading the Thai script. We have made it easier for you by writing each word separately.

You may wish to skip this exercise for the time being and concentrate on the sentences section. It is up to you, however!

แล้ว ชอบ เล่น กับ เพื่อน มากๆ – **แล้ว** บอก ว่า – ฉัน กับ **มา – ได้** และ **ไป** อยาก ทำ ให้ ทุก คน เข้า ใจ ว่า – บาง ครั้ง การ กระทำ ที่ ยัง ไม่ เสร็จ สิ้น จะ ต้อง ดำ เนิน ต่อ ไป – ฉัน จะ อธิบาย ให้ คุณ เข้า ใจ เอง

lɛ́ɛu tʃɔ̂ɔp lên *kàp* phûɯan mâak-mâak – **lɛ́ɛu** bɔ̀ɔk wâa – tʃán kàp **maa – dâai** lé *pai* yàak tham hâi thúk-khon khâu-tsai wâa – baang khráng *kaan-kràtham* thîi yang mâi *sèt-sîn* tsà tông *dam-nəən* tɔ̀ɔ pai – tʃán tsà athíbaai hâi khun khâu-tsai *eeng*

Words:

kàp	กับ	*with* is translated in this context as *and*
kaan-kràtham	การ กระทำ	*act, action*

sèt-sîn	เสร็จ สิ้น	to end, to finish, to come to an end
dam-nəən	ดำ เนิน	to proceed
eeng	เอง	oneself, here the meaning is *myself*

2. Spoken sentences and the duration of time

Listen to the audio several times and see if you understand the above sentences and how Thai people express the *duration of time* and *ongoing actions*.

Here are some grammatical words and expressions which may be helpful.

lέεu แล้ว as a *time indicator*

1. Ongoing actions "up to now"

naan lέεu	นาน แล้ว	*for a long time*
maa-naan lέεu	มา นาน แล้ว	*for a long time (having it)*
dâai-naan lέεu	ได้ นาน แล้ว	*for a long time (getting it)*
maa-dâai-naan lέεu	มา ได้ นาน แล้ว	*for a long time (having and getting)*
pai-naan lέεu	ไป นาน แล้ว	*for a long time (slightly negative, or loosing time)*

2. Point of time in the past:

| tâng-tὲε | ตั้ง แต่ | *since* |
| lăng-tsàak | หลัง จาก | *after* |

3. lέεu แล้ว and *ongoing actions,* the *duration of time "up to now"*

In the previous Secret 3, we have been focusing on actions that happen at the *time of speaking* or *now*. Now, we are focusing on the actions that started *before now* and are *still going on*.

When the *time indicator* **lɛ́ɛu** แล้ว is placed after the *duration of time*, usually at the end of the sentence, the sentence normally expresses the continuation of the action at least *"up to now"*. The action may continue even longer.

If you have some difficulty to understand **lɛ́ɛu** แล้ว in different contexts, just think how the English word *already* behaves in similar situations, and you will get it.

In fact, **lɛ́ɛu** แล้ว is a far more expressive and important word in Thai than the adverb *already* in English. The difference is that **lɛ́ɛu** แล้ว has many more meanings than the English word *already*, and it plays several grammatical functions as well.

Word order:

When **lɛ́ɛu** แล้ว is used as a *time indicator*, it normally comes at the end of the sentence and after the *duration of time*.

Thai time aspects

In Thai, we normally talk about the three main time aspects:
- **pàt-tsùbanna-kaan** ปัจจุบัน กาล *present time, now* or *nowadays*
- **adìitta-kaan** อดีต กาล *past time, completed actions*
- **anaakhótta-kaan** อนาคต กาล *future time, future planning* or *prediction*

Ongoing time aspect

In this Secret, the focus is on *ongoing actions:* **pàt-tsùbanna-kaan** ปัจจุบัน กาล and the *duration of time*.

Depending on the context, additional indicators, such as **maa** มา, **dâai** ได้, **maa-dâai** มา ได้ or **pai** ไป are normally placed *before* the *duration of time*.

lɛ́ɛu แล้ว connects the *ongoing action* with the *past*. When the *duration of time* is dropped, the time normally changes.

Natural time aspect

The *basic sentences* that denote the *natural time aspect,* are normally translated into *English in italics*.

English tense:

When **lɛ́ɛu** แล้ว is placed after the *duration of time*, the English tense is usually the *Present Perfect* or *Present Perfect Continuous*. The preposition *for* is placed before the duration of time in English.

English translations

Often there are two translations into English: one with *time words* or *tense markers* and one without them.

4. Overall meaning – natural time aspect and verb groups 1-5

Normally, when **lɛ́ɛu** แล้ว *already* is placed after the *duration of time*, the sentence reflects an *ongoing action*. It expresses a continuation of an action or a state. An action has started in the past, and it may still continue a while longer. Depending on the context, the meaning can be translated into English as *so far, up to now, already*.

lɛ́ɛu แล้ว connects the *ongoing state* with the *past*. We are here *now* looking into the *past*.

maa มา, **dâai** ได้, **maa-dâai** มา ได้ or **pai** ไป can be placed before the *duration of time* in order to give the statement more flow and flavour.

When the action has been going on from the certain *point of time* in the past, we can use **tâng-tɛ̀ɛ** ตั้ง แต่ *since* before the *point of time*.

In this section, the duration of time is made clear by **naan** นาน *long*, **hâa-pii** ห้า ปี *five years* and **nùng-tʃûua-moong** หนึ่ง ชั่ว โมง *one hour*, **tâng-tɛ̀ɛ-dèk** ตั้ง แต่ เด็ก *since I was a child* and **sɔ̌ɔng-pii** สอง ปี *two years*.

When the *duration of time phrases* and *tense markers* are omitted, the *Thai time aspect* normally changes.

The *basic sentences* denote the *natural time aspect,* which are translated into *English in italics*.

Examples

1. Group 1 – *Adjectives*, which are used as *state verbs*
   There is no need to have any separate verb or subject as we need to have in English.

Example

thúk-yàang thîi mɯɯang-thai *dii* **maa naan** *lέɛu*
ทุก อย่าง ที่ เมือง ไทย ดี มา นาน แล้ว
every-kind at state-Thai good come long already

Everything in Thailand has been good already **for a long time**. *Everything in Thailand is already good. / Everything in Thailand is good now.*

Duration of time
- When **lέɛu** แล้ว is placed after the *duration of time* **naan** นาน *long time*, the meaning is *already for a long time*.
- **lέɛu** แล้ว connects the *ongoing state* with the *past*.

Time aspect
- The time aspect is understood from the *duration of time* and **lέɛu** แล้ว. The time aspect refers to the *ongoing action*, which has started in the past.
- The English tense is the *Present Perfect*.

Natural time aspect
- The *duration of time* also affects the Thai time aspect.
- Without the *duration of time,* the *natural time aspect* refers to the *present state* since **dii** ดี *to be good* is a *non-action verb* (Group 1).
- *Now it is good! Before, it was not good.*
- The English tense is the *Present Simple*.

Notes
- **lέɛu** แล้ว connects the *present state* with the *past*.
- The adjective **dii** ดี *to be* good also plays the role of a verb.
- The helping verb **maa** มา *to come* is placed *before* the *duration of time* to emphasise the fact that the condition has started *before now*.

2. Group 2 – *State verbs* are verbs, which describe a state or condition

The time indicator **lɛ́ɛu** แล้ว can be used together with *non-action verbs* (also called state verbs) to express the present time condition that has been *attained, reached* or *obtained; it is already the case!*

Example

phǒm *rúu-tsàk* kháu **maa hâa-pii** *lɛ́ɛu*
ผม รู้ จัก เขา มา ห้า ปี แล้ว
I know he come five-year-already

I have already known him **for five years**.
I already know him. / I know him now.

Duration of time
- When **lɛ́ɛu** แล้ว is placed after the duration of time **hâa-pii** ห้า ปี *five years*, the meaning is *already for five years.*
- **lɛ́ɛu** แล้ว connects the *ongoing state* with the *past*.
- The English tense is the *Present Perfect.*

Time aspect
- The time aspect is understood from the *duration of time* and by **lɛ́ɛu** แล้ว. The time aspect refers to the *ongoing action*, which has started in the past.

Natural time aspect
- The *duration of time* also affects the Thai time aspect.
- Without the *duration of time*, the *natural time aspect* refers to the *present state* since the *non-action verb* **rúu-tsàk** รู้ จัก *to know someone* (Group 2) is used as a main verb.
- **lɛ́ɛu** แล้ว connects the *present state* with the *past.*
- *Now I know him. Before, I did not know him.*
- The English tense is the *Present Simple.*

Notes
- The helping verb **maa** มา *to come* is placed *before* the *duration of time* to emphasise the fact that the condition has started before now.

3. Group 3 – *General action verbs* may be conveniently used together with **lέεu** แล้ว.

Action verbs are used when something happens or when somebody is performing an action. The *action verbs* are more dynamic; they usually express a movement.

State verbs, on the other hand, express a quality or condition of something or somebody.

Example

tʃán *tɔ̀ɔ-khiu* **pai nὑng-tʃûua-moong** *lέεu*
ฉัน ต่อ คิว ไป หนึ่ง ชั่ว โมง แล้ว
I extend-queue go one-during-hour already

I have already been queuing **up for an hour**.
I am already standing in the queue. / I am standing in the queue now.

Duration of time

- When **lέεu** แล้ว is placed after the duration of time **nὑng-tʃûua-moong** หนึ่ง ชั่ว โมง an *hour*. The meaning is *already for an hour*.
- **lέεu** แล้ว connects the *ongoing action* with the *past*.

Time aspect

- The time aspect is understood from the *duration of time* and by **lέεu** แล้ว. The time aspect refers to the *ongoing action*, which has started in the past.
- The English tense is the *Present Perfect Continuous*.

Natural time aspect

- The *duration of time* also affects the Thai time aspect.
- Without the *duration of time*, the *natural time aspect refers* to the *present state* since **tɔ̀ɔ-khiu** ต่อ คิว *to queue up* is a *general action verb* (Group 3).
- **lέεu** แล้ว connects the *present state* with the *past*.
- *I am already standing in the queue. Before, it was not the case.*
- The English tense is the *Present Continuous*.

Notes
- The helping verb **pai** ไป *to go* is placed before the duration of time to emphasise the fact that so much time has already passed.

4. Group 4 – *Specific action verbs*

   When **lɛ́ɛu** แล้ว is used with some *specific action verbs*, the statement usually refers to *completed actions* in the past.

Example

tʃán *kin* phǒnlámáai yɔ́ – **maa tâng-tɛ̀ɛ-dèk** *lɛ́ɛu*
ฉัน กิน ผลไม้ เยอะ – มา ตั้ง แต่ เด็ก แล้ว
I eat fruit much – come set-from child already

I have been eating a lot of fruits **since I was a child.**
I have already eaten a lot of fruits.
I eat a lot of fruits now. *

Duration of time
- When **lɛ́ɛu** แล้ว is placed after the duration of time **tâng-tɛ̀ɛ-dèk** ตั้ง แต่ เด็ก *since I was a child,* the sentence refers to the *past.*
- **lɛ́ɛu** แล้ว connects the *ongoing state* with the *past.*

Time aspect
- The time aspect is understood from the *duration of time* and by **lɛ́ɛu** แล้ว. The time aspect refers to the *ongoing action*, which has started in the past.
- The English tense is the *Present Perfect Continuous.*

Natural time aspect
- The *duration of time* also affects the *Thai time aspect.*
- Without the *duration of time*, the *natural time aspect* refers to a *completed action* in the past since the *specific action verb* **kin** กิน *to eat* (Group 4) is used as a main verb.
- **lɛ́ɛu** แล้ว connects the *present state* with the *past.*
- The English tense is the *Present Perfect.*

* However, when the *specific action verb* **kin** กิน *to eat* (Group 4) is used in a *general sense,* the sentence can also refer to the *present time, I eat a lot of fruits.*

Then the English tense is the *Present Simple*.

Notes

- The helping verb **maa** มา *to come* is placed *before* the *time phrase* to emphasise the fact that the condition has started before now.

5. Group 5 – *Direction verbs*

   lέεu แล้ว can also be used with *direction verbs* such as **sòng** ส่ง *to send*. Without additional indicators, the statement usually refers to *completed actions* in the past.

Example

tʃǎn *sòng* tsòt-mǎai hâi kháu **maa sɔ̌ɔng-pii** *lέεu*
ฉัน ส่ง จด หมาย ให้ เขา มา สอง ปี แล้ว
I send letter give he come two-year already

I have already been sending letters to him **for two years**.
I have already sent a letter to him.

Duration of time

- When **lέεu** แล้ว is placed after the *duration of time* **sɔ̌ɔng-pii** สอง ปี *two years*, the meaning is *already for two years*.
- **lέεu** แล้ว connects the *ongoing state* with the *past*.

Time aspect

- The time aspect is understood from the *duration of time* and by **lέεu** แล้ว. The time aspect refers to the *ongoing action*, which has started in the past.
- The English tense is the *Present Perfect Continuous*.

Natural time aspect

- The *duration of time also* affects the Thai time aspect.
- In this sentence, the *direction verb* **sòng** ส่ง *to send* (Group 5) is used together with **lέεu** แล้ว.
- Without the *duration of time*, the *natural time aspect* refers to a *completed action* in the past.
- **lέεu** แล้ว connects the present *state* with the *past*.
- *The letter has been sent now! Before, it was not done.*
- The English tense is the *Present Perfect*.

Notes

- The helping verb **maa** มา *to come* is placed *before* the *duration of time* to emphasise the fact that the condition has started *before now*.

5. Spoken sentences translated and grammar explained

Study the details of each sentence in this Secret and make sure that you understand all the words and how Thai people express the *duration of time*. Every sentence is translated into English with grammatical explanations.

We have also given "word-for-word" translations. Transliterations, how words are pronounced in Thai, can be used alongside with the spoken audio file. You should be able to get the correct tone from the spoken audio file. It can also be checked from the transliterations since they have tone marks.

This is an excellent exercise to find out what happens to the *time aspect* when different verbs (Groups 1–5) are used, and when the time words are omitted.

When there is more than one translation, the first translation denotes the *duration of time aspect,* and the second reflects the *natural time aspect* without the *duration of time.*

1. Using *léɛu* แล้ว alone after the duration of time

In this section, the time aspect is understood from the *duration of time* **naan** นาน *long time,* **tsèt wan** เจ็ด วัน *seven days,* **nùng pii** หนึ่ง ปี *one year* and from **léɛu** แล้ว.

When the *duration of time phrases* and *tense markers* are omitted, the *Thai time aspect* normally changes.

The *basic sentences* denote the *natural time aspect,* which are translated into *English in italics.*

Examples

1.1 kháu khàp rót-théksîi **naan** *léɛu*
เขา ขับ รถ แท็กซี่ นาน แล้ว
he drive a car-taxi long already

He has already been driving a taxi **for a long time.**
He is driving a taxi now.

1.2 tʃán yùu thîi-nîi **tsèt wan** *léɛu*
ฉัน อยู่ ที่ นี่ เจ็ด วัน แล้ว
I stay place-this seven day already

I have already been staying here **for seven days**.
I am staying here now.

1.3 tʃán tʃái prookrɛɛm níi **nùng pii** *léɛu*
ฉัน ใช้ โปรแกรม นี้ หนึ่ง ปี แล้ว
I use programme this one year already

I have already been using this programme **for a year**.
I am using this programme now.

Duration of time
- **léɛu** แล้ว is placed at the end of the sentence after the *duration of time* **naan** นาน *long time*, **tsèt wan** เจ็ด วัน *seven days* and **nùng pii** หนึ่ง ปี *one year.*
- The Thai sentences refer to the actions that have been going on *for so long "up to now".*

Time aspect
- The time aspect is understood from the *duration of time* and **léɛu** แล้ว.
- It refers to the *ongoing action*, which has started in the past.
- The English tense is the *Present Perfect Continuous.*

Natural time aspect
- Without the *duration of time phrase*, the *natural time aspect* refers to the *ongoing action* since the main verbs **khàp** ขับ *to drive*, **yùu** อยู่ *to stay, to live* and **tʃái** ใช้ *to use* are *general action verbs* (Group 3).

- The English tense is the *Present Continuous*.

Notes

- Omitting the *duration of time phrase* affects the *time aspect*.
- Sometimes, it is better to translate **lέεu** แล้ว *already* into English as *now*.

2. Using **maa** and **lέεu** มา แล้ว

In this section, the *duration of time* is made clear by **sìi pii** สี่ ปี *four years*, **sìp duuan** สิบ เดือน *ten months* and **naan** นาน *long time* and **lέεu** แล้ว.

When the *duration of time phrases* and *tense markers* are omitted, the *Thai time aspect* normally changes.

The *basic sentences* denote the *natural time aspect*, which are translated into *English in italics*.

Examples

2.1 **tɔɔn-níi** tʃán pen khruu **maa sìi pii** *lέεu*
ตอน นี้ ฉัน เป็น ครู มา สี่ ปี แล้ว
at-this I be teacher come four year already

Now, I have already been a teacher **for four years**.
I am a teacher now.

2.2 kháu pen nák-sùksǎa **maa pràmaan sìp duuan** *lέεu*
เขา เป็น นักศึกษา มา ประมาณ สิบ เดือน แล้ว
he be person-study come about ten month already

He has already been a student **for about ten months**.
He is a student now.

2.3 tʃán pháyaayaam tham man **maa naan** *lέεu*
ฉัน พยายาม ทำ มัน มา นาน แล้ว
I try do it come long already

I have already been trying to do it **for a long time**.
I have already tried to do it.

Duration of time

- **maa** มา *to come* before the *duration of time* emphasises that the action is coming from the *past*.
- **léɛu** แล้ว is placed at the end of the sentence after the duration of time **sìi pii** สี่ ปี *four years*, **sìp dwuan** สิบ เดือน *ten months* and **naan** นาน *long time*.

Time aspect

- The time aspect is understood from the *duration of time* and **léɛu** แล้ว.
- It refers to the *ongoing action*, which has started in the past.
- In the sentence 2.1, the *present time* has been emphasised by the *present time word* **tɔɔn-níi** ตอน นี้ *now*.
- The English tense is the *Present Perfect Continuous*.

Natural time aspect

- Without the *duration of time phrase* and **maa** มา *to come*, the *natural time aspect* refers to *present time* since the main verb **pen** เป็น *to be* is a *non-action verb* (Group 2)
- The English tense is the *Present Simple*.
- However, in the sentence 2.3, the time aspect refers to a *completed action* in the past since **pháyaayaam** พยายาม *to try* and **tham** ทำ *to do* are *specific action verbs* (Group 4).
- The English tense is the *Present Perfect*.

Notes

- Omitting the *duration of time phrase* affects the *Thai time aspect*.
- Sometimes, it is better to translate **léɛu** แล้ว *already* into English as *now*.

3. Using **dâai** ได้ or **maa-dâai** มา ได้ and **léɛu** มา แล้ว

We can use **dâai** ได้ *to get* or **maa-dâai** มา ได้ *to come-get* instead of **maa** มา *to come* before the duration of time to emphasise the fact that the ongoing action is possible.

In this section, the duration of time is made clear by **hòk pii** หก ปี *six years*, **sìi pii** สี่ ปี *four years* and **sɔ̌ɔng wan** สอง วัน *two days* and by **léɛu** แล้ว.

When the *duration of time phrases* and *tense markers* are omitted, the *Thai time aspect* normally changes.

The *basic sentences* denote the *natural time aspect,* which are translated into *English in italics.*

Examples

3.1 tʃán yùu udɔɔn-thaanii **dâai hòk pii** lέεu
ฉัน อยู่ อุดรธานี ได้ หก ปี แล้ว
I live Udon Thani get six year already

I have already been living in Udon Thani **for six years**.
I am already living in Udon Thani. / I am living in Udon Thani now.

3.2 tʃán riian phaasǎa-thai **maa-dâai klâi-tsà-khróp sìi pii** lέεu
ฉัน เรียน ภาษา ไทย มา ได้ ใกล้ จะ ครบ สี่ ปี แล้ว
I study language Thai come-get close-will-fully one year already

I have already been studying Thai **for almost four years**.
I am already studying Thai. / I am studying Thai now.

3.3 kháu mâi sàbaai **maa-dâai sɔ̌ɔng wan** lέεu
เขา ไม่ สบาย มา ได้ สอง วัน แล้ว
he no well come-get two day already

He has not been feeling well **for two days**.
He is not feeling well now.

Duration of time
- The helping verbs **dâai** ได้ *to get* or **maa-dâai** มา ได้ *to come-get* are placed before the *duration of time* to emphasise the fact that the action is possible.
- **lέεu** แล้ว is placed at the end of the sentence after the *duration of time* **hòk pii** หก ปี *six years,* **sìi pii** สี่ ปี *four years* and **sɔ̌ɔng wan** สอง วัน *two days.*

Time aspect

- The time aspect is understood from the *duration of time* and from **lɛ́ɛu** แล้ว.
- It refers to the *ongoing action*, which has started in the past.
- The English tense is the *Present Perfect Continuous*.

Natural time aspect

- Without the *duration of time phrase* and **dâai** ได้ *to get* or **maa-dâai** มา ได้ *to come-get*, the *natural time aspect* refers to the *present time*, since the main verbs, **yùu** อยู่ *to live, to stay* and **riian** เรียน *to study* are *general action verbs* (Group 3), and the adjective **sàbaai** สบาย *to be well* is a *non-action verb* (Group 1).
- The English tense is the *Present Continuous*.

Notes

- Omitting the *duration of time phrase* affects the *Thai time aspect*.
- Sometimes, it is better to translate **lɛ́ɛu** แล้ว *already* into English as *now*.

4. Using **pai** and **lɛ́ɛu** ไป แล้ว

In this section, the duration of time is made clear by **săam tʃûua moong**, สาม ชั่ว โมง *three hours*, **yîi-sìp naa-thii** ยี่ สิบ นาที *twenty minutes* and **sìp naathii** สิบ นาที *ten minutes* and by **lɛ́ɛu** แล้ว.

When the *duration of time phrases* and *tense markers* are omitted, the *Thai time aspect* normally changes.

The *basic sentences* denote the *natural time aspect,* which are translated into *English in italics.*

Examples

4.1 nɯ̀ɯai tsang – tʃǎn tham-ngaan **pai săam tʃûua moong** *lɛ́ɛu*
เหนื่อย จัง – ฉัน ทำ งาน ไป สาม ชั่ว โมง แล้ว
tired very – I do-work go three during-hour already

I am dead tired. I have already been working **for three hours**.
I am dead tired. I am working now.

4.2 tʃán rɔɔ kháu **pai yîi-sìp naa-thii** *lɛ́ɛu*
ฉัน รอ เขา ไป ยี่ สิบ นาที แล้ว
I wait he go twenty minute already

I have already been waiting for him **for twenty minutes.**
I am already waiting for him. / I am waiting for him now.

4.3 **pàan-pai sìp naathii lɛ́ɛu** – man yang mâi kə̀ət-khûn
ผ่าน ไป สิบ นาที แล้ว – มัน ยัง ไม่ เกิด ขึ้น
pass-go ten minute already – it yet no happen-rise

Ten minutes have already passed, but it has not happened yet.
It has not happened yet.

Duration of time

- We have placed the helping verb **pai** ไป *to go* or **pàan-pai** ผ่าน ไป *to pass* before the *duration of time* to express the *indifferent* or slightly *negative* attitude.
- **lɛ́ɛu** แล้ว is placed at the end of the sentence after the *duration of time* **sǎam tʃûua moong,** สาม ชั่ว โมง *three hours,* **yîi-sìp naa-thii** ยี่ สิบ นาที *twenty minutes* and **sìp naathii** สิบ นาที *ten minutes.*

Time aspect

- The time aspect is understood from the *duration of time* and **lɛ́ɛu** แล้ว.
- It refers to the *ongoing action,* which has started in the past.
- The English tense is the *Present Perfect Continuous.*

Natural time aspect

- Without the duration of time and **pai** ไป *to go* or **pàan-pai** ผ่าน ไป *to pass,* the *natural time aspect* refers to the *present time* in the sentences 4.1–4. 2, since the main verbs **tham-ngaan** ทำ งาน *to work,* **rɔɔ** รอ *to wait* are *general action verbs* (Group 3).
- The English tense is the *Present Continuous.*
- In the sentence 4.3, the *natural time aspect* refers to an *action,* which has not yet happened. **kə̀ət-khûn** เกิด ขึ้น is a *specific action verb* (Group 4).
- The English tense is the *Present Perfect.*

Notes

- Omitting the *duration of time phrase* affects the *Thai time aspect*.
- Sometimes, it is better to translate **lɛ́ɛu** แล้ว *already* into English as *now*.

5. Point of time in the past – using *tâng-tɛ̀ɛ* ตั้ง แต่ and *lăng-tsàak* หลัง จาก

   In order to express activities which have started at a certain point in the *past*, we can use **tâng-tɛ̀ɛ** ตั้ง แต่ *since* before the *point of time*.

   In this section, the point of time is expressed by **tâng-tɛ̀ɛ** ตั้ง แต่ phrases such as **tâng-tɛ̀ɛ mûua-rai** ตั้ง แต่ เมื่อไร *since when?* **tâng-tɛ̀ɛ pii-thîi-lɛ́ɛu** ตั้ง แต่ ปี ที่ แล้ว *since last year,* **lăng-tsàak duuan-thanwaa-khom** ตั้ง หลัง จาก เดือน ธันวาคม *since January*.

   When the **tâng-tɛ̀ɛ** ตั้ง แต่ *time phrases* and *tense markers* are omitted, the *Thai time aspect* normally changes.

   The *basic sentences* denote the *natural time aspect,* which are translated into *English in italics*.

Examples

5.1 khun yùu thîi-nîi – **tâng-tɛ̀ɛ mûua-rai** *lɛ́ɛu*
    คุณ อยู่ ที่ นี่ – ตั้ง แต่ เมื่อไร แล้ว
    you stay place this – set-from when already

   Since when have you been staying here?
   You are staying here now. Right?

5.2 kháu tham-ngaan thîi lɔɔndɔɔn – **tâng-tɛ̀ɛ pii kɔ̀ɔn** *lɛ́ɛu*
    เขา ทำ งาน ที่ ลอนดอน – ตั้ง แต่ ปี ก่อน แล้ว
    he do work at London – set-from year before already

   He has been working in London **since last year**.
   He is working in London now.

5.3 lăng-tsàak dʉʉan-thanwaa-khom pen-tôn-maa – aakàat thîi krungthêep năau

หลัง จาก เดือน ธันวาคม เป็น ต้น มา – อากาศ ที่ กรุงเทพ หนาว

after-from month-January be-start-come-weather-that-Bangkok-cold

The weather in Bangkok has been cold **since December**.
The weather in Bangkok is cold.

Point of time
- We have placed **tâng-tɛ̀ɛ** ตั้ง แต่ *since* before the *point of time*, which is in the past.
- When the point of time refers to the past, we need to have time words such as **mʉ̂ua-rai** เมื่อไร *when?* **pii kɔ̀ɔn** ปี ก่อน *last year*, **dʉʉan-thanwaa-khom** เดือน ธันวาคม *December* to tell that since that time *it has been like that*.

Time aspect
- The sentences refer to the *ongoing action*, which has started at a *certain point* in the past.
- The English tenses are the *Present Perfect Continuous* and *Present Perfect*.

Natural time aspect
- The *point of time* also affects the *Thai time aspect*.
- Without **tâng-tɛ̀ɛ** ตั้ง แต่ *time phrase*, the *natural time aspect* (sentences 5.1 and 5.2) refers to the *present time* since **yùu** อยู่ *to live, to stay*, **tham-ngaan** ทำ งาน *to work* are *general action verbs* (Group 3).
- The English tense is the *Present Continuous*.
- The sentence 5.3 refers to the *present time* since **năau** หนาว *to be cold* is a *non-action verb* (Group 1).
- The English tense is the *Present Simple*.

Notes
- In the sentence 5.3, **lăng-tsàak** หลัง จาก is used instead of **tâng-tɛ̀ɛ** ตั้ง แต่. It has a similar meaning.

- We could also just use **pen-ton-maa** เป็น ต้น มา alone after the *duration of time*, and the meaning would be the same or very similar.

C. Language hints

When the time indicator **lɛ́ɛu** แล้ว is placed at the end of the sentence and after the duration of time, it normally expresses the continuation of the action: *so far, up to now, already.*

There are basically three kinds of actions which have a connection to the past.

  a) Actions that have started in the past and are still *going on*.
  b) Ongoing actions, which refer to a *certain point of time* in the past.
  c) Actions *completed* in the past.

In this Secret, we shall concentrate on a) and b) only. Actions that have been *completed* in the past are reviewed extensively in the next Secret 5.

Normally, when **lɛ́ɛu** แล้ว *already* is placed after the *duration of time*, the sentence reflects the *ongoing action*.

a) Actions that have started in the past and are still *going on*.

In this section, the duration of time is made clear by **naan** นาน *long* and **kâau-duuan** เก้า เดือน *nine months*.

When the *duration of time phrases* and *tense markers* are omitted, the *Thai time aspect* normally changes.

The *basic sentences* denote the *natural time aspect,* which are translated into *English in italics.*

Examples

1. **pen phûuan kan** เป็น เพื่อน กัน *to be friends*

1.1 pen phûuan kan **maa naan** *lέεu*
เป็น เพื่อน กัน มา นาน แล้ว
be friend together come long already

We have already been friends **for a long time.**
We are already friends. / We are friends now.

1.2 pen phûuan kan **dâai naan** *lέεu*
เป็น เพื่อน กัน ได้ นาน แล้ว
be friend together get long already

We have already been friends for **a long time.**
We are already friends. / We are friends now.

1.3 pen phûuan kan **maa-dâai naan** *lέεu*
เป็น เพื่อน กัน มา ได้ นาน แล้ว
be friend together come-get long already

We have already been friends **for a long time**.
We are already friends. / We are friends now.

1.4 pen phûuan kan **pai naan** *lέεu*
เป็น เพื่อน กัน ไป นาน แล้ว
be friend together go long already

We have already been friends **for a long time.**
We are already friends. / We are friends now.

Duration of time
- **lέεu** แล้ว is placed after the *duration of time*, here **naan** นาน *for a long time*.

Time aspect
- The time aspect is understood from the *duration of time* and from **lέεu** แล้ว.
- It refers to the *ongoing action*, which has started in the past.
- The English tense is the *Present Perfect*.

Natural time aspect
- The *duration of time* has also an effect on the *Thai time aspect*.

- Without the duration of time, the sentences refer to the *present time* since **pen** เป็น *to be* is a *non-action verb* (Group 2).
- The English tense is the *Present Simple*.

Notes
- The above sentences are translated into English the same even though in Thai there is a subtle difference. For example, when **pai** ไป is placed before the *duration of time*, it implies a slightly *negative* or *indifferent* attitude.
- It is difficult to translate all the nuances accurately into English. In English, the difference is normally made clear by changing the voice.
- See also the next section!

2. **ɔ̀ɔk-kamlang-kaai** ออก กำลัง กาย *to exercise*

Examples

2.1 phǒm ɔ̀ɔk-kamlang-kaai **maa kâau-duuan** lέεu
 ผม ออก กำลัง กาย มา เก้า เดือน แล้ว
 I produce strength-body come nine-month-already

 I have already been exercising **for nine months**.
 I have already exercised.

2.2 phǒm ɔ̀ɔk-kamlang-kaai **dâai kâau-duuan** lέεu
 ผม ออก กำลัง กาย ได้ เก้า เดือน แล้ว
 I produce strength-body get nine-month already

 I have already been exercising **for nine months**.
 I have already exercised.

2.3 phǒm ɔ̀ɔk-kamlang-kaai **maa-dâai kâau-duuan** lέεu
 ผม ออก กำลัง กาย มา ได้ เก้า เดือน แล้ว
 I produce strength-body come-get nine-month already

 I have already been exercising **for nine months**.
 I have already exercised.

2.4 phǒm ɔ̀ɔk-kamlang-kaai **pai kâau-duuan** *lɛ́ɛu*
ผม ออก กำลัง กาย ไป เก้า เดือน แล้ว
I produce strength-body go nine-month already

I have already been exercising **for nine months.**
I have already exercised.

Duration of time
- **lɛ́ɛu** แล้ว is placed after the *duration of time*, here **kâau-duuan** เก้า เดือน *nine months.*

Time aspect
- The time aspect is understood from the *duration of time* and from **lɛ́ɛu** แล้ว.
- It refers to the *ongoing action*, which has started in the past.
- The English tense is the *Present Perfect Continuous.*

Natural time aspect
- The *duration of time* has also an effect on the *Thai time aspect*.
- Without the duration of time, the sentences reflect the *completed* action in the past since **ɔ̀ɔk-kamlang-kaai** ออก กำลัง กาย *to exercise* is a *specific action verb* (Group 4).
- The English tense is the *Past Perfect.*

Notes
- The above sentences 2.1–2.4 are translated into English the same even though in Thai there is a subtle difference.
- The following helping verbs can be placed *before the duration of time* to give the sentence more flavour and clarity.
- All these helping verbs are optional here, however.
- **maa** มา emphasises the fact that the action has started in the past. **maa** มา is the most common word used before the *duration of time*. It is more neutral than the other three expressions, which express feelings such as:
- **dâai** ได้ *can, to get* (feeling of getting it)
- **maa-dâai** มา ได้ *to come and get* (feeling of having it and getting it)
- **pai** ไป *to go* (slightly negative feeling or being indifferent).

b) Ongoing actions which refer to a *certain point of time* in the past. The point of time is expressed by **tâng-tɛ̀ɛ** ตั้ง แต่ phrases such as **tâng-tɛ̀ɛ wan-nán** ตั้ง แต่ วัน นั้น *since that day* **tâng-tɛ̀ɛ pii 2015** ตั้ง แต่ ปี 2015 *since year 2015* and **tâng-tɛ̀ɛ tɛ̀ɛng-ngaan** ตั้ง แต่ แต่ง งาน *since I got married*.

When the **tâng-tɛ̀ɛ** ตั้ง แต่ *time phrases* and *tense markers* are omitted, the *Thai time aspect* normally changes.

The *basic sentences* denote the *natural time aspect,* which are translated into *English in italics.*

Examples

1. tʃán nɯ̀ɯai maa **tâng-tɛ̀ɛ wan-nán** *lɛ́ɛu*
   ฉัน เหนื่อย มา ตั้ง แต่ วัน นั้น แล้ว
   I tired come set-from day that already

   I have already been tired **since that day.**
   I am already tired.

2. phɯ̂ɯan tʃán pen khruu-phaasǎa-angkrìt **tâng-tɛ̀ɛ pii 2015 pen-tôn-maa** *lɛ́ɛu*
   เพื่อน ฉัน เป็น ครู ภาษา อังกฤษ ตั้ง แต่ ปี 2015 เป็น ต้น มา แล้ว
   friend I be teacher-language-English *set-from* year 2015 be-start-come *already*

   A friend of mine has already been an English teacher **since 2015.**
   A friend of mine is already an English teacher.

3. **tâng-tɛ̀ɛ tʃán tɛ̀ɛng-ngaan** – yang mâi-khəəi dâai pai thîiau *ləəi*
   ตั้ง แต่ ฉัน แต่ง งาน – ยัง ไม่ เคย ได้ ไป เที่ยว เลย
   set-from I prepare-ceremony – still no-once get go trip beyond

   Since I got married, I have not had a possibility to go on holiday at all.
   I have not had a possibility to go on holiday at all.

Point of time
- **tâng-tɛ̀ɛ** ตั้ง แต่ is placed before the *point of time* to express the fact that the action has been going on since that time.
- The point of time in the past is identified as **wan-nán** วัน นั้น *that day,* **pii 2015** ปี 2015 *year 2015* and **tɛ̀ɛng-ngaan** แต่ง งาน *to be married.*

Time aspect
- The sentences refer to the *ongoing action*, which has started at a *certain point* in the past.
- The English tense is the *Present Perfect.*

Natural time aspect
- The *point of time* affects the *Thai time aspect.*
- Without the *point of time phrase,* the *natural time aspect* refers to the *present time* in the sentences 2.1–2.2 since the main verbs **nùuai** หน่วย *to be tired* and **pen** เป็น *to be* are *non-action verbs* (Groups 1–2).
- The English tense is the *Present Simple.*
- However, the sentence 2.3 refers to a state, which has not happened yet since the *negative tense marker,* **mâi-khəəi** ไม่ เคย *never* is used.
- The English tense is the *Past Perfect.*

Notes
- In the sentence 2.2, **pen-tôn-maa** เป็น ต้น มา *up to now* is placed after the *duration of time* to mark the fact that the action has started in the past and has been going on *"up to now".* It is, however, optional here.
- We cannot use **pen-tôn-pai** เป็น ต้น ไป here. The rule of thumb is that **pen-tôn-maa** เป็น ต้น มา is used when the translation into English is *"up to now"* and **pen-tôn-pai** เป็น ต้น ไป when translation into English is *from now onwards.*

D. Conclusion

Key: Place the time indicator **lɛ́ɛu** แล้ว at the end of the sentence and after the *duration of time* to emphasise the *continuation* of an action or a state. The meaning is *so far, up to now, already*. The function of **lέεu** แล้ว is to connect *ongoing actions* with the *past*.

We may place helping verbs **maa** มา, **dâai** ได้, **maa-dâai** มา ได้ or **pai** ไป before the *duration of time* in order to give the statement more flavour and flow.

Unfamiliar expression
Start reading the sentences of this book out loud to yourself. There is a wide range of different sentences and expressions. Soon, you are going to speak Thai fluently.

Once you know the Thai way, you can forget about the grammar rules. To get the pronunciation and tones right is the key. That way, the structure of the Thai language sinks into your consciousness. You gain confidence in speaking Thai correctly and intuitively.

Sometimes, it is not possible to translate directly subtle nuances into English. Using helping verbs **maa** มา, **dâai** ได้, **maa-dâai** มา ได้ or **pai** ไป before the duration of time can be challenging in the beginning.

Examples

> 1. tʃǎn kin plaa **pai** kâau-dɯɯan *lέεu*
> ฉัน กิน ปลา ไป เก้า เดือน แล้ว
> I eat fish go nine-month already
>
> *I have been eating fish already for nine months.*

- This sentence is grammatically correct, but...
- If your intention is to make a general statement, then the above sentence is incorrect in Thai.
- When **pai** ไป *to go* is placed before the time phrase, this sentence would refer to the fact that one has been eating fish *unwillingly* for nine months already. The action has not been enjoyable.
- The above statement has a negative connotation.

2. tʃán kin plaa **maa** kâau-dɯɯan *lɛ́ɛu*
   ฉัน กิน ปลา มา เก้า เดือน แล้ว
   I eat fish come nine-month already

   I have been eating fish already for nine months.

   - This sentence is correct.
   - Place **maa** มา *to come* before the time phrase to tell someone that you have been eating fish for nine months already. Then, it is a *neutral statement* and does not tell anything about your preferences.

3. tʃán kin plaa **dâai** kâau-dɯɯan *lɛ́ɛu*
   ฉัน กิน ปลา ได้ เก้า เดือน แล้ว
   I eat fish get nine-month already

   I have been eating fish already for nine months.

   - This sentence is correct.
   - Place **dâai** ได้ *to get* before the time phrase to tell someone that you have been *enjoying eating* fish for nine months already.
   - One has achieved one's goal.

4. tʃán kin plaa **maa-dâai** kâau-dɯɯan *lɛ́ɛu*
   ฉัน กิน ปลา มา ได้ เก้า เดือน แล้ว
   I eat fish come-get nine-month already

   I have been eating fish already for nine months.

   - This sentence is correct.
   - Place **maa-dâai** มา ได้ *to come* and *to get* before the time phrase to tell someone that you have been *enjoying eating* fish for nine months already. It is more expressive than the sentences 2 and 3.

5. tʃán kin plaa kâau-dɯɯan *lɛ́ɛu*
   ฉัน กิน ปลา เก้า เดือน แล้ว
   I eat fish nine-month already

   I have been eating fish already for nine months.

   - This sentence is correct.

- When *time indicator* **lέεu** แล้ว is placed at the end of the sentence, we can drop helping words.
- However, the sentence is lacking some special flavour. It has a similar meaning as the sentence 2.

E. Simple advice

In this Secret, much emphasis has been placed on the actions that have started in the past and are still going on, at least *"up to now"*. Then, **lέεu** แล้ว is normally placed after the *duration of time* and at the end of the sentence. The function of **lέεu** แล้ว is to connect *ongoing actions* with the *past*.

When **lέεu** แล้ว is placed after the *duration of time,* it indicates that the action has started in the *past* and has been going on *up to now*. Omitting **lέεu** แล้ว after the *duration of time*, can change the Thai time aspect.

We may place helping verbs **maa** มา, **dâai** ได้, **maa-dâai** มา ได้ or **pai** ไป before the *duration of time* in order to give the statement slightly distinct emphasis.

Whether you wish to use **maa** มา, **dâai** ได้, **maa-dâai** มา ได้ or **pai** ไป before the duration of time is optional. Sometimes, it may be justified to use them to give the action a certain flavour or special emphasis. They can be dropped as well, and the sentences would be grammatically correct. **maa** มา is the most common indicator used by Thais to emphasise the fact that the action has started sometime in the past.

maa มา *to come*, **dâai** ได้ *to get* and **pai** ไป *to go* can also be used as *main verbs*, but then the grammatical function is totally different.

Use **tâng-tὲε** ตั้ง แต่ *since* when the sentence is referring to an *ongoing action,* which has started at a certain *point of time* in the past.

One more thing
It is often said that the *Thai time aspect* is mainly understood from the *context*. However, this book explains what are the underlying factors behind the *natural time aspect* – the way Thai people *naturally*

understand the *time aspect* when *time words* or *tense markers* are omitted.

lέεu แล้ว is a magic word. It makes the *Thai time aspect clear*. In this Secret, it tells that the action has already been going on *for so long "up to now"*.

Secret 5

Looking into the past!

Focusing on completed actions.

เกี่ยว กับ อดีตกาล – **แล้ว** ไม่ ค่อย กังวล เท่าไร – **แล้ว** บอก ว่า – ฉัน อยาก ให้ ทุก คน เข้า ใจ ว่า – อดีตกาล ผ่าน ไป แล้ว – มัน กลาย มา เป็น ประสบการณ์ – เข้า ใจ ได้ แต่ เปลี่ยน ไม่ ได้ – อย่า กังวล กับ มัน เลย – ถ้า อยาก เข้า ใจ เรื่อง นี้ มาก ขึ้น – เรา มา คุย กับ เพื่อน ฉัน ที่ ชื่อ **เคย** และ **เพิ่ง** กัน เถอะ

kìiau-kàp *adìitta-kaan* – **lɛ́ɛu** mâi khôi *kang-won* thâu-rai – **lɛ́ɛu** bɔ̀ɔk wâa – tʃán yàak hâi thúk-khon khâu-tsai wâa – *adìit-ta-kaan* phàan pai lɛ́ɛu – man *klaai-maa-pen pràsòp-kaan* – khâu-tsai dâai tɛ̀ɛ plìian mâi dâai – yàa *kang-won* kàp man ləəi – thâa yàak khâu-tsai rûuang níi *mâak-khûn* – rau maa khui kàp phûuan tʃán thîi tʃûu **khəəi** lɛ́ **phûng** kan thə̀

A. lɛ́ɛu แล้ว and the past times words and tense markers

1. Using *basic sentences* and *lɛ́ɛu* แล้ว

1.1 kháu pai tham-ngaan lɛ́ɛu
เขา ไป ทำ งาน แล้ว

1.2 dii-tsai tsang-ləəi – kháu maa lɛ́ɛu
ดี ใจ จัง เลย – เขา มา แล้ว

1.3 tʃán bɔ̀ɔk thəə lɛ́ɛu
ฉัน บอก เธอ แล้ว

2. Using past time words

2.1 *mûua-waan* เมื่อ วาน
mûua-waan kháu tham man sèt lɛ́ɛu
เมื่อ วาน เขา ทำ มัน เสร็จ แล้ว

2.2 *sɔ̌ɔng tʃûua-moong kɔ̀ɔn* สอง ชั่ว โมง ก่อน
sɔ̌ɔng tʃûua-moong kɔ̀ɔn – kháu yùt tham-ngaan lɛ́ɛu
สอง ชั่ว โมง ก่อน – เขา หยุด ทำ งาน แล้ว

2.3 *mûua-sàk-khrûu* เมื่อ สัก ครู่
fǒn yùt tòk *mûua-sàk-khrûu* lɛ́ɛu
ฝน หยุด ตก เมื่อ สัก ครู่ แล้ว

3. Using past tense markers *khəəi* เคย and *phûng* เพิ่ง

3.1 tʃán *khəəi* riian phaasăa-tsiin lɛ́ɛu
ฉัน เคย เรียน ภาษา จีน แล้ว

3.2 khun *khəəi* lɔɔng lên kiilaa hɔ̀kkîi lɛ́ɛu-rɯ̌ɯ-yang
คุณ เคย ลอง เล่น กีฬา ฮอกกี้ แล้ว หรือ ยัง

3.3 kháu *phûng* tham sèt lɛ́ɛu
เขา เพิ่ง ทำ เสร็จ แล้ว

4. Point of time and completed actions in the past using *tâng-tèe* ตั้ง แต่ and *lăng-tsàak* หลัง จาก

4.1 tʃán sòng tsòt măai *tâng-tèe sìp naa-thii thîi-lɛ́ɛu*
ฉัน ส่ง จดหมาย ตั้ง แต่ สิบ นาที ที่ แล้ว

4.2 *tâng-tèe kháu tsàak-pai lɛ́ɛu* – tʃán rúu-sùk yɛ̂ɛ
ตั้ง แต่ เขา จาก ไป แล้ว – ฉัน รู้ สึก แย่

4.3 *lăng-tsàak phŏm phóp khun* – kɔ̂ɔ rúu lɛ́ɛu wâa – rau pen phɯ̂ɯan kan dâai
หลัง จาก ผม พบ คุณ – ก็ รู้ แล้ว ว่า – เรา เป็น เพื่อน กัน ได้

B. How the language works
– mɯ̂ɯa-kɔ̀ɔn เมื่อ ก่อน, khəəi เคย, phûng เพิ่ง

The following five exercises have been constructed for you to go deeper into the Thai language with **lɛ́ɛu** แล้ว and to understand how Thais express actions, which have been *completed* in the past.

1. **lɛ́ɛu** แล้ว shares her wisdom
2. Spoken sentences and *completed actions* in the past
3. **lɛ́ɛu** แล้ว with *past time words* and *past tense markers*
4. Overall meaning – the *natural time aspect* and *verb groups 1–5*
5. Spoken sentences translated and grammar explained

It all depends on your personal preferences and your level of the Thai language skills on how to use these exercises. You may study each section in an orderly manner or skip any section and then come back later as you wish.

Sometimes, you may just wish to read Thai sentences only and skip explanations and grammar altogether. That way you can facilitate your intuitive expression of the Thai language and learn new words and language skills.

1. **lɛ́ɛu** แล้ว shares her wisdom

Listen to the audio several times and see if you can make the meaning clear to yourself what **lɛ́ɛu** แล้ว says. There are not any English translations in this section. However, we shall translate some keywords.

This is also an excellent exercise for those who wish to practise reading the Thai script. We have made it easier for you by writing each word separately.

You may wish to skip this exercise for the time being and concentrate on the sentences section. It is up to you, however!

เกี่ยว กับ อดีตกาล – **แล้ว** ไม่ ค่อย กังวล เท่าไร – **แล้ว** บอก ว่า – ฉัน อยาก ให้ ทุก คน เข้า ใจ ว่า – อดีตกาล ผ่าน ไป แล้ว – มัน กลาย มา เป็น ประสบการณ์ – เข้า ใจ ได้ แต่ เปลี่ยน ไม่ ได้ – อย่า กังวล กับ มัน เลย – ถ้า อยาก เข้า ใจ เรื่อง นี้ มาก ขึ้น – เรา มา คุย กับ เพื่อน ฉัน ที่ ชื่อ **เคย** และ **เพิ่ง** กัน เถอะ

kìiau-kàp *adìitta-kaan* – **lɛ́ɛu** mâi khôi *kang-won* thâu-rai – **lɛ́ɛu** bɔ̀ɔk wâa – tʃán yàak hâi thúk-khon khâu-tsai wâa – *adìit-ta-kaan* phàan pai lɛ́ɛu – man *klaai-maa-pen pràsòp-kaan* – khâu-tsai dâai tɛ̀ɛ pliian mâi dâai – yàa *kang-won* kàp man ləəi – thâa yàak khâu-tsai rûuang níi *mâak-khûn* – rau maa khui kàp phûuan tʃán thîi tʃûu **khəəi** lé **phŵng** kan thə̀

Words:

adìitta-kaan	อดีต กาล	*past time, completed actions*
kang-won	กังวล	*to worry, to feel anxious*
klaai-maa-pen	กลาย มา เป็น	*to become, to turn into*

pràsòp-kaan	ประสบการณ์	*to experience*
mâak-khûn	มาก ขึ้น	*better*
khəəi	เคย	*once, used to*
phûng	เพิ่ง	*just, a moment ago*

2. Spoken sentences and completed actions in the past

Listen to the audio several times and see if you can understand all the above sentences and how Thai people express the *completed time aspect*. Here are some grammatical words and expressions which may be helpful.

• **lέεu** แล้ว as the *time indicator*

Past time words:

mûua-waan	เมื่อ วาน	*yesterday*
pii-thîi-lέεu	ปี ที่ แล้ว	*last year*
mûua-kɔ̀ɔn	เมื่อ ก่อน	*before, previously*

Past tense markers:

khəəi	เคย	*once, used to*
phûng	เพิ่ง	*just, a moment ago*

Point of time in the past

tâng-tɛ̀ɛ	ตั้ง แต่	*since, after*
lăng-tsàak	หลัง จาก	*after*

3. lέεu แล้ว with past time words and past tense markers

Often, Thai people use only a *basic sentence* without *time words* or *tense markers*. Yet, there is not any difficulty in understanding whether the sentence refers to the *present, past* or even to *future time*. The meaning is understood from the context and from the type of main verb **lέεu** แล้ว is used with. **lέεu** แล้ว functions as the bridge between the *present state* and the *previous state* in the past.

In this Secret, we can turn all kinds of sentences into *completed actions in the past* by using *past time words* or *past tense markers*.

Normally, when **lɛ́ɛu** แล้ว is used with *specific action verbs* such as **kin** กิน *to eat* (Group 4) or with *direction verbs* such as **pai** ไป *to go* and **maa** มา *to come* (Group 5), the *natural time aspect* refers to *completed* actions in the past.

The *past tense markers* such as **khɔ̌ɔi** เคย *once, used to* and **phûng** เพิ่ง *just, a moment ago* can be used to give the statement some extra emphasis. The exact timing of an action can be given by *past time words* such as **pii-thîi-lɛ́ɛu** ปี ที่ แล้ว *last year*.

Word order

When **lɛ́ɛu** แล้ว is used as a *time indicator* it normally comes at the end of the sentence.

In Thai, time words such as **mûua-waan** เมื่อวาน *yesterday* are often placed at the beginning of the sentence. Depending on the context, time words can also be placed at the end of the sentence.

The past tense markers such as **khɔ̌ɔi** เคย *once, used to* and **phûng** เพิ่ง *just, a moment ago* are always placed *before the main verb*.

Thai time aspects

In Thai, we normally talk about the three main time aspects as follows:
- **pàt-tsùbanna-kaan** ปัจจุบัน กาล *present time, now* or *nowadays*
- **adìitta-kaan** อดีต กาล *past time, completed actions*
- **anaakhɔ́tta-kaan** อนาคต กาล *future time, future planning* or *prediction*

Past time aspect

In this Secret, the focus is on the *completed actions* in the past – **adìitta-kaan** อดีต กาล *past time, completed actions*.

The focus can be made clear by *past time words* or *past tense markers* to reflect *completed* actions in the past.

Natural time aspect

Without *time words* or *tense markers*, the focus falls *naturally* on *completed actions* in the past when the verb groups 4–5 are used.

The *basic sentences* denote the *natural time aspect* and are translated into *English in italics*.

If *non-action verbs* (Groups 1–2) or *general action verbs* (Group 3) are used, the *natural time aspect* normally reflects the *present time*. Then, *past time words* or *past tense markers* change the time aspect to denote *completed actions* in the past.

English tense
In this Secret, the English tenses are the *Past Simple* or *Present Perfect*.

English translations
Often there are two translations into English: one with *time words* or *tense markers* and one without them.

4. Overall meaning – natural time aspect and verb groups 1-5

Try to make clear to yourself what overall meaning **lɛ́ɛu** แล้ว plays in this Secret as far as the Thai time aspect is concerned.

Much depends on the context and the type of verbs **lɛ́ɛu** แล้ว is used with. The function of **lɛ́ɛu** แล้ว is to connect the *present state* with the *past*. **lɛ́ɛu** แล้ว functions as the bridge between the *present state* and the *previous state* in the past.

When there is more than one translation, the first translation denotes the *time aspect* when *time words* or *tense markers* are used. The second reflects the *natural time aspect* without them.

This is an excellent exercise to find out what happens to the *time aspect* with different verbs (Groups 1–5) when the *time words are omitted*.

In this section, the past time aspect is made clear by the *past tense markers* such as **khɔ̂ɔi** ซอบ *once, used to* and **phûŋ** เพิ่ง *just, a moment ago*.

When the *time words* and *tense markers* are omitted, the *Thai time aspect* normally changes.

The *basic sentences* denote the *natural time aspect,* which are translated into *English in italics.*

1. Group 1 – *Adjectives,* which are used as *state verbs*
   When **lɛ́ɛu** แล้ว is used with *non-action verbs,* the *natural time aspect* usually refers to the *present time.*

   The *past tense marker* **khɤɤi** เคย *once, used to* changes the *time aspect* to reflect the *completed action* in the past.

Example

kháu **khɤɤi** *khɛ̌ng-rɛɛng* mâak *lɛ́ɛu**
เขา เคย แข็ง แรง มาก แล้ว
he once strong-power very already

He **used to** be very strong.
He is very strong now.

Past time aspect
- The past time aspect is made clear by the *past tense marker* **khɤɤi** เคย *once, used to*.
- Depending on the context, the *time indicator* **lɛ́ɛu** แล้ว at the end of the sentence can be dropped.

* To include **lɛ́ɛu** แล้ว sounds *unnatural* with the *past tense marker* **khɤɤi** เคย *once, used to* when *non-action verbs* (Group 1) are used.
- The English tense is the past with *used to*.

Natural time aspect
- In the absence of the *past tense marker* **khɤɤi** เคย, the *natural time aspect* refers to the *present state (now)* since the adjective **khɛ̌ng-rɛɛng** แข็ง แรง *to be strong* is *a non-action verb* (Group 1).
- **lɛ́ɛu** แล้ว is included at the end of the sentence to emphasise a change in the state.
- The English tense is the *Present Simple.*

Notes

- Sometimes, the adjective **khɛ̌ng-rɛɛng** แข็ง แรง (Group 1) *to be strong* can be translated into English as *to be well*. It also plays the role of a verb here.

2. Group 2 – *State verbs* are *non-action verbs*, which describe a state or condition.

    When **lɛ́ɛu** แล้ว is used with *non-action verbs,* the *natural time aspect* usually refers to the *present time.*

    The *past tense marker* **khəəi** เคย *once, used to* changes the *time aspect* to reflect the *completed action* in the past.

    Good examples of state verbs (non-action verbs) in English are: *to like, to love, to hate, to want, to need, to hear, to see,* etc.

Example

kháu **khəəi** tʃɔ̂ɔp duu rót-khɛ̀ɛng *lɛ́ɛu**
เขา เคย ชอบ ดู รถ แข่ง แล้ว
he once like watch car-racing already

He **used to** enjoy watching car racing.
He already enjoys watching car racing.

Past time aspect

- The past time aspect is made clear by the *past tense marker* **khəəi** เคย *once, used to.*
- Depending on the context, the *time indicator* **lɛ́ɛu** แล้ว at the end of the sentence can be dropped.

* To include **lɛ́ɛu** แล้ว sounds *unnatural* with the *past tense marker* **khəəi** เคย *once, used to* when *non-action verb* **tʃɔ̂ɔp** ชอบ *to like, to enjoy* (Group 2) is used.
- The English tense is the past with *used to.*

Natural time aspect

- In the absence of the tense markers, the *natural time aspect* refers to the *present time* since **tʃɔ̂ɔp** ชอบ *to like* is a *non-action verb* (Group 2).

- **lɛ́ɛu** แล้ว is included at the end of the sentence to emphasise a change in the state.
- The English tense is the *Present Simple*.

Notes
- The *past tense marker* **khɔ̌ɔi** เคย *once, used to,* which is always placed before the main verb, emphasises the fact that the statement refers to the *past*.

3. Group 3 – *General action verbs* can be conveniently used together with **lɛ́ɛu** แล้ว.

   Action verbs are used when something happens or when somebody is performing an action.

   When **lɛ́ɛu** แล้ว is used with *general action verbs,* the *natural time aspect* usually refers to the *present time*.

   The *past tense marker* **khɔ̌ɔi** เคย *once, used to* changes the *time aspect* to reflect the *completed action* in the past.

Example

thúk-khon **khɔ̌ɔi** sài sûɯa-phâa thîi sùphâap lɛ́ sǔuai-ngaam *lɛ́ɛu*
ทุก คน เคย ใส่ เสื้อ ผ้า ที่ สุภาพ และ สวย งาม แล้ว
every-person once wear shirt-cloth that well-mannered and beautiful-pretty already

Everybody **used to** wear beautiful clothes.
Everybody is wearing beautiful clothes now.

Past time aspect
- The *past tense marker* **khɔ̌ɔi** เคย *once, used to* emphasises the fact the action refers to the *past*.
- With action verbs **khɔ̌ɔi** เคย and **lɛ́ɛu** แล้ว can be used in the same sentence, and the statement sounds good.
- **lɛ́ɛu** แล้ว is included at the end of the sentence to emphasise a change in the state.
- The English tense is the past with *used to*.

Natural time aspect

- In the absence of the *past tense marker*, the *natural time aspect* refers to the *present time* since **sài** ใส่ *to wear* is a *general action verb* (Group 3).
- **lɛ́ɛu** แล้ว is included at the end of the sentence to emphasise the change in a state.
- The English tense is the *Present Continuous*.

Notes

- **lɛ́ɛu** แล้ว connects the *present state* with the *past*.

4. Group 4 – *Specific action verbs*

When **lɛ́ɛu** แล้ว is used with *specific action verbs,* the *natural time aspect* usually refers to the past.

Example

tʃán **khəəi** *tʃûuai* kháu maa yə́ *lɛ́ɛu*
ฉัน เคย ช่วย เขา มา เยอะ แล้ว
I once help he come much already

I **used to** help him a lot.
I have already helped him a lot.

Past time aspect

- The *past tense marker* **khəəi** เคย *once, used to* emphasises the *past time aspect*.
- We have also used the helping verb **maa** มา before the adverb **yə́** เยอะ *much* to emphasise the fact that the action has started in the past.
- However, depending on the context, the sentence can denote the action, which has started in the past and is *still continuing*.
- The English tense is the past with *used to*.

Natural time aspect

- Without **khəəi** เคย, the *natural time aspect* would still refer to a *completed action* in the past since **tʃûuai** ช่วย *to help* is a *specific action verb* (Group 4).
- The English tense is the *Present Perfect*.

Notes
- With action verbs **khəəi** เคย and **lέεu** แล้ว can be used in the same sentence, and the statement sounds good.
- **lέεu** แล้ว connects the *present state* with the *past*. *Before, I used to help him a lot. Now, I do not help him anymore.*

5. Group 5 – *Direction verbs*

lέεu แล้ว can also be used with *direction verbs* such as **thoo-hăa** โทร หา *to call*. Then, the *natural time aspect* usually refers to *completed actions* in the past.

Example

kháu **phûng** thoo-hăa tʃǎn *lέεu**
เขา เพิ่ง โทร หา ฉัน แล้ว
he just call-search I already

He has **just** called me. / He **just** called me.
He has already called me.

Past time aspect
- Some additional information has been given by the *past tense marker* **phûng** เพิ่ง *just*.

* The *time indicator* **lέεu** แล้ว at the end of a sentence is normally dropped. Native speakers point out that to include **lέεu** แล้ว here sounds *unnatural*.
- The *past tense marker* **phûng** เพิ่ง *just, a moment ago* would be enough to express the past time aspect.
- The English tense is the *Present Perfect* or *Past Simple*.

Natural time aspect
- In the absence of the *past tense marker* **phûng** เพิ่ง *just, a moment ago*, the *natural time aspect* would still refer to the *completed action* in the past since the main verb **thoo-hăa** โทร หา *to call* is a *direction verb* (Group 5).
- **lέεu** แล้ว is included at the end of the sentence to emphasise a change in the state.
- The English tense is the *Present Perfect*.

Notes

- It seems that when the *past tense markers* **khəəi** เคย *once, used to* and **phûng** เพิ่ง *just, a moment ago* are used, then **lɛ́ɛu** แล้ว is not necessary. In some context, it sounds *unnatural*, particularly when *non-action verbs* (Groups 1–2) are used.

5. Spoken sentences translated and grammar explained

Study the details of each sentence in this Secret and make sure that you understand all the words and how Thai people use *past time words* and *past tense markers*. Every sentence is translated into English with grammatical explanations.

We have also given "word-for-word" translations. Transliterations, how words are pronounced in Thai, can be used alongside with the spoken audio file. You should be able to get the correct tone from the spoken audio file. You can also check the pronunciation and tones from the transliterations since they have tone marks.

A. Sentences – completed actions

1. Using basic sentences and **lɛ́ɛu** แล้ว

Usually, when **lɛ́ɛu** แล้ว is used with *direction verbs* such as **pai** ไป *to go* and **maa** มา *to come* or with *specific action verbs* such as **kin** กิน *to eat*, the past tense is understood from the context.

We do not need any other indicators to tell that the action has been *completed* in the past. Hence, there is only one translation into English in this section.

Examples

1.1 kháu *pai* tham-ngaan *lɛ́ɛu*
เขา ไป ทำ งาน แล้ว
he go do-work already

He has already gone to work.

1.2 dii-tsai tsang-ləəi – kháu *maa lɛ́ɛu*
ดี ใจ จัง เลย – เขา มา แล้ว
good-heart very-excess – he come already

I am very happy that he has already arrived.

1.3 tʃǎn *bɔ̀ɔk* thəə *lɛ́ɛu*
ฉัน บอก เธอ แล้ว
I tell she already

I have already told her.

Time aspect
- In the above sentences, there are not any *time words* or *tense markers*. Therefore, the time aspect is understood from the context. That is called the *natural time aspect*.

Natural time aspect
- In the above sentences, there are not any *past time words* or *past tense markers*.
- The *natural time aspect* refers to *completed* actions in the past since the main verbs **pai** ไป *to go,* **maa** มา *to come* and **bɔ̀ɔk** บอก *to tell* are *direction verbs* (Group 5).
- The English tense is the *Present Perfect*.

Notes
- With **lɛ́ɛu** แล้ว, the *natural time aspect* is clear. When the *specific action verbs* or *direction verbs* (Groups 4–5) are used, the *natural time aspect* refers to *completed actions* in the past.
- **lɛ́ɛu** แล้ว connects the *past* with the *present time*. The action has been *completed*. Now, it is *done*.

2. Using past time words

In this section, the *past time action* is made clear by the *past time words* such as **mûua-waan** เมื่อวาน *yesterday,* **sɔ̌ɔng tʃûua-moong kɔ̀ɔn** สอง ชั่ว โมง ก่อน *two hours ago* and **mûua-sàk-khrûu** เมื่อ สัก ครู่ *a moment ago.*

When the *time words* and *tense markers* are omitted, the *Thai time aspect* normally changes.

The *basic sentences* denote the *natural time aspect,* which is translated into *English in italics.*

Examples

2.1 **mûua-waan** เมื่อ วาน *yesterday*
mûua-waan kháu *tham* man *sèt-léɛu*
เมื่อวาน เขา ทำ มัน เสร็จ แล้ว
yesterday he do it finish already

He already finished it **yesterday**.
He has already finished it.

2.2 **sɔ̌ɔng tʃûua-moong kɔ̀ɔn** สอง ชั่ว โมง ก่อน *two hours ago*
sɔ̌ɔng tʃûua-moong kɔ̀ɔn – kháu *yùt* tham-ngaan *léɛu*
สอง ชั่ว โมง ก่อน – เขา หยุด ทำ งาน แล้ว
two during-hour before – he stop do-work already

He already stopped working **two hours ago**.
He has already stopped working.

2.3 **mûua-sàk-khrûu** เมื่อ สัก ครู่ *a moment ago*
fǒn *yùt* tòk **mûua-sàk-khrûu** *léɛu*
ฝน หยุด ตก เมื่อ สัก ครู่ แล้ว
rain stop fall when-just-moment already

It already stopped raining **a moment ago**.
It has already stopped raining.

Past time aspect

- The *exact time* of the *past time* action is given by the *past time words* such as **mûua-waan** เมื่อวาน *yesterday,* **sɔ̌ɔng tʃûua-moong kɔ̀ɔn** สอง ชั่ว โมง ก่อน *two hours ago* and **mûua-sàk-khrûu** เมื่อ สัก ครู่ แล้ว *a moment ago.*
- The English tense is the *Past Simple.*

Natural time aspect

- The main verbs **tham** ทำ *to do* and **yùt** หยุด *to stop* are *specific action verbs* (Group 4).

- When the *specific action verbs* or *direction verbs* (Groups 4–5) are used with **lɛ́ɛu** แล้ว, the *natural time aspect* refers to *completed actions* in the past.
- The English tense is the *Present Perfect*.

Notes
- **lɛ́ɛu** แล้ว is placed at the end of the sentence to confirm that "*it is already the case*".
- With **lɛ́ɛu** แล้ว the *natural time aspect* is *clear*.

3. Using past tense markers **khəəi** เคย *once, used to* and **phûng** เพิ่ง *just, a moment ago*

   In this section, the *past time action* is made clear by the *past tense markers* such as **khəəi** เคย *once, used to* and **phûng** เพิ่ง *just, a moment ago*.

   When the *time words* and *tense markers* are omitted, the *Thai time aspect* normally changes.

   The *basic sentences* denote the *natural time aspect*, which is translated into *English in italics*.

Examples

3.1 tʃán **khəəi** riian phaasǎa itaalii *lɛ́ɛu*
     ฉัน เคย เรียน ภาษา อิตาลี แล้ว
     I once study language Italy already

   I **have already** studied Italian. / I **used to** study Italian.
   I am studying Italian now.

3.2 khun **khəəi** lɔɔng lên kiilaa hɔ́kkîi *lɛ́ɛu rǔu-yang*
     คุณ เคย ลอง เล่น กีฬา ฮอกกี้ แล้ว หรือ ยัง
     you once try play sport hockey already or not

   Have you **ever** tried playing hockey?
   Have you already tried playing hockey?

3.3 kháu **phûng** *tham* sèt *lɛ́ɛu**
เขา เพิ่ง ทำ เสร็จ แล้ว
he just do finish already

He has **just** finished it.
He has already finished it.

Past time aspect

- The *past tense markers* **khəəi** เคย *once, used to* and **phûng** เพิ่ง *just, a moment ago* are used here to emphasise the fact that these actions have been *completed* in the past.
- Place *tense markers* always before the main verbs.

* With the *past tense marker* **phûng** เพิ่ง *just, a moment ago* (sentence 3.3), **lɛ́ɛu** แล้ว is often dropped.
Native speakers normally do not use **lɛ́ɛu** แล้ว together with **phûng** เพิ่ง. It *sounds unnatural.* It is grammatically correct, however.
- The English tense is the *Present Perfect.*

Natural time aspect

- If we drop the *past tense markers,* the *natural time aspect* would reflect the *present time* in the sentence 3.1 since the main verb **riian** เรียน *to study* is a *general action verb* (Group 3).
- The English tense is the *Present Continuous.*
- In the sentences 3.2–3.3, the *natural time aspect* refers to *completed actions* in the past since **lɔɔng** ลอง *to try* and **tham** ทำ *to do* are *specific action verbs* (Group 4).
- The English tense is the *Present Perfect.*

Notes

- *Past tense markers* are used to place more emphasis on the *past time.*
- They are placed before the main verb.

4. Point of time and completed actions in the past using **tâng-tɛ̀ɛ** ตั้ง แต่ *since* and **lăng-tsàak** หลัง จาก *after that*

In order to express activities which have started at a *certain point* in the *past,* we normally use **tâng-tɛ̀ɛ** ตั้ง แต่ *since* before the point of time.

In this section, the point of time is made clear by the **tâng-tɛ̀ɛ** ตั้ง แต่ *time phrases* such as **tâng-tɛ̀ɛ sìp naa-thii kɔ̀ɔn** ตั้ง แต่ สิบ นาที ก่อน *ten minutes ago,* **tâng-tɛ̀ɛ kháu tsàak-pai** ตั้ง แต่ เขา จาก ไป *since he left* and **lăng-tsàak phŏm phóp khun** หลัง จาก ผม พบ คุณ *after I met you.*

When the **tâng-tɛ̀ɛ** ตั้ง แต่ *time phrases* and *tense markers* are omitted, the *Thai time aspect* normally changes.

The *basic sentences* denote the *natural time aspect,* which are translated into *English in italics.*

Examples

4.1 tʃán *sòng* tsòt-măai **tâng-tɛ̀ɛ sìp naa-thii kɔ̀ɔn** *lɛ́ɛu*
ฉัน ส่ง จด หมาย ตั้ง แต่ สิบ นาที ก่อน แล้ว
I send write-notice set-from ten minute-time before already

I have already sent the letter **ten minutes ago**.
I have already sent the letter.

4.2 **tâng-tɛ̀ɛ kháu tsàak-pai lɛ́ɛu** – tʃán *rúu-sùk* yɛ̂ɛ
ตั้ง แต่ เขา จาก ไป แล้ว – ฉัน รู้ สึก แย่
set-from he out-go already – I feel terrible

Since he has left, I have been feeling lonely / terrible.
I feel lonely.

4.3 **lăng-tsàak phŏm phóp khun** – phŏm kɔ̂ɔ *rúu-lɛ́ɛu-wâa* – rau *pen* phɯ̂ɯan kan *dâai*
หลัง จาก ผม พบ คุณ – ผม ก็ รู้ แล้ว ว่า – เรา เป็น เพื่อน กัน ได้
after-from I meet you – I also know already that – we be friend together can

After I met you, I knew already that we can be friends.
I already knew that we can be friends.

Point of time

- When the point of time refers to the *past*, we need to have a *time word* to tell that since that time *it has been like that.*

Time aspect
- **tâng-tὲε** ตั้ง แต่ *since* and **lăng-tsàak** หลัง จาก *after* are placed before the *point of time*, which refers to the *past*.
- The English tenses are the *Present Perfect* and *Past Simple*.

Natural time aspect
- If we drop the **tâng-tὲε** ตั้ง แต่ *time phrases* and use the basic sentences, the *natural time aspect* refers to a *completed* action in the past in the sentence 4.1 since **sòng** ส่ง *to send* is a *direction verb* (Group 5).
- The English tense is *Present Perfect*.
- In the sentence 4.2, the *natural time aspect* refers to the *present time* since **rúu-sùk** รู้ สึก *to feel* is a *non-action verb* (Group 2).
- The English tense is *Present Simple*.
- In the sentence 4.3, the *natural time aspect* is slightly complex. The phrase **rúu-lέεu-wâa** รู้ แล้ว ว่า *I knew that* refers to the *past* even thought **rúu** is a *non-action verb* (Group 2).

  The second clause refers to the *present time* since **pen** เป็น *to be* and **dâai** ได้ *to be able to* are *non-action verbs* (Group 2).
- The English tenses are the *Past Simple* and *Present Simple*.

Notes
- In the basic sentence, we need to drop also **kɔ̂ɔ** ก็ (sentence 4.3).
- **lăng-tsàak** หลังจาก *after* can be used instead of **tâng-tὲε** ตั้ง แต่.

C. Language hints

We have previously pointed out in Secrets 2–4 that **lέεu** แล้ว is commonly used as a *time indicator* in the *present time* activities. In this Secret, we demonstrate how **lέεu** แล้ว can be used in the *past time sentences* in different ways.

1. Basic sentences and **lέεu** แล้ว without *time words or tense markers*.

   In this section, there is only one translation into English, since the sentences are constructed without *time words* or *tense markers*.

Examples

1.1 kháu *pai léɛu*
เขา ไป แล้ว
he go already

He has already gone.

1.2 ngaan-níi *sèt-léɛu*
งาน นี้ เสร็จ แล้ว
job-this finish already

This job has already been done.

1.3 pai kan thə̀ – fǒn *yùt léɛu*
ไป กัน เถอะ – ฝน หยุด แล้ว
go together let's – rain stop already

Let's go! The rain has already stopped.

Past time aspect
- In the above sentences, there are not any *time words* or *tense markers*. Therefore, the *past time aspect* is understood naturally from the context. That is called the *natural time aspect*.

Natural Time aspect
- The focus is on the *completed actions* in the past since **pai** ไป *to go* is a *direction verb* (Group 5), **sèt** เสร็จ *to finish, to complete* and **yùt** หยุด *to stop* are *specific action verbs* (Group 4).
- The English tense is the *Present Perfect*.

Notes
- When **léɛu** แล้ว *already* is placed after *specific action verbs* or *direction verbs* (Groups 4–5), the *natural time aspect* normally reflects *completed actions* in the past.

2. Actions *completed at a certain time* in the past
   When we wish to tell that the action has been completed in the past, we can use *time words* or *past tense markers* with **léɛu** แล้ว.

In this section, the *past time aspect* is made clear by the *past time words* such as **aathít-kɔ̀ɔn** อาทิตย์ ก่อน *last week,* **sìp-naathii thîi-kɔ̀ɔn** สิบ นาที ก่อน *ten minutes ago* or by the *past tense marker* **phʉ̂ŋ** เพิ่ง *just, a moment ago.*

When the *time words* and *tense markers* are omitted, the *Thai time aspect* normally changes.

The *basic sentences* denote the *natural time aspect,* which are translated into *English in italics.*

Examples

2.1 **aathít kɔ̀ɔn** tʃán *pai-hăa* phɔ̂ɔ-mɛ̂ɛ *lɛ́ɛu*
อาทิตย์ ก่อน ฉัน ไป หา พ่อ แม่ แล้ว
week before I go-meet father-mother already

I already visited my parents **last week**.
I have already visited my parents.

2.2 kháu *yùu* thîi nîi **sìp-naathii kɔ̀ɔn** *lɛ́ɛu*
เขา อยู่ ที่ นี่ สิบ นาที ก่อน แล้ว
he be place-this ten minute before already

He was here **ten minutes ago**.
He is here already.

2.3 phʉ̂ʉan tʃán **phʉ̂ŋ** *pai lɛ́ɛu**
เพื่อน ฉัน เพิ่ง ไป แล้ว
friend I just go already

My friend **just** left.
My friend has already left.

Past time aspect
- When *past time words* or *past tense markers* are used, the sentences *clearly* refer to the *completed actions* in the past.
- The timing of actions are given by the *past time words* such as **aathít-kɔ̀ɔn** อาทิตย์ ก่อน *last week,* **sìp-naathii kɔ̀ɔn** สิบ นาที ก่อน *ten minutes ago* and by the *past tense marker* **phʉ̂ŋ** เพิ่ง

just, a moment ago, which tells that the action has taken place *recently, just now.*
- The English tense is the *Past Simple.*

Natural time aspect
- Without *past time words* or *tense markers*, the *natural time aspect* refers to the *past time* in the sentences 2.1 and 2.3 since the main verbs **pai** ไป *to go* and **pai-hăa** ไป หา *to visit* are *direction verbs* (Group 5).
- The English tense is the *Present Perfect.*
- However, in the sentence 2.2, the *natural time aspect* refers to the *present time* since **yùu** อยู่ *to stay, to live* is a *general action verb* (Group 3).
- The English tense is *Present Continuous.*

Notes
- **lɛ́ɛu** แล้ว connects the *present state* with the *past.*
* With the *past tense marker* **phûng** เพิ่ง *just, a moment ago*, (sentence 2.3) **lɛ́ɛu** แล้ว is often dropped. For natives, it sounds *unnatural.*
- **sìp-naathii thîi-kɔ̀ɔn** สิบ นาที ก่อน is used instead of **sìp-naathii thîi-lɛ́ɛu** สิบ นาที ที่ แล้ว *ten minutes ago* because repeating **lɛ́ɛu** แล้ว twice sounds weird, **sìp-naathii thîi-lɛ́ɛu-lɛ́ɛu** สิบ นาที ที่ แล้ว แล้ว *already ten minutes ago*

3. *Completed actions* in the past – *no time given*

   In this section, the *past time action* is made clear by the *past tense markers* **khɔɔi** เคย *once, used to.*

   When the *time words* and *tense markers* are omitted, the *Thai time aspect* normally changes.

   The *basic sentences* denote the *natural time aspect,* which are translated into *English in italics.*

Examples

3.1 khun **khəəi** *pai* niuyɔ̀ɔk lɛ́ɛu rʉ̆ʉ-yang
คุณ เคย ไป นิวยอร์ก แล้ว หรือ ยัง
you once go New York already-or-not

Have you **ever** been to New York?
Have you been to New York?

3.2 tʃán **khəəi** *pai* pràthêet fàràngsèet *lɛ́ɛu*
ฉัน เคย ไป ประเทศ ฝรั่งเศส แล้ว
I once go country France already

I have **already** been to France.
I have already been to France.

3.3 phǒm **khəəi** *pai* pràthêet filíppin sǎam-khráng *lɛ́ɛu*
ผม เคย ไป ประเทศ ฟิลิปปินส์ สาม ครั้ง แล้ว
I once go country Philippines three-time already

I **have** already been to the Philippines three times.
I have already been to the Philippines three times.

Past time aspect
- The *past time aspect* is understood from the context and from the *past tense marker* **khəəi** เคย *once, used to.*
- The *past tense marker* **khəəi** เคย tells that the action has taken place *at least once* in the past.
- The English tense is the *Present Perfect*.

Natural time aspect
- We can drop the *past tense marker* **khəəi** เคย, and the sentences would still refer to the *past* since the verb **pai** ไป *to go* is a *direction verb* (Group 5).
- The English tense is the *Present Perfect*.

Notes
- **khəəi** เคย can be dropped, but the translations into English would be the same or similar.

- The question with **khəəi** เคย becomes *have you ever been to...* instead of *have you been to...*
- We have previously hinted that using **khəəi** เคย and **lɛ́ɛu** แล้ว in one sentence sometimes sounds unnatural. However, with the *direction verb* **pai** ไป *to go* it is perfectly fine.

4. More examples with **khəəi** เคย

   In this section, the *past time action* is made clear by the *past tense markers* **khəəi** เคย *once, used to.*

   When the *time words* and *tense markers* are omitted, the *Thai time aspect* normally changes.

   The *basic sentences* denote the *natural time aspect,* which are translated into *English in italics.*

Examples

4.1 kháu **khəəi** tɛ̀ɛng-ngaan *lɛ́ɛu*
เขา เคย แต่ง งาน แล้ว
she once prepare-ceremony already

She **has** already been married.
She is already married.

4.2 kháu mâi **khəəi** tɛ̀ɛng-ngaan ləəi
เขา ไม่ เคย แต่ง งาน เลย
she no once prepare-ceremony beyond

She has **never** been married (at all).
She is not married (at all).

4.3 tʃán mâi **khəəi** pai pràthêet fàràngsèet ləəi
ฉัน ไม่ เคย ไป ประเทศ ฝรั่งเศส เลย
I no once go country France beyond

I have **never** been to France (at all).
I have not been to France (at all).

Past time aspect
- The *past time aspect* is understood from the context and from the *past tense marker* **khəəi** เคย *once, used to.*
- The English tense is the *Present Perfect.*

Natural time aspect
- We can drop the *past tense marker* **khəəi** เคย, and the sentences 4.1–4.2 refer to the *present time* since **tɛ̀ɛng-ngaan** เคย แต่ง *to get married* is a *general action verb* (Group 3).
- The English tense is the *Present Simple.*
- However, the sentence 4.3 refers to the *past* since the main verb **pai** ไป *to go* is a *direction verb* (Group 5).
- The English tense is the *Present Perfect.*

Notes
- **khəəi tɛ̀ɛng-ngaan lɛ́ɛu** เคย แต่ง งาน แล้ว is translated into English as *has already been married.*
- **mâi khəəi tɛ̀ɛng-ngaan ləəi** ไม่ เคย แต่ง งาน เลย is translated as *has never been married (at all).*
- In the negative sentence, **ləəi** เลย is normally used as an intensifier. To use **lɛ́ɛu** แล้ว in this context would be grammatically wrong.

5. Point of time with **tâng-tɛ̀ɛ** ตั้ง แต่ *from, since, because*

In this section, the point of time is made clear by the **tâng-tɛ̀ɛ** ตั้ง แต่ *time phrases* such as **tâng-tɛ̀ɛ-rɛ̂ɛk** แต่ แรก *from the beginning,* **tâng-tɛ̀ɛ tʃǎn yaai** ตั้ง แต่ ฉัน ย้าย *since I moved* and **tâng-tɛ̀ɛ khun mâi maa** ตั้ง แต่ คุณ ไม่ มา *since you did not come.*

When the **tâng-tɛ̀ɛ** ตั้ง แต่ *time phrases* and *tense markers* are omitted, the *Thai time aspect* normally changes.

The *basic sentences* denote the *natural time aspect,* which are translated into *English in italics.*

Examples

5.1 phǒm *rúu* **tâng-tὲɛ-rêɛk** *lɛ́ɛu-wâa* – kháu *pen* khon *dii*
ผม รู้ ตั้ง แต่ แรก แล้ว ว่า – เขา เป็น คน ดี
I know set-from original already that – he be person good

I knew from the beginning that he was a good person.
I knew already that he is a good person.

5.2 **tâng-tὲɛ tʃán yaai-maa krungthêep** – mɔɔtɘ̂ɘsai tʃán hăai-pai sɔ̌ɔng khráng *lɛ́ɛu*
ตั้ง แต่ ฉัน ยาย มา กรุงเทพ – มอเตอร์ไซค์ ฉัน หาย ไป สอง ครั้ง แล้ว
set-from I move-come Bangkok – motorcycle I disappear-go two time already

Since I moved to Bangkok, my motorcycle has already disappeared twice.
My motorcycle has already disappeared twice.

5.3 **tâng-tὲɛ khun mâi maa** – phǒm kɔ̂ɔ *yùt* tham-ngaan *lɛ́ɛu*
ตั้ง แต่ คุณ ไม่ มา ผม ก็ หยุด ทำ งาน แล้ว
set-from you no come I also stop do-work already

Since (because) you did not come, I have already stopped working.
I have already stopped working.

Past time aspect
- The point of time is in the past.
- When the action has been *completed* in the past, we can use **tâng-tὲɛ** ตั้ง แต่ before the point of time as follows: **tâng-tὲɛ-rêɛk** แต่ แรก *from the beginning*, **tâng-tὲɛ tʃán yaai** ตั้ง แต่ ฉัน ยาย *since I moved*, **tâng-tὲɛ khun mâi maa** ตั้ง แต่ คุณ ไม่ มา *since you did not come*.
- The English tenses are the *Past Simple* and *Present Perfect*.

Natural time aspect
- In the sentence 5.1, the *natural time aspect* is slightly complex. The phrase **rúu-lɛ́ɛu-wâa** รู้ แล้ว ว่า *I knew that* refers to the *past*

even though **rúu** is a *non-action verb* (Group 2). **lɛ́ɛu-wâa** แล้ว ว่า *already that* is a special expression.
- The second clause refers to the *present time* since **pen** เป็น *to be* and **dii** ดี *to be good* are *non-action verbs* (Groups 1–2)
- The English tense is the *Past Simple.*
- In the sentences 5.2 and 5.3, the *natural time aspect* refers to *completed actions* in the past since **hăai-pai** หายไป *to disappear* is a *direction verb* (Group 5) and **yùt** หยุด *to stop* is a *specific action verb* (Group 4).
- The English tense is the *Present Perfect.*

Notes
- In the basic sentence 5.3, also **kɔ̂ɔ** ก็ needs to be dropped.
- One particular feature of **tâng-tɛ̀ɛ** ตั้งแต่ is that depending on the context, it can be translated into English as *since* or *because*. See the sentence 5.3 where there is a *causative relationship* between the two clauses.
- However, if the *causative* connection is to be emphasised, we need to use **phrɔ́-wâa** เพราะว่า instead of **tâng-tɛ̀ɛ** ตั้งแต่ since **tâng-tɛ̀ɛ** ตั้งแต่ is only used to refer to *time phrases* in Thai.

D. Conclusion

Key: Place **lɛ́ɛu** แล้ว *already* at the end of the sentence to express the fact that a certain state *has been reached, obtained* or *attained*; the meaning is similar to the phrase *it is already the case*. **lɛ́ɛu** แล้ว functions as the *bridge between* the *present state* and the *previous state* in the past.

Verb groups
The meaning in Thai is normally understood from the *context* and from the *type of verbs* **lɛ́ɛu** แล้ว is used with. When we use *basic sentences* without *additional time words* or *tense markers* (Groups 1–5), the *natural time aspect* is *clear*.

When the *non-action verbs* (Groups 1–2) or *general action verbs* (Group 3) are used, the focus falls *naturally* on the *present state*.

When *specific action verbs* (Group 4) or *direction verbs* (Group 5) are used, the focus falls *naturally* on the *completed* actions in the past.

Time words

If we want to give the *exact timing* of an action, it can be made clear by *past time words*.

Place the *past time word* such as **mûua-waan** เมื่อ วาน *yesterday* at the beginning of the sentence and **lɛ́ɛu** แล้ว at the end of the sentence to emphasise the fact that the action took place *yesterday*. Depending on the emphasis, the *time words* in Thai can also be placed at the *end* of the sentence.

When the exact time of the action is given, the English tense is normally the *Past Simple*.

Tense markers

If we want to emphasise the fact that the action refers to *completed actions* in the past, we can also use the *past tense markers*.

Place the *past tense marker* such as **khɔɔi** เคย *once, used to* before the main verb and **lɛ́ɛu** แล้ว at the end of the sentence to emphasise the fact that the action has taken place in the past. The English tense is then usually the *Present Perfect*.

The *past tense marker* **phûng** เพิ่ง *just, a moment ago* before the main verb expresses the fact that the action has taken place *recently*. The English tense is usually the *Present Perfect*.

Changing the time aspect

If you want to change the focus of the sentence that does not *naturally* reflect the *past time* or you may want to place some *extra emphasis* on the *past time* or to give the *exact timing* of an action; then, it is well justified to use *past time words* or *tense markers*. It is always a good idea to use *past time words* and *past tense markers* to avoid misunderstanding.

Unfamiliar expressions

Some words sound unnatural if used together when referring to the past.

a) Sometimes, **khəəi** เคย *once, used to* and **phûng** เพิ่ง *just, a moment ago* sound unnatural when used in the past time sentences *together with* **lɛ́ɛu** แล้ว.

Examples

> 1. tɔɔn-dèk khău **khəəi** nâa-rák **lɛ́ɛu**
> ตอน เด็ก เขา เคย น่า รัก แล้ว
> when-child she once able-love already
> *When she was a child, she was cute.*
>
> 2. mûɯa-kɔ̀ɔn khău **khəəi** tʃɔ̂ɔp pai duu rót-khɛ̀ɛng **lɛ́ɛu**
> เมื่อ ก่อน เขา เคย ชอบ ไป ดู รถ แข่ง แล้ว
> when-before he once like go watch car-racing already
> *Before, he used to enjoy watching car racing.*

- These sentences 1 and 2 are grammatically correct but...
- When **khəəi** เคย and **lɛ́ɛu** แล้ว are used together with *non-action verbs*, the sentence may sound *unnatural* to the Thai ear.
- It would be better to omit **lɛ́ɛu** แล้ว since **nâa-rák** น่า รัก *to be cute* and **tʃɔ̂ɔp** ชอบ *to enjoy, to like* are *non-action verbs* (Groups 1–2).

3. tʃán **khəəi** pai pràthêet fàràngsèet *lɛ́ɛu*
ฉัน ไม่ เคย ไป ประเทศ ฝรั่งเศส แล้ว
I once go country France already

I have already been to France.

- This sentence is correct.
- **khəəi** กำลัง *once, used to* and the *time indicator* **lɛ́ɛu** แล้ว work best together with *action verbs* (Groups 3–5).

b) The negative sentences with **khəəi** เคย *once, used to* and **lɛ́ɛu** แล้ว

> 1. tʃán **mâi khəəi** pai pràthêet fàràngsèet *lɛ́ɛu*
> ฉัน ไม่ เคย ไป ประเทศ ฝรั่งเศส แล้ว
> I no once go country France already
>
> *I have never been to France.*

- This sentence is incorrect.
- In negative sentences with **khəəi** เคย and **lɛ́ɛu** แล้ว together sound *unnatural*. The sentence 1 is considered to be grammatically wrong. It would sound strange to the Thai ear.

2. tʃán **mâi-khəəi** pai pràthêet fàràngsèet *ləəi*
ฉัน ไม่ เคย ไป ประเทศ ฝรั่งเศส เลย
I no once go country France beyond

I have never been to France at all.

- This sentence is correct.
- However, when **lɛ́ɛu** แล้ว is replaced by **ləəi** เลย, the sentence sounds fine. **ləəi** เลย is used as an intensifier here.

3. tʃán **mâi-khəəi** pai pràthêet fàràngsèet
ฉัน ไม่ เคย ไป ประเทศ ฝรั่งเศส
I no once go country France

I have never been to France.

- This sentence is correct.
- The intensifier here **ləəi** เลย can be dropped as well, and the sentence sounds good.

c) **phûng** เพิ่ง *just, a moment ago* and **lɛ́ɛu** แล้ว as a *time indicator* are not commonly used together in the same sentence.

Example

> 1. khău **phɯ̂ng** thoo-hăa tʃán *lɛ́ɛu*
> เขา เพิ่ง โทร หา ฉัน แล้ว
> he just call-search I already
>
> *He has just called me.*

- This sentence is grammatically correct but...
- However, for natives, this sentence sounds *unnatural*.
- The issue is more related to the usage of language than to grammatical reasons.

2. kháu **phɯ̂ng** thoo-hăa tʃán
   เขา เพิ่ง โทร หา ฉัน
   he just call-search I.

   He has just called me.

3. kháu thoo-hăa tʃán *lɛ́ɛu*
   เขา โทร หา ฉัน แล้ว
   he call-search I already.

   He has already called me.

- The above sentences 2 and 3 are correct.
- In order to make the sentence 1 to sound more *natural* in Thai, one should omit **phɯ̂ng** เพิ่ง *just, a moment ago* or **lɛ́ɛu** แล้ว.

E. Simple advice

In absence of any *time words* or *tense markers*, the genuine nature of **lɛ́ɛu** แล้ว is uncovered.

In order to understand the *time indicator* **lɛ́ɛu** แล้ว, just think in terms that it always has some connection to the *present state*. We are "here and now" looking into the *past, previous state*.

a) When **lɛ́ɛu** แล้ว is placed after a *specific action verb* or a *direction verb*, the meaning is understood from the context and from the main verbs (Groups 4–5) **lɛ́ɛu** แล้ว is used with.

Then, the focus falls *naturally* on the *completed actions* in the past. **lɛ́ɛu** แล้ว connects the *present state* with the *past*. The English tense is normally the *Present Perfect*.

Examples

kin lɛ́ɛu	กิน แล้ว	*I have already eaten.* (Group 4)
pai lɛ́ɛu	ไป แล้ว	*He has already gone.* (Group 5)
maa lɛ́ɛu	มา แล้ว	*He has already come.* (Group 5)

b) However, without *time words* or *tense markers*, when **lɛ́ɛu** แล้ว is used together with *non-action verbs,* also called *state verbs* including adjectives (Groups 1–2), the focus falls *naturally* on the *present state* (now) in relation to the *previous state*. English tense is normally the *Present Simple*.

When **lɛ́ɛu** แล้ว is used together with *general action verbs* (Group 3), the focus falls *naturally* on the *present state* (now) in relation to the *previous state*. **lɛ́ɛu** แล้ว connects the *present state* with the *past*. English tense is normally the *Present Continuous*.

Examples

di-lɛ́ɛu	ดี แล้ว	*It is good now.* (Group 1)
khâu-tsai-lɛ́ɛu	เข้า ใจ แล้ว	*I understand now.* (Group 2)
hǔuarɔ́-lɛ́ɛu	หัวเราะ แล้ว	*He is already laughing.* (Group 3)

c) The *timing of an action* can be given by *past time words*

Examples of past time words

mûua-waan	เมื่อวาน	*yesterday*
mûua-kɔ̀ɔn	เมื่อก่อน	*before, previously*
aathít-thîi-lɛ́ɛu	อาทิตย์ ที่ แล้ว	*last week*
sìp naathii thîi-lɛ́ɛu	สิบ นาที ที่ แล้ว	*ten minutes ago*

d) Using the *past tense markers*

Examples of past tense markers

khəəi	เคย	*used to, once*
khəəi...mái	เคย... ไหม	*have you ever?*

mâi-khəəi	ไม่ เคย	*I have never*
phûng	เพิ่ง	*just, a moment ago*

One more thing

With **lɛ́ɛu** แล้ว, there is always a *change* in a state. **lɛ́ɛu** แล้ว changes an action to become "*state* or *condition*", which is true *now*. **lɛ́ɛu** แล้ว functions as the *bridge* between the *present state* and *previous state*.

Even if an action has been *completed* in the past, **lɛ́ɛu** แล้ว always reflects the *present state* in relation to the *past*. Something has been *reached* or *attained*. Now it is like this, before it was different.

A similar expression to **lɛ́ɛu** แล้ว can be found in many Asian languages like Laos, Cambodian, Mandarin or other Chinese dialects. The Thai language uses many words, which have been borrowed from Chinese. **lɛ́ɛu** แล้ว is one of them.

Secret 6

Dreaming and thinking!

Focusing on anticipated future actions.

แล้ว คิด ว่า อนาคตกาล สลับ ซับ ซ้อน นิด หน่อย – เพราะ เรา ไม่ แน่ใจ ว่า มัน จะ เป็น ยังไง – **แล้ว** บอก ว่า – ฉัน อยาก ทำ ให้ ทุก คน เข้า ใจ ว่า อนาคต เป็น แค่ ความ คิด เท่า นั้น – ยัง มา ไม่ ถึง – คิด ได้ – จินตนาการ ได้ – แต่ แตะ ต้อง ไม่ ได้ – เพื่อ ที่ จะ เข้า ใจ เรื่อง นี้ ให้ ดี ขึ้น เรา **ควร** จะ ถาม เพื่อน ฉัน ที่ ชื่อ จะ – **กำลัง จะ** หรือ **อยาก จะ**

lɛ́ɛu khít wâa *anaakhótta-kaan sàlàp-sáp-sɔ́ɔn* nít-nɔ̀i – phrɔ́ rau mâi nɛ̂ɛ-tsai wâa man tsà pen yang-ngai – **lɛ́ɛu** bɔ̀ɔk wâa – tʃán yàak tham hâi thúk-khon khâu-tsai wâa anaakhót pen khɛ̂ɛ khwaam khít thâu-nán – yang maa mâi thŭng – khít dâai – *tsintànaa-kaan* dâai – tɛ̀ɛ tè-tôŋ mâi dâai – phûɯan thîi tsà khâu-tsai rûɯang níi hâi dii khûn rau **khuuan-tsà** thăam phûɯan tʃán thîi tʃûɯ **tsà – kamlang-tsà** rŭɯ **yàak-tsà**

A. lɛ́ɛu แล้ว and future time words and tense markers

1. Simple future tense with time words and *tsà* จะ

1.1 *phrûng-níi* พรุ่งนี้
    khít wâa *phrûng-níi tsà* sèt *lɛ́ɛu*
    คิด ว่า พรุ่งนี้ จะ เสร็จ แล้ว

1.2 *ìik-hâa-naa-thii* อีก ห้า นาที
    ìik hâa naa-thii tʃán *tsà* dùɯm kaafɛɛ *lɛ́ɛu*
    อีก ห้า นาที ฉัน จะ ดื่ม กาแฟ แล้ว

1.3 *pii-nâa* ปี หน้า
    pii-nâa kháu *tsà* riian năngsɯ̆ɯ thîi máhăa-wíttháyaalai *lɛ́ɛu*
    ปี หน้า เขา จะ เรียน หนังสือ ที่ มหาวิทยาลัย แล้ว

2. Future with *kamlang-tsà* กำลัง จะ and *thâa* ถ้า *if clause*

2.1 tʃán *kamlang-tsà* pai nɔɔn *lɛ́ɛu*
    ฉัน กำลัง จะ ไป นอน แล้ว

2.2 *thâa* kháu mâi maa nai khrûng tʃûɯa-moong – tʃán *tsà* pai *lɛ́ɛu*
    ถ้า เขา ไม่ มา ใน ครึ่ง ชั่วโมง – ฉัน จะ ไป แล้ว

2.3 *thâa* khun mâi mii ngən – rau *tsà* pai mâi-dâai ìik lέεu
ถ้า คุณ ไม่ มี เงิน – เรา จะ ไป ไม่ ได้ อีก แล้ว

3. Future with *yàak-tsà* อยาก จะ, *khuuan-tsà* ควร จะ, *tsà-tɔ̂ng* จะ ต้อง

3.1 *yàak-tsà* อยาก จะ
tʃán *yàak-tsà* dâai kràpăư bai mài lέεu
ฉัน อยาก จะ ได้ กระเป๋า ใบ ใหม่ แล้ว

3.2 *khuuan-tsà* ควร จะ
kháu *khuuan-tsà* pai lέεu
เขา ควร จะ ไป แล้ว

3.3 *tsà-tɔ̂ng* จะ ต้อง
rau *tsà-tɔ̂ng* yùt ngaan níi lέεu
เรา จะ ต้อง หยุด งาน นี้ แล้ว

4. Point of time with *tâng-tὲε* ตั้ง แต่ and *lăng-tsàak* หลัง จาก

4.1 *tâng-tὲε phrûng-níi* – aakàat *tsà* plìian lέεu
ตั้ง แต่ พรุ่ง นี้ – อากาศ จะ เปลี่ยน แล้ว

4.2 *tâng-tὲε khráng-nâa* – *tsà* rîiap-rɔ́ɔi lέεu
ตั้ง แต่ ครั้ง หน้า – จะ เรียบ ร้อย แล้ว

4.3 *lăng-tsàak máruun-níi* – rau *tsà* yùt thálɔ́-kan rûuang níi lέεu
หลัง จาก มะรืน นี้ เรา จะ หยุด ทะเลาะ กัน เรื่อง นี้ แล้ว

B. How the language works – khráng-nâa ครั้ง หน้า, yàak-tsà อยาก จะ, kamlang-tsà กำ ลัง จะ

The following five exercises have been constructed for you to go deeper into the Thai language with lέεu แล้ว and to understand how Thais express the *future*.

It all depends on your personal preferences and your level of proficiency in the Thai language. You may study each section in an orderly manner or skip any section and then come back later as you wish.

Sometimes, you may just wish to read Thai sentences only and skip explanations and grammar altogether. That way you can facilitate your intuitive expression of the Thai language and learn naturally extra words and language skills.

1. lέεu แล้ว shares her wisdom
2. Spoken sentences and the *future*
3. lέεu แล้ว with the *future time words* and *future tense markers*
4. Overall meaning –the *future time aspect* and *verb groups 1–5*
5. Spoken sentences translated and grammar explained

1. lέεu แล้ว shares her wisdom

Listen to the audio several times and see if you can make the meaning clear to yourself what **lέεu** แล้ว says. There are not any English translations in this section. However, we shall translate some words, which can be helpful to you.

This is also an excellent exercise for those who wish to practise reading the Thai script. It has been made easier for you by writing each word separately.

You may wish to skip this exercise for the time being and concentrate on the sentences section. It is up to you, however!

แล้ว คิด ว่า อนาคตกาล สลับ ซับ ซ้อน นิด หน่อย – เพราะ เรา ไม่ แน่ ใจ ว่า มัน จะ เป็น ยังไง – **แล้ว** บอก ว่า – ฉัน อยาก ทำ ให้ ทุก คน เข้า ใจ ว่า อนาคต เป็น แค่ ความ คิด เท่า นั้น – ยัง มา ไม่ ถึง – คิด ได้ – จินตนาการ ได้ – แต่ แตะ ต้อง ไม่ ได้ – เพื่อ ที่ จะ เข้า ใจ เรื่อง นี้ ให้ ดี ขึ้น เรา **ควร จะ** ถาม เพื่อน ฉัน ที่ ชื่อ จะ – **กำลัง จะ** หรือ **อยาก จะ**

lέεu khít wâa *anaakhótta-kaan sàlàp-sáp-sɔ́ɔn* nít-nɔ̀i – phrɔ́ rau mâi nɛ̂ɛ-tsai wâa man tsà pen yang-ngai – **lέεu** bɔ̀ɔk wâa – tʃán yàak tham hâi thúk-khon khâu-tsai wâa anaakhót pen khɛ̂ɛ khwaam khít thâu-nán – yang maa mâi thŭng – khít dâai – *tsintànaa-kaan* dâai – tὲɛ *tὲ-tɔ̂ŋ* mâi dâai – phɯ̂an thîi tsà khâu-tsai rɯ̂ang níi hâi dii khûn rau **khuuan-tsà** thăam phɯ̂an tʃán thîi tʃɯ̂ɯ **tsà – kamlang-tsà** rɯ̌ɯ **yàak-tsà** Words

anaakhótta-kaan	อนาคตกาล	*future time, future planning* or *prediction*
sàlàp-sáp-sɔ́ɔn	สลับ ซับ ซ้อน	*to be complicated, to be complex*
tsintànaa-kaan	จินตนา การ	*to imagine, imagination*
tɛ̀-tɔ̂ng	แตะ ต้อง	*to touch*
tsà	จะ	*will*
kamlang-tsà	กำลัง จะ	*just about*
khuan-tsà	ควร จะ	*should*
yàak-tsà	อยาก จะ	*would like to*

2. Spoken sentences and the *future*

Listen to the audio several times and see if you understand all the sentences and how Thai people express the *future*. Here are some grammatical words and expressions which can be helpful to you.

lɛ́ɛu แล้ว as a *time indicator*

Future time words

phrûng-níi	พรุ่ง นี้	*tomorrow*
máruun-níi	มะรืน นี้	*day after tomorrow*
ìik-hâa-naa-thii	อีก ห้า นา ที	*in five minutes*
pii-nâa	ปี หน้า	*next year*
khráng-nâa	ครั้ง หน้า	*next time*

Future tense markers

tsà	จะ	*will*
kamlang-tsà	กำลัง จะ	*just about*

If clause

thâa	ถ้า	*if*

Modal verbs

yàak-tsà	อยาก จะ	*would like to*
khuan-tsà	ควร จะ	*should*
tsà-tɔ̂ng	จะ ต้อง	*have to, need to*

Point of time in the future

tâng-tɛ̀ɛ	ตั้ง แต่	*after, from, starting from, onwards*
lăng-tsàak	หลัง จาก	*after*

3. lɛ́ɛu แล้ว with the *future time words* and *future tense markers*

Often, Thai people use only a *basic sentence* without *time words* or *tense markers*. Yet, there is not any difficulty in understanding whether the sentence refers to the *present* or *past*. The meaning is understood from the *context* and from the type of *main verbs* **lɛ́ɛu** แล้ว is used with.

However, for the future actions, Thais normally prefer to use the *future tense marker* **tsà** จะ *will* in order to make the focus clear. That is because depending on the context, the focus falls *naturally* either on the *present state* (Groups 1–3) or on the *completed* actions in the past (Groups 4–5) when the *basic sentences* with **lɛ́ɛu** แล้ว are used.

With *future time words* such as **phrûng-níi** พรุ่งนี้ *tomorrow* or *future tense markers* such as **tsà** จะ *will* or **kamlang-tsà** กำลัง จะ *just about,* the *future time aspect* is made clear.

Just to avoid confusion, the *future tense marker* **tsà** จะ *will* is used *frequently* in Thai to mark the fact that the action is *anticipated* to happen in the future. Thais prefer to use it for all *kinds of sentences* that refer to the *future*. After all, the future is only a *plan, prediction* or *wishful thinking.* The *present* and *past* are more *real.*

Word order

When **lɛ́ɛu** แล้ว is used as a *time indicator* after the main verb, it normally comes at the end of the sentence.

In Thai, *time words* such as **phrûng-níi** พรุ่งนี้ *tomorrow* are often placed at the beginning of the sentence. Depending on the context, time words can be sometimes placed at the end of the sentence before **lɛ́ɛu** แล้ว.

The *tense markers* such as **tsà** จะ *will* are always placed before the main verb.

Thai time aspect

In Thai, we normally talk about the three main time aspects as follows.

pàt-tsùbanna-kaan	ปัจจุบัน กาล	*present time, now* or *nowadays*
adìitta-kaan	อดีต กาล	*past time, completed actions*
anaakhótta-kaan	อนาคต กาล	*future time, future planning* or *prediction*

Future time aspect

In this Secret, the focus is on **anaakhótta-kaan** อนาคต กาล *future time, future planning* or *prediction*.

The focus is made clear by the *future time words* and *future tense markers* to reflect *anticipated* future actions.

Natural time aspect

The term *natural time aspect* does not normally apply to *future* sentences.

Thai people prefer to use *future time words* or the *future tense marker* **tsà** จะ *will* when sentences or statements refer to the future. Sometimes, Thais use *basic sentences* without additional indicators also for the *future time*.

Then, the meaning is totally understood from the *context* and not directly from the main verbs (Groups 1–5) and **lɛ́ɛu** แล้ว. This is often the case when you reply to *questions*.

The *basic sentences,* which denote the *natural time aspect,* are translated into *English in italics*.

English Tenses

In fact, the Thai way to express the *future* is much simpler. The English language uses several tenses to express the future. For example, the *Future Simple* with *will*, the future with *going to*, the future with the *Future Perfect* and the future with the *Present Simple* or *Present Continuous,* are all used to talk about the *future.*

However, if you express the *future tense* only with the English helping word *will,* then it is quite similar to the Thai way.

Some linguists argue that the English language has only two main tenses, *present* and *past.* If that is the case, then the term *natural time aspect,* which works well for the *present time* and for *completed* actions in the past in Thai, falls well within that definition.

English translations

Often there are two translations into English: one with *time words* or *tense markers* and one without them.

The *basic sentences* denote the *natural time aspect* and are translated into *English in italics.*

4. Overall meaning – future time aspect and verb groups 1–5

When **lɛ́ɛu** แล้ว is used in sentences that refer to the future time, we usually need to add a *future time word* or the *future tense marker* **tsà** จะ *will* to make the meaning clear. However, when the future time is clearly understood from the context, there is no need for any additional indicators in Thai.

lɛ́ɛu แล้ว functions as the bridge between the *present state* and the *anticipated future state.*

With the help of *future time words* or *future tense markers,* we can turn all kinds of sentences to denote the *future time.* The English tenses may be slightly confusing since the future in English is expressed by several tenses.

We give here some examples to clarify the difference between the *natural time aspect* and how the *future time words* and the *future tense marker* **tsà** จะ *will* affect the focus and how sentences are understood by Thais.

This is an excellent exercise to find out how different verbs (Groups 1–5) affect the time aspect when the time words are omitted.

In the following sections, the future time is made clear by the *future time words* such as **dʉʉan-nâa** เดือน หน้า *next week*, **ìik-mâi-naan** อีก ไม่ นาน *soon*, **phrûng-níi** พรุ่งนี้ *tomorrow* and **máruun-níi** มะรืน นี้ *the day after tomorrow* and by the *future tense markers* such as **tsà** จะ *will* and **kamlang-tsà** กำลัง จะ *just about*.

When the *time words* and *tense markers* are omitted, the *Thai time aspect* normally changes.

The *basic sentences* denote the *natural time aspect,* which are translated into *English in italics*.

1. Group 1 – *Adjectives*, which are used as *state verbs*

   Often in Thai, the subject is omitted while in English, it is normally needed.

Example

kamlang-tsà *dii lɛ́ɛu*
กำลัง จะ ดี แล้ว
being-will good already

It is already **getting** better.
It is already good. / It is good now.

Future time aspect
- The *future tense marker* **kamlang-tsà** กำลัง จะ *just about* can be translated into English here as *getting*.
- The English tense is the *Present Continuous*.

Natural time aspect
- Without the *tense marker*, the focus falls *naturally* on the *present state* since the main verb **dii** ดี *to be good* is a *non-action verb* (Group 1).
- The English tense is the *Present Simple*.

Notes
- With **lɛ́ɛu** แล้ว, there is always a change in a *state*. It expresses the fact that a certain state *has been reached* or *will be reached*.
- **lɛ́ɛu** แล้ว connects the *present state* with the *previous state* or with the *next state* in the future.

2. Group 2 – *State verbs* describe a *state* or *condition*

   The time indicator **lέεu** แล้ว can be used together with *state verbs*, also called *non-action verbs*.

Example

2.2 **duuan-nâa** phŏm **tsà** *mii* mɔɔtɔ̂ɔsai săam khan *lέεu*
   เดือน หน้า ผม จะ มี มอเตอร์ไซค์ สาม คัน แล้ว
   month-next, I will have motorcycles three vehicle already

   Next month, I **will** already have three motorcycles.
   I already have three motorcycles.

Future time aspect
- The *future time aspect* is made clear by the *future time word* **duuan-nâa** เดือน หน้า *next month* and by the *future tense marker* **tsà** จะ *will* to reflect the *future time*.
- The English tense is the *Future Simple*.

Natural time aspect
- Without *future time words* or *future tense markers*, the focus falls *naturally* on the *present time* since the main verb **mii** มี *to have* is a *non-action verb* (Group 2).
- The English tense is the *Present Simple*.

Notes
- With **lέεu** แล้ว there is always a *change* in a state. It expresses the fact that a certain state *has been reached* or *will be reached*.
- **lέεu** แล้ว connects the *present time* with the *previous state* in the past or with the *next state* in the future.

3. Group 3 – *General action verbs* may be conveniently used together with **lέεu** แล้ว

   Action verbs are used when something happens or when somebody is performing an action.

Example

ìik-mâi-naan kháu **tsà** *hǔuarɔ́ lɛ́ɛu*
อีก ไม่ นาน เขา จะ หัวเราะ แล้ว
more-no-long he will laugh already

Soon, he **will** be laughing.
He is already laughing.

Future time aspect

- The *future time* is made clear by using the *future time word* **ìik-mâi-naan** อีก ไม่ นาน *soon* and the *future tense marker* **tsà** จะ *will*, which is always placed before the main verb.
- The English tense is the *Future Continuous*.

Natural time aspect

- Without *time words* or *tense markers,* the focus falls *naturally* on the *present time* since the main verb **hǔuarɔ́** หัวเราะ *to laugh* is a *general action verb* (Group 3).
- The English tense is the *Present Continuous.*

Notes

- With **lɛ́ɛu** แล้ว there is always a *change* in a state. It expresses the fact that a certain state *has been reached* or *will be reached.*
- **lɛ́ɛu** แล้ว connects the *present time* with the *previous state* in the past or the *next state* in the future.

4. Group 4 – *Specific action verbs*

When **lɛ́ɛu** แล้ว is used with *specific action verbs*, the *natural time aspect* refers to *completed* actions in the *past*. The situation is normally expressed in English by the *Present Perfect.*

Example

phrûng-níi tsà *phɔ̌ɔi lɛ́ɛu*
พรุ่งนี้ จะ เผย แล้ว
tomorrow will reveal secret already

Tomorrow, the secret **will** be revealed.
The secret has been revealed already.

Future time aspect

- The *future time aspect* is made clear by the *future time word* **phrûng-níi** พรุ่งนี้ *tomorrow* and *future tense marker* **tsà** จะ *will*, which is always placed before the main verb.
- The sentence reflects the *future*.
- The English tense is the *Future Simple*.

Natural time aspect

- Without *time words* or *tense markers*, the focus falls *naturally* on a *completed* action in the past since the main verb **phɔ̌ɔi** เผย *to reveal a secret* is a *specific action verb* (Group 4).
- The English tense would be the *Present Perfect*.

Notes

- With **lɛ́ɛu** แล้ว, there is always a *change* in a state. It expresses the fact that a certain state *has been reached* or *will be reached*.
- **lɛ́ɛu** แล้ว connects the *present time* with the *previous state* in the past or with the *next state* in the future.

5. Group 5 – *Direction verbs*

   lɛ́ɛu แล้ว is frequently used with *direction verbs* such as **maa** มา *to come* and **pai** ไป *to go*.

   When **lɛ́ɛu** แล้ว is used with *direction verbs*, the *natural time aspect* refers to *completed* actions in the *past*. The situation is normally expressed in English by the *Present Perfect*.

Example

kháu **tsà** *klàp-maa* **máruun-níi** *lɛ́ɛu*
เขา จะ กลับ มา มะรืน นี้ แล้ว
he will return-come day-after-tomorrow already

He **will** return the **day after tomorrow**.
He has already returned.

Future time aspect

- The future time aspect is made clear by the *future time word* **máruun-níi** มะรืน นี้ *day after tomorrow* and *future tense marker* **tsà** จะ *will*, which is always placed before the main verb.

- The sentence reflects the *future*.
- The English tense is the *Future Simple*.

Natural time aspect

- Without *time words* or *tense markers*, the focus falls *naturally* on a *completed* action in the past since the main verb **klàp-maa** กลับ มา *to return* is a *direction verb* (Group 5).
- The English tense is the *Present Perfect*.

Notes

- With **lɛ́ɛu** แล้ว, there is always a *change* in a state. It expresses the fact that a certain state *has been reached* or *will be reached*.
- **lɛ́ɛu** แล้ว connects the *present time* with the *previous state* in the past or with the *next state* in the future.

5. Spoken sentences translated and grammar explained

Study the details of each sentence in this Secret and make sure that you understand all the words and how Thai people use the *future time words* and *future tense markers*. Every sentence is translated into English with grammatical explanations.

We have also given "word-for-word" translations. Transliterations, how words are pronounced in Thai, can be used alongside with the spoken audio file. You can also check the pronunciation and tones from the transliterations since they have tone marks.

The term *natural time aspect* does not apply very well to the future sentences. We shall focus here mainly on the *future time words* and future *tense markers*. You may also wish to refer to the previous section 4, overall meaning, where we clarify the difference between the *natural time aspect* and the *future time*.

A. Sentences – anticipated future actions

1. Simple future with *time words* and **tsà** จะ

   In this section, the future time is made clear by the *future time words* such as **phrûng-níi** พรุ่งนี้ *tomorrow*, **ìik-hâa-naa-thii** อีก ห้า นา ที *in five minutes* and **pii-nâa** ปี หน้า *next year* and by the *future tense markers* such as **tsà** จะ *will*.

When the *time words* and *tense markers* are omitted, the *Thai time aspect* normally changes.

The *basic sentences* denote the *natural time aspect,* which are translated into *English in italics.*

Examples

1.1 **phrûng-níi** พรุ่งนี้ *tomorrow*
khít wâa **phrûng-níi tsà** sèt *lɛ́ɛu*
คิด ว่า พรุ่ง นี้ จะ เสร็จ แล้ว
think that tomorrow will finish already

I think it will be finished by tomorrow.
I think it has been finished.

1.2 **ìik-hâa-naa-thii** อีก ห้า นาที *in five minutes*
ìik-hâa-naa-thii tʃán **tsà dùum** kaafɛɛ *lɛ́ɛu*
อีก ห้า นา ที ฉัน จะ ดื่ม กาแฟ แล้ว
more five minute I will drink coffee already

In five minutes, I **will** already be drinking coffee.
I have already been drinking coffee.

1.3 **pii-nâa** ปี หน้า *next year*
pii-nâa kháu **tsà** riian năngsɯ̌ɯ thîi máhăa-wítthayaalai *lɛ́ɛu*
ปี หน้า เขา จะ เรียน หนังสือ ที่ มหาวิทยาลัย แล้ว
next-year he will study book at university already

Next year, he **will** already be studying at the University.
He is already studying at the University.

Future time aspect

- The *future time aspect* has been made clear by the *future time words* **phrûng-níi** พรุ่ง นี้ *tomorrow,* **ìik-hâa-naa-thii** อีก ห้า นา ที *in five minutes* and **pii-nâa** ปี หน้า *next year.*
- We have also placed the *future tense marker* **tsà** จะ *will* before the main verbs **sèt** เสร็จ *to finish,* **dùum** ดื่ม *to drink* and **riian** เรียน *to study.*
- The English tenses are the *Future Simple* and the *Future Continuous.*

Natural time aspect
- If the *future time words* or *tense markers* are dropped, the *time aspect* will change.
- Sentences 1.1 and 1.2 refer to a *completed* action in the past since **sèt** เสร็จ *to finish* and **dùum** ดื่ม *to drink* are *specific action verbs* (Group 4).
- The English tense is the *Present Perfect*.
- However sentence 1.3 reflects the *present time* since **riian** เรียน *to study* is a *general action verb* (Group 3).
- The English tense is the *Present Continuous*.

Notes
- **lɛ́ɛu** แล้ว makes the bridge between the *present time* and *future time*.
- The *term natural time aspect* does not apply very well to the *future*. Therefore, when we are talking about the future, the *future time words* or the *future tense markers* are normally necessary.
- The *natural time aspect* works best when we talk about the *present time* or *completed* actions in the past.

2. Future with **kamlang-tsà** กำลัง จะ and **thâa** ถ้า *if clause*

In this section, the future time is made clear by the *future tense markers* such as **tsà** จะ *will* and **kamlang-tsà** กำลัง จะ *just about*.

In addition, the *if clause* **thâa** ถ้า has a strong connotation regarding the *future time*.

When the *time words* and *tense markers* and *if clauses* are omitted, the *Thai time aspect* normally changes.

The *basic sentences* denote the *natural time aspect,* which are translated into *English in italics*.

Examples

2.1 **kamlang-tsà** กำลัง จะ *just about*

2.1 tʃán **kamlang-tsà** pai nɔɔn *lɛ́ɛu*
ฉัน กำลัง จะ ไป นอน แล้ว
I being-will go sleep already

I am just about going to sleep already.
I have gone to sleep already.

2.2 **thâa...** ถ้า... *if*
thâa kháu mâi maa nai khrûng tʃûua-moong – tʃán tsà pai *lɛ́ɛu*
ถ้า เขา ไม่ มา ใน ครึ่ง ชั่วโมง ฉัน จะ ไป แล้ว
if he no come in half during-hour I will go already

If he does not come within half an hour, I will have left already.
I have left already.

2.3 **thâa...** ถ้า... *if*
thâa khun mâi mii ŋən – rau tsà pai mâi-dâai *ìik-lɛ́ɛu*
ถ้า คุณ ไม่ มี เงิน – เรา จะ ไป ไม่ ได้ อีก แล้ว
if you no have money – we will go no-can more-already

If you do not have any money, we cannot go there anymore.
We cannot go there anymore.

Future time aspect
- The *future time aspect* is understood from **kamlang-tsà** กำลัง จะ *just about* and from the *future tense marker* **tsà** จะ *will*.
- We can also talk about the future time by using the *if clause* **thâa** ถ้า.
- When the sentence starts with **thâa** ถ้า *if,* the second clause *normally* has a future connotation.
- The English tenses are the *Future with going to* (2.1), *Future Perfect* (2.2), *Future Simple* (2.3).

Natural time aspect

- If the *future tense markers* and *if clauses* are dropped, the *time aspect* will change.
- The sentences 2.1–2.2 would refer to *completed actions* in the past since **pai** ไป *to go* is a *direction verb* (Group 5).
- The English tenses is the *Present Perfect*.
- However, the sentence 2.3 reflects the *present time* since **mâi-dâai** ไม่ ได้ *cannot* denotes the *present time state*.
- The English tense is the *Present Simple*.

Notes

- In the negative context, **ìik-lɛ́ɛu** อีก แล้ว is normally translated into English as *not anymore*.

3. Future with **yàak-tsà** อยาก จะ, **khuuan-tsà** ควร จะ, **tsà-tɔ̂ng** จะ ต้อง.

In this section, the future time is made clear with the *modal verbs* such as **yàak-tsà** อยาก จะ *would like to*, **khuuan-tsà** ควร จะ *should* and **tsà-tɔ̂ng** จะ ต้อง *must, have to*.

When the *modal verbs* and *tense markers* are omitted, the *Thai time aspect* normally changes.

The *basic sentences* denote the *natural time aspect,* which are translated into *English in italics*.

Examples

3.1 **yàak-tsà** อยาก จะ *would like to, to want*
tʃán **yàak-tsà** dâai kràpăo bai mài *lɛ́ɛu*
ฉัน อยาก จะ ได้ กระเป๋า ใบ ใหม่ แล้ว
I want-will get bag piece new already

I **would like to** get a new bag now / already.
I have already got a new bag.

3.2 **khuuan-tsà** ควร จะ *should, ought to*
   kháu **khuan-tsà** pai *lέεu*
   เขา ควร จะ ไป แล้ว
   he should-will go already

   He **should** go now.
   He has already gone.

3.3 **tsà-tɔ̂ng** จะ ต้อง *must, have to*
   rau **tsà-tɔ̂ng** yùt ngaan níi *lέεu*
   เรา จะ ต้อง หยุด งาน นี้ แล้ว
   we will-need stop work this already

   We **will have** to quit this project now.
   We have already quit this project.

Future time aspect
- Normally, modal verbs have a future connotation.
- The following verb combinations **yàak-tsà** อยาก จะ *would like to*, **khuan-tsà** ควร จะ *should* and **tsà-tɔ̂ng** จะ ต้อง *must, have to* are used to denote the desired *future goal*.
- The *future tense marker* **tsà** จะ is included to emphasise the *future*.
- The English sentences refer to the *future* with the modal verbs such as *would like to*, *should* and *have to*.

Natural Time aspect
- If the modal verbs and the future *tense marker* **tsà** จะ are dropped, the *time aspect* will change.
- The *natural time aspect* refers to *completed actions* in the past since **dâai** ได้ *to get* and **pai** ไป *to go* are *direction verbs* (Group 5) and **yùt** หยุด *to stop, to quit* is a *specific action verb* (Group 4).
- The English tense is the *Present Perfect*.

Notes
- We can drop the *future tense marker* **tsà** จะ and use only **yàak** อยาก *to want*, **khuan** ควร *should* and **tɔ̂ng** ต้อง *must, have to*

and the time aspect would *not change* since the modal verbs are normally used to talk about the *future*.

4. Point of time with **tâng-tɛ̂ɛ** ตั้ง แต่

In order to express activities, which will start at a certain time in the *future*, **tâng-tɛ̂ɛ** ตั้ง แต่ *from* is placed before the *point of time*.

When the action refers to the certain point of time in the future, we normally translate **tâng-tɛ̂ɛ** ตั้ง แต่ into English as *from, starting from, onwards*.

In Thai, we often place the phrase **pen-tôn-pai** เป็น ต้น ไป *onwards* after the time word.

In this section, the point of time is made clear by *future time words* such as **phrûng-níi** พรุ่ง นี้ *tomorrow*, **máruun-níi** มะรืน นี้ *day after tomorrow* and **khráng-nâa** ครั้ง หน้า *next time* to tell that something will happen in the future *"from that point onwards"*.

The *future tense marker* **tsà** จะ is used in the second clause to emphasise the future time aspect.

When the **tâng-tɛ̂ɛ** ตั้ง แต่, *time phrases* and *tense markers* are omitted, the *Thai time aspect* normally changes.

The *basic sentences* denote the *natural time aspect,* which are translated into *English in italics*.

Examples

4.1 **tâng-tɛ̂ɛ phrûng-níi** ตั้ง แต่ พรุ่ง นี้ *from tomorrow onwards*
   tâng-tɛ̂ɛ phrûng-níi – aakàat **tsà** pliian *lɛ́ɛu*
   ตั้ง แต่ พรุ่ง นี้ – อากาศ จะ เปลี่ยน แล้ว
   set-from tomorrow – weather will change already

   From tomorrow onwards, the weather **will** change.
   The weather has already changed.

4.2 **tâng-tèɛ khráng-nâa** ตั้ง แต่ ครั้ง หน้า *from the next time onwards*
tâng-tèɛ khráng-nâa – **tsà** rîiap-rɔ́ɔi *lɛ́ɛu*
ตั้ง แต่ ครั้ง หน้า – จะ เรียบ ร้อย แล้ว
set-from time next – will smooth-together-already

From the next time onwards, it **will** be fine.
It is fine now.

4.3 **lăng-tsàak máruun-níi** หลัง จาก มะรืน นี้ *after the day after tomorrow*
lăng-tsàak máruun-níi – rau **tsà** yùt thálɔ́-kan rûuang níi *lɛ́ɛu*
หลัง จาก มะรืน นี้ เรา จะ หยุด ทะเลาะ กัน เรื่อง นี้ แล้ว
start-from day after tomorrow – we will stop fight together matter this already

Starting from the day after tomorrow, we **will** stop arguing about this matter.
We have stopped arguing about this matter already.

Point of time
- When the *point of time* is in the future, we need to have *future time words* such as **phrûng-níi** พรุ่ง นี้ *tomorrow,* **máruun-níi** มะรืน นี้ *day after tomorrow* and **khráng-nâa** ครั้ง หน้า *next time* to tell that something will happen in the future *"from that point onwards".*

Future time aspect
- **tâng-tèɛ** ตั้ง แต่ is normally placed before the *point of time.*
- In addition, the *future tense marker* **tsà** จะ is placed before the main verbs to emphasise the fact that the action will happen in the *future.*
- The English tense is the *Future Simple.*

Natural time aspect
If the *future time phrases* with **tâng-tèɛ** ตั้ง แต่ and *future tense marker* **tsà** จะ are omitted, then the *natural time aspect* refers to a *completed* action in the past in the sentences 4.1 and 4.3 since

plìian เปลี่ยน *to change* and **yùt** หยุด *to stop* are *specific action verbs* (Group 4).
- The English tense is the *Present Perfect*.
- However, the sentence 4.2 would refer to the *present time* since **rîiap-rɔ́ɔi** เรียบ ร้อย *to be ready* is a *non-action verb* (Group 1).
- The English tense is the *Present Simple*.

Notes
- We can use here another Thai word **lăng-tsàak** หลัง จาก *after* instead of **tâng-tὲε** ตั้ง แต่, and the meaning is the same or very similar.
- **lέεu** แล้ว is normally placed at the end of the sentence to emphasise a change in a state.
- **tâng-tὲε** ตั้ง แต่ cannot be translated here as *since* into English when talking about the future. It is better translated as *from, starting from, onwards*.

C. Language hints

To express the future in Thai is relatively simple compared to English. However, it can be expressed in a few different ways. We give here more examples of the future sentences with **lέεu** แล้ว *already*.

a) **tsà** จะ *will* for the simple future

In this section, the future is made clear by the *future tense markers* **tsà** จะ *will* and by the adverb **dĭiau ná** เดี๋ยว นะ *just a moment*.

When the *time words* and *tense markers* are omitted, the *Thai time aspect* normally changes.

The *basic sentences* denote the *natural time aspect,* which are translated into *English in italics*.

Examples

1. rau **tsà** riian phaasăa thai *lέεu*
   อีก ไม่ นาน เรา จะ เรียน ภาษา ไทย แล้ว
   we will study language Thai already

   We **will** be studying Thai already.
   We are studying Thai now.

2. **tsà** pai *lέεu*
   จะ ไป แล้ว
   will go already

   He **will** be going now / already.
   He has already gone.

3. **dĭiau ná** – rau **tsà** tham man sèt *lέεu*
   เดี๋ยว นะ – เรา จะ ทำ มัน เสร็จ แล้ว
   moment ná – we will do it finish already

   Just a moment, we **will** finish it now.
   We have already finished it.

Future time aspect

- The future is made clear by *future tense marker* **tsà** จะ *will* before the main verb to denote the fact that the action will happen in the future
- **dĭiau ná** เดี๋ยว นะ *just a moment* is normally used to refer to the *future*. It cannot be used in the sentences that refer to the *past time*.
- The English tenses are the *Future Continuous Tense* and the *Future Simple*.

Natural time aspect

- Without *future time words* and *future tense marker* **tsà** จะ *will*, the focus falls *naturally* either in the *past* or *present time*.
- In the sentence 1, the focus falls *naturally* on the *present time* since **riian** เรียน *to study* is a *general action verb* (Group 3).
- The English tense is the *Present Continuous*.

- In the sentences 2 and 3, the focus falls *naturally* on the *completed action* in the past since **pai** ไป *to go* is a *direction verb* (Group 5) and **tham** ทำ *to do* is a *specific action verb* (Group 4).
- The English tense is the *Present Perfect.*

Notes

- **lɛ́ɛu** แล้ว functions as the bridge between the *present, past* or *future time*. A certain state *has been reached* or *will be reached.*
- In the sentence 3, we must also omit **dǐiau ná** เดี๋ยว นะ *just a moment* for the sentence to be correct.

b) **tsà** จะ as *getting, becoming*

We may place **tsà** จะ *will* before adjectives; the meaning is that the certain state is *becoming* true. In English, we express this by the verb form *getting, becoming.*

When the *time words* and *tense markers* are omitted, the *Thai time aspect* normally changes.

The *basic sentences* denote the *natural time aspect,* which are translated into *English in italics.*

Examples

1. aakàat **tsà** yen *lɛ́ɛu*
   อากาศ จะ เย็น แล้ว
   weather will cool already

   The weather is already **getting** cool.
   The weather is already cool.

2. kháu **tsà** kèng *lɛ́ɛu*
   เขา จะ เก่ง แล้ว
   he will skilful already

   He is already **becoming** an expert.
   He is already an expert.

3. phûu-yǐng khon nán **tsà** sǔuai *lέεu*
   ผู้หญิง คน นั้น จะ สวย แล้ว
   person-women person-that will beautiful already

   That girl is already **becoming** beautiful.
   That girl is already beautiful. / That girl is beautiful now.

Future Time aspect

- We have placed the *future time* by placing **tsà** จะ *will* before the adjectives **yen** เย็น *to be cool*, **kèng** เก่ง *to be skilful* and **sǔuai** สวย *to be beautiful*.
- This structure describes a process, which can be translated into English as *"getting"* or *"becoming"*.
- The English is the *Present Continuous*.

Natural time aspect

- Without the *future tense marker* **tsà** จะ *will*, the focus falls *naturally* on the *present time* since **yen** เย็น ไป *to be cool*, **kèng** เก่ง *to be skilful* and **sǔuai** สวย *to be beautiful* are *non-action verbs* (Group 1).
- The English tense is the *Present Simple*.

Notes

- **lέεu** แล้ว functions as the bridge between the *present, past* or *future time*. A certain state *has been reached* or *will be reached*.
- Thai people use the adjective **kèng** เก่ง *to be skilful, to be proficient, to be talented* frequently, but it is not so easy to translate it into English. We use the noun an *expert* here.

c) Future with future time words

In this section, the future time is made clear by the *future time words* such as **ìịk-sɔ̌ɔng-aathít** อีก สอง อาทิตย์ *in two weeks* and **phrûng-níi** พรุ่งนี้ *tomorrow* and by the *future tense marker* **tsà** จะ *will*.

When the *time words* and *tense markers* are omitted, the *Thai time aspect* normally changes.

The *basic sentences* denote the *natural time aspect*, which are translated into *English in italics*.

Examples

1. **ìik-sɔ̌ɔng-aathít** tʃán tsà pai *lɛ́ɛu*
   อีก สอง อาทิตย์ ฉัน จะ ไป แล้ว
   more-two-week I will go already

   In two weeks, I **will** be gone.
   I have already left.

2. **phrûng-níi** ngaan-níi tsà sèt *lɛ́ɛu*
   พรุ่ง นี้ งาน นี้ จะ เสร็จ แล้ว
   tomorrow work-this will finish already

   Tomorrow, this work **will** be finished.
   This work has already been finished.

Future time aspect
- The *future tense marker* **tsà** จะ *will* is included to emphasise the *future time aspect*.
- The *future time words* **ìik-sɔ̌ɔng-aathít** อีก สอง อาทิตย์ *in two weeks* and **phrûng-níi** พรุ่ง นี้ *tomorrow* are placed at the beginning of the sentence to refer to the future.
- The English tense is the *Future Simple*.

Natural time aspect
- Without *time words* or *tense markers*, the focus falls *naturally* on a *completed action* in the past, since **pai** ไป *to go* is a *direction verb* (Group 5) and **sèt** เสร็จ *to finish* is a *specific action verb* (Group 4).
- The English tense is the *Present Perfect*.

Notes
- **lɛ́ɛu** แล้ว functions as the bridge between the *present, past* or *future time*. A certain state *has been reached* or *will be reached*.
- When the future is understood from the context, we may omit the future tense marker **tsà** จะ *will*.

d) Future with modal verbs

In this section, the future time is made clear by the *modal verbs* such as **nâa-tsà** น่า จะ *should, had better* and **thêɛp-tsà** แทบ จะ *almost, nearly* and the *tense marker* **kamlang-tsà** กำลัง จะ *just about*.

When the *modal verbs* and *tense markers* are omitted, the *Thai time aspect* normally changes.

The *basic sentences* denote the *natural time aspect,* which are translated into *English in italics*.

Examples

1. tʃán **nâa-tsà** pai *lɛ́ɛu*
   ฉัน น่า จะ ไป แล้ว
   I should-will go already

   I **should be** leaving now / already.
   I have left already.

2. tʃán **thêɛp-tsà** lóm *lɛ́ɛu*
   ฉัน แทบ จะ ล้ม แล้ว
   I almost-will fall already

   I am **almost going to** fall.
   I already fell.

3. tʃán **kamlang-tsà** tham *lɛ́ɛu*
   ฉัน กำลัง จะ ทำ แล้ว
   I being-will do already

   I am **just about going to** do it.
   I have done it already.

Future time aspect

We have placed **nâa-tsà** น่า จะ *should, had better,* **thêɛp-tsà** แทบ จะ *almost, nearly* and **kamlang-tsà** กำลัง จะ *just about* before the main verbs.
- The sentences reflect the *future time.*
- The English tenses are the future with *should be* and the future with *almost going to* and *just about going to.*

Natural time aspect
- Without the *future tense marker* and *future modal verbs*, the focus falls *naturally* on a *completed action* in the past since **pai** ไป *to go* and **lóm** ล้ม *to fall* are *direction verbs* (Group 5) and **tham** ทำ *to do* is a *specific action verb* (Group 4).
- The English tenses are the *Present Perfect* and *Past Simple*.

Notes
- **lɛ́ɛu** แล้ว functions as the bridge between the *present, past* or *future time*. A certain state *has been reached* or *will be reached*.

e) Talking about the future with **thâa** ถ้า *if*

In this section, the *future tense marker* **tsà** จะ *will* is used to make the *future time aspect* clear. **thâa** ถ้า in the first clause is used to spell out the *if* condition. It is used in the similar way as the English word *if*.

When the *if clauses* and *tense markers* are omitted, the *Thai time aspect* normally changes.

The *basic sentences* denote the *natural time aspect,* which are translated into *English in italics*.

Examples

1. **thâa khon yə́** – tʃán **tsà** mâi pai *lɛ́ɛu*
   ถ้า คน เยอะ – ฉัน จะ ไม่ ไป แล้ว
   if person many – I will no go already

   If there are many people, I **will** not go.
   I am not going anymore.

2. **thâa kháu tsà klàp bâan** – rau kɔ̂ɔ mâi tông hùuang *ìik-lɛ́ɛu*
   ถ้า เขา จะ กลับ บ้าน – เรา ก็ ไม่ ต้อง ห่วง อีก แล้ว
   if he will return home – we also no must worry more-already

   If he comes home, we do not need to worry anymore.
   We do not need to worry anymore.

3. **thâa khun rɔɔ ìik-sàk-nɔ̀i** – man **kɔ̂ɔ tsà** rîiap-rɔ́ɔi *lɛ́ɛu*
ถ้า คุณ รอ อีก สัก หน่อย มัน ก็ จะ เรียบ ร้อย แล้ว
if you wait more-just-little – it also will smooth-together already

If you wait a little, it **will** be ready.
It is ready now.

Future time aspect

- The *future tense marker* **tsà** จะ *will* is placed before the main verb to emphasise the *future time aspect*.
- When the sentence starts with **thâa** ถ้า *if*, it has usually some future connotation.
- These sentences reflect the *future time clearly*.
- **lɛ́ɛu** แล้ว functions as the bridge between the *present* and *future time*.
- The English tense is the *Future Simple*.

Natural time aspect

- Without the **thâa** ถ้า *if* clause and the *future tense marker* **tsà** จะ *will*, the time aspect falls *naturally* on the *present time* since the negative statements in the sentences 1–2 **mâi-pai** ไม่ ไป *not going* and **mâi-tɔ̂ŋ** ไม่ ต้อง *no need*, refer to the *present time conditions*.
- Sentence 3 reflect also the *present time* since **rîiap-rɔ́ɔi** เรียบ ร้อย *to be fine* is a *non-action verb* (Group 1).
- The English tenses are the *Present Continuous* and the *Present Simple*.

Notes

In sentences 2 and 3, we must add **kɔ̂ɔ** ก็ *also* in the second clause to facilitate flow and make the sentence to sound smooth.

However, **kɔ̂ɔ** ก็ is dropped in the second clause when basic sentences are used without *tense makers*.

f) The future understood from the context

When the *future tense* is understood from the *context*, Thais often leave the *future tense marker* **tsà** จะ out. There is no need for any additional indicators. This is often the case when *"face to face"* with someone or when you reply to a question.

Examples

1. khun **tsà** pai năi
   คุณ จะ ไป ไหน
   you will go where
   Where are you going to?

2. khun pai năi
   คุณ ไป ไหน
   you go where
   Where are you going to?

3. khun pai năi maa
   คุณ ไป ไหน มา
   you go where come
   Where have you been to?

4. kháu **tsà** pai *lέεu*
   เขา จะ ไป แล้ว
   he will go already
   *He **will** be going now. / He **will** go now.*

5. kháu pai *lέεu*
   เขา ไป แล้ว
   he go already
   He has already gone.

Notes

- When you are *face to face* with someone, much is understood from the context. The *future tense marker* **tsà** จะ can be omitted as in the sentences 2 and 3, and the time aspect remains the same.
- When we are talking about the third person and place the *future tense marker* **tsà** จะ *will* before the main verb and **lέεu** แล้ว at the end of the sentence 4, the time aspect refers to the *present time* with the *future connotation*.

- However, when the *future tense marker* **tsà** จะ *will* is dropped, the sentence refers to the *past* since **pai** ไป *to go* is a *direction verb* (Group 5). See the sentence 5.

g) The future with **tâng-tɛ̀ɛ** ตั้ง แต่ *from, starting from*

The point of time is made clear by the **tâng-tɛ̀ɛ** ตั้ง แต่ *time phrases* such as **aathít-nâa** อาทิตย์ หน้า *next week* or **phrûng-níi** พรุ่ง นี้ *tomorrow* to tell that something will happen in the future *"from that point onwards"*. In addition, the *future tense marker* **tsà** จะ is placed before the main verb.

When the **tâng-tɛ̀ɛ** ตั้ง แต่ *time phrases* and *tense markers* are omitted, the *Thai time aspect* normally changes.

The *basic sentences* denote the *natural time aspect,* which are translated into *English in italics*.

Examples

1. **tâng-tɛ̀ɛ aathít-nâa pen-tôn-pai** – phǒm **tsà** yùu thîi pràthêet ùun lɛ́ɛu
ตั้ง แต่ อาทิตย์ หน้า เป็น ต้น ไป – ผม จะ อยู่ ที่ ประเทศ อื่น แล้ว
set-from week-next be-start-go – I will stay at country other already
Starting from next week, I **will** already be in another country.
I am already in another country.

2. **tâng-tɛ̀ɛ phrûng-níi pen-tôn-pai lɛ́ɛu** – tʃán **tsà** mii wan-yùt aathít-lá sɔ̌ɔng khráng
ไม่ ได้ ค่ะ – ตั้ง แต่ พรุ่ง นี้ เป็น ต้น ไป แล้ว – ฉัน จะ มี วัน หยุด อาทิตย์ ละ สอง ครั้ง
set-from tomorrow be-start-go already – I will have day-stop week two time
Starting already from tomorrow, I **will** have a day off twice a week.
I have a day off twice a week.

Point of time
- The point of time is in the *future*.
- In the future sentences, **tâng-tɛ̀ɛ** ตั้ง แต่ is normally placed before the *future time words* such as **aathít-nâa** อาทิตย์ หน้า *next week* or **phrûng-níi** พรุ่ง นี้ *tomorrow*.

Future time aspect
- The *future tense marker* **tsà** จะ *will* is placed before the main verb **mii** มี *to have* to emphasise the fact that the sentence refers to the *future*.
- The English tense is the *Future Simple*.

Natural Time aspect
- If the *future time phrases* with **tâng-tɛ̀ɛ** ตั้ง แต่ and the *future tense marker* **tsà** จะ are omitted, then the sentences would refer to the *present time* since **yùu** อยู่ *to live, to stay* is a *general action verb* (Group 3), and **mii** มี *to have* is a *non-action verb* (Group 2).
- The English tense is the *Present Simple*.

Notes
- In the future sentences, **tâng-tɛ̀ɛ** ตั้ง แต่ is translated into English as *starting from* or *from that time onwards*.
- We can also place **pen-tôn-pai** เป็น ต้น ไป after the *future point of time* to emphasise the continuation of the action in the future. It is optional, however.
- It is also possible to omit **tâng-tɛ̀ɛ** ตั้ง แต่ and use only **pen-tôn-pai** เป็น ต้น ไป. The meaning is the same or very similar.
- We could also use another Thai word **lăng-tsàak** หลัง จาก *after* instead of **tâng-tɛ̀ɛ** ตั้ง แต่, and the meaning would be the same or similar.

D. Conclusion

Key: Place the *future time word* such as **pii-nâa** ปี หน้า *next year* at the beginning of the sentence or *future tense marker* **tsà** จะ *will* before the main verb in order to express the *future time* in Thai.

Place **lɛ́ɛu** แล้ว at the end of the sentence to express the fact that a certain state will be *reached, obtained* or *attained* in the future. Then, **lɛ́ɛu** แล้ว functions *as the bridge* between the *present state* and the *anticipated future state*.

Basic sentences

In the basic sentences without additional indicators, and when **lɛ́ɛu** แล้ว is used with *non-action verbs* (Groups 1–2) or *general action verbs* (Group 3), the *natural time aspect* denotes the *present time* in relation to the past.

When we use **lɛ́ɛu** แล้ว with *specific action verbs* (Group 4) or *direction verbs* (Group 5), the focus falls *naturally* on *completed actions* in the past.

Natural time aspect

The *future time aspect* is not *naturally* understood from the main verbs (Groups 1–5). Normally, the *future* is expressed by the *future time words* or by the *future tense marker* **tsà** จะ *will*.

In Thai, the *future tense marker* **tsà** จะ *will* is usually used for all kinds of future sentences. This is important since many times *basic sentences* refer to the *present time* or *completed actions* in the past in Thai.

It is better to use the *future time words* or *future tense markers* when talking about the *future*.

English tenses

We would like to remind you of the fact that English tenses, which are very sophisticated, do not help you in understanding how Thai people express the *present, past* or *future time*.

Unfamiliar expressions

It is estimated that already about 70% of English language used today in the world is spoken by *non-native speakers*. Hence, you will hear all kinds of English sentences influenced by different languages. That does not seem to be a big problem. Native English speakers are already used to it.

However, the same does not apply to the Thai language. Thai is not a world language. You are advised to learn to speak Thai as *Thai people do,* otherwise you are *not easily understood* in Thailand when you speak Thai.

Examples

a) **tông** ต้อง *must* and **tsà** จะ *will*

> 1. rau *tông-tsà* yùt ngaan níi *léɛu*
> เรา ต้อง จะ หยุด งาน นี้ แล้ว
> we need-will stop work this already
>
> *We must stop this project now / already.*

- This sentence is incorrect.
- The *future tense marker* **tsà** จะ *will* must be placed before the *modal verb* **tông** ต้อง.

2. rau **tsà-tông** yùt ngaan níi *léɛu*
เรา จะ ต้อง หยุด งาน นี้ แล้ว
we will need stop work this already

We must stop this project now / already.

- This sentence is correct.
- When **tông** ต้อง *must* and **tsà** จะ *will* are used together to refer to the future, the *future tense marker* **tsà** จะ is always placed before the *modal verb* **tông** ต้อง.

b) **mâi** ไม่ *not* and **tsà** จะ *will*

> 1. thâa kháu tsà klàp bâan – rau *mâi-tsà* hùuang *iik-léɛu*
> ถ้า เขา จะ กลับ บ้าน – เรา ไม่ จะ ห่วง อีก แล้ว
> if he will return home – we will not worry more-already
>
> *If he comes home, we will not worry anymore.*

- This sentence is grammatically correct but...
- Some Thais feel that this sentence is unnatural; it does not sound smooth.

- **mâi** ไม่ *not* is not normally placed before the *future tense marker* **tsà** จะ.
- It should be pointed out, however, that for some Thais this sentence sounds good and is correct.

2. thâa kháu tsà klàp bâan – rau *tsà-mâi* hùuang *ìik-lɛ́ɛu*
   ถ้า เขา จะ กลับ บ้าน – เรา จะ ไม่ ห่วง อีก แล้ว
   if he will return home – we will not must worry more-already

   If he comes home, we will not worry anymore.

- This sentence is grammatically correct.
- The *future tense marker* **tsà** จะ is normally placed before **mâi** ไม่.
- The sentence sounds smoothe and is correct.

c) **kɔ̂ɔ** ก็ *also*, **mâi-tɔ̂ng** ต้อง *no need* and **tsà** จะ *will*

> 1. thâa kháu tsà klàp bâan – rau *mâi-tɔ̂ng* hùuang *ìik-lɛ́ɛu*
>   ถ้า เขา จะ กลับ บ้าน – เรา ไม่ ต้อง ห่วง อีก แล้ว
>   if he will return home – we no-must worry more-already
>
>   *If he comes home, we do not need to worry anymore.*

- This sentence is grammatically correct but...
- Some Thais feel that this sentence is unnatural; it does not sound smooth.
- There is something missing.
- It should be pointed out, however, that for some Thais this sentence sounds good and is correct.

2. thâa kháu tsà klàp bâan – rau *kɔ̂ɔ-mâi-tɔ̂ng* hùuang *ìik-lɛ́ɛu*
   ถ้า เขา จะ กลับ บ้าน – เรา ก็ ไม่ ต้อง ห่วง อีก แล้ว
   if he will return home – we-also no-must worry more-already

   If he comes home, we do not need to worry anymore.

- This sentence is correct.
- **kɔ̂ɔ** ก็ has been included to facilitate the flow.
- It sounds good and is easy to understand.
- The phrase **kɔ̂ɔ-mâi-tɔ̂ng** ก็ ไม่ ต้อง *not have to*... has the same meaning as **mâi-tɔ̂ng** ไม่ ต้อง in the sentence 1.

3. thâa kháu tsá klàp bâan – rau *kɔ̂ɔ-tsà-mâi-tɔ̂ng* hùuang *ìik-lɛ́ɛu*
ถ้า เขา จะ กลับ บ้าน – เรา ก็ จะ ไม่ ต้อง ห่วง อีก แล้ว
if he will return home – we-also will-no-must worry more-already

If he comes home, we do not need to worry anymore.

- This sentence is correct.
- It sounds good and is easy to understand.
- The phrase **kɔ̂ɔ-tsà-mâi-tɔ̂ng** ก็ จะ ไม่ ต้อง *will not have to...* is, however, a more complex way to express the same meaning as in the sentences 1 and 2.
- **kɔ̂ɔ** ก็ has been included to facilitate the flow.
- The *future time marker* **tsà** จะ *will* emphasises the *future time aspect*.

How to use **kɔ̂ɔ** ก็ in Thai is somewhat sophisticated. **kɔ̂ɔ** ก็ is a very mysterious word. It is an art to use **kɔ̂ɔ** ก็ correctly.

There will be a book about **kɔ̂ɔ** ก็ in the future.

More information about the Thai learning books can be found in the website:
www.thaibooks.net

E. Simple advice

When talking about the future, English uses several tenses such as the *Future Simple* with *will*, *Future* with *going to*, *Present Simple*, *Present Continuous*, *Future Continuous Tense* etc. Actually, it is an art to use English tenses correctly.

Therefore, it is not a very good idea to try to understand the *Thai future time aspect* by using English tenses. In Thai, we just place the *future tense marker* **tsà** จะ *will* before the *main verb* when talking about the *future* or use the *future time words* when the *exact timing* of an action is given.

If you use only one helping verb *will* to express the *future* in English, then the Thai way is similar to English.

There is not really any clear *natural future time aspect* in Thai. The term *natural time aspect* suits better when the sentences refer to the *present time of affaires* or *completed actions* in the past. However, **lɛ́ɛu** แล้ว can be *conveniently* used in the sentences that refer to the *future*. **lɛ́ɛu** แล้ว makes the bridge *between* the *present state* and the *future*.

When the *future time aspect* is understood from the context, it is not always necessary to use the *future tense marker* **tsà** จะ *will*. However, many Thais prefer to use it whenever they are talking about the future.

The *future tense marker* **tsà** จะ *will* is also used as the compound verb construction with *modal verbs* such as **khuan-tsà** ควร จะ *should*, **àat-tsà** อาจจะ *maybe, perhaps,* etc.

When **lɛ́ɛu** แล้ว is used in the future sentence, it often refers to the *near future* or *now*. **tsà-pai-lɛ́ɛu** จะ ไป แล้ว is best translated into English as *I am going now, I will go now* or *I will be going now*.

When the *future tense marker* **tsà** จะ *will* is used with *non-action verbs* (Group 1), the focus is normally on the *present state*. Then the meaning is often translated into English as *getting* or *becoming*.

One more thing
To speak a foreign language like Thai fluently and correctly is challenging. You may speak grammatically correctly, but Thais may not understand you. On the other hand, you may speak grammatically incorrectly, and Thais could understand you without difficulty. Since words in Thai are not conjugated, the choice of words and the order in the sentence becomes important.

The aim of this book is to give you the tools so that you will be able to speak Thai *fluently* and *also grammatically correctly*. Then, you are on the way to speak Thai as native speakers do. It will take a lot of practise and repetition on your part. If you really want, you can get there.

Secret 7

Reviewing the Thai tenses with เคย แล้ว

Present, past and future.

จริง ๆ แล้ว – แล้ว คิด ว่า กาล ใน ภาษา ไทย ไม่ ค่อย ยาก – แล้ว เป็น คน ที่ เปลี่ยน ความ หมาย ตัว เอง ได้ ง่าย ๆ – แล้ว บอก ว่า – ฉัน ชอบ ปัจจุบันกาล มาก ที่ สุด – แต่ ว่า บาง ครั้ง เรา ต้อง คุย กัน เกี่ยว กับ เรื่อง อดีต กาล หรือ อนาคต กาล ด้วย – เพราะ ว่า พวก เขา มี ผล ต่อ ปัจจุบัน กาล – นั่น คือ ธรรมชาติ ของ ชีวิต

tsing-tsing lέεu – **lέεu** khít wâa kaan nai phaasǎa thai *mâi-khɔ̌i-yâak* – **lέεu** pen khon thîi plìian *khwaam-mǎai* tuua-eeng dâai ngâai-ngâai – **lέεu** bɔ̀ɔk wâa – t∫án t∫ɔ̂ɔp pàt-tsùban-na-kaan mâak thîi-sùt – tὲε-wâa baang-khráng rau tôŋ khui kan *kìiau-kàp* rûuang adìit-ta-kaan rǔu anaakhót-ta-kaan dûuai – phrɔ́-wâa phûuak-kháu *mii-phǒn-tɔ̀ɔ* pàt-tsùban-na-kaan – nân khuu *tham-má-t∫âat* khɔ̌ɔng t∫iiwít

A. Review of the Thai time aspect

1. Using basic sentences

1.1 Present

Question
    au ìik mái khá
    เอา อีก ไหม คะ

Reply
    khɔ̀ɔp-khun khâ – *phɔɔ lέεu* khâ
    ขอบ คุณ ค่ะ – พอ แล้ว ค่ะ

1.2 Past

Question
    khau pai nǎi *lέεu* khá
    เขา ไป ไหน แล้ว คะ

Reply
    pai duu nǎng *lέεu* khâ
    ไป ดู หนัง แล้ว ค่ะ

1.3 Future

Question
>khun hĭu mái khá
>คุณ หิว ไหม คะ

Reply
>hĭu khâ – tông pai kin khâau *lɛ́ɛu* khâ
>หิว ค่ะ – ต้อง ไป กิน ข้าว แล้ว ค่ะ

2. Using time words

2.1 Present – *tɔɔn-níi* ตอน นี้

Question
>kháu phûut phaasăa arai khá
>เขา พูด ภาษา อะไร คะ

Reply
>*tɔɔn-níi* kháu phûut phaasăa thai *lɛ́ɛu* khâ
>ตอน นี้ เขา พูด ภาษา ไทย แล้ว ค่ะ

2.2 Past – *mûɯa-waan* เมื่อ วาน

Question
>khun dâai-ráp wiisâa khun *lɛ́ɛu* rɯ̆ɯ-yang khá
>คุณ ได้ รับ วีซ่า คุณ แล้ว หรือ ยัง คะ

Reply
>*mûɯa-waan* tʃán dâai-ráp *lɛ́ɛu* khâ
>เมื่อ วาน ฉัน ได้ รับ แล้ว ค่ะ

2.3 Future – *phrûng-níi* พรุ่ง นี้

Question
>*phrûng-níi* kháu pìt-thəəm *lɛ́ɛu* – tʃâi-mái khá
>พรุ่ง นี้ เขา ปิด เทอม แล้ว – ใช่ ไหม คะ

Reply
>tʃâi khâ – *phrûng-níi* kháu pìt-thəəm *lɛ́ɛu* khâ
>ใช่ ค่ะ – พรุ่ง นี้ เขา ปิด เทอม แล้ว ค่ะ

3. Using tense markers

3.1 Present

Question
    kháu *kamlang* tham arai *yùu* khá
    เขา กำลัง ทำ อะไร อยู่ คะ

Reply 1
    kháu *kamlang* tham-ngaan *lέεu* khâ
    เขา กำลัง ทำ งาน แล้ว ค่ะ

Reply 2
    kháu tham-ngaan *yùu* khâ
    เขา กำลัง ทำ งาน อยู่ ค่ะ

3.2 Past

Question
    khun *khəəi* pai thîiau pràthêet kamphuutʃaa mái
    คุณ เคย ไป เที่ยว ประเทศ กัมพูชา ไหม

Reply
    tʃán *khəəi* pai *lέεu* khâ
    ฉัน เคย ไป แล้ว ค่ะ

3.3 Future

Question
    khun *tsà* tham man sèt mûɯa-rài khá
    คุณ จะ ทำ มัน เสร็จ เมื่อไหร่ คะ

Reply
    ìik-sǎam-wan tsà sèt *lέεu* khâ
    อีก สาม วัน จะ เสร็จ แล้ว ค่ะ

4. Point of time – using *tâng-tὲε* ตั้ง แต่

4.1 Present
Question
>   *pàt-tsùban-níi* khwaam tɔ̀əp-too thaang sèet-thàkìt khɔ̌ɔng pràthêet-thai pen yang-ngai
>   ปัจจุบันนี้ ความ เติบ โต ทาง เศรษฐกิจ ของ ประเทศ ไทย เป็น ยังไง

Reply
>   dii khûn *lέεu* – lέ *tâng-tὲε pii-níi pen-tôn-pai* – kɔ̂ɔ *tsà* tsàrəən khûn yàang-rûuat-reu
>   ดี ขึ้น แล้ว – และ ตั้ง แต่ ปี นี้ เป็น ต้น ไป – ก็ จะ เจริญ ขึ้น อย่าง รวด เร็ว

4.2 Past
Question
>   kháu ɔ̀ɔk-pai *tâng-tὲε mɯ̂ɯa-rài* khráp
>   เขา ออก ไป ตั้ง แต่ เมื่อไหร่ ครับ

Reply
>   kháu ɔ̀ɔk-pai *tâng-tὲε yîisìp naa-thii thîi-lέεu*
>   เขา ออก ไป ตั้ง แต่ ยี่ สิบ นา ที ที่ แล้ว

4.3 Future
Question
>   khun *tsà* dâai khûn-ngən-dɯɯan *mɯ̂ɯa-rài* khá
>   คุณ จะ ได้ ขึ้น เงินเดือน เมื่อไหร่ คะ

Reply
>   *tsà* dâai – *lăng-tsàak dɯɯan-nâa pen-tôn-pai lέεu* khâ
>   จะ ได้ – หลัง จาก เดือน หน้า เป็น ต้น ไป แล้ว ค่ะ

B. How the language works – Present, past and future

In this Secret, the Thai time aspect is reviewed with *questions* and *replies*. It helps the reader to understand better how Thais express the *present*, *past* and the *future time*. The grammatical comments apply to the replies only.

The following five exercises have been constructed for you to go deeper into the Thai language with **แล้ว แล้ว**, and to understand how Thais express the *time aspect*, called tenses in English. It all depends on your personal preferences and your level of the Thai language skills how to use these exercises.

1. **แล้ว แล้ว** shares her wisdom
2. Spoken sentences – *present, past* and *future*
3. Review of the *Thai time aspect* and **แล้ว แล้ว**
4. Overall meaning – the *Thai time aspect* and *verb groups 1–5*
5. Spoken sentences translated and grammar explained

You may study each section in an orderly manner or bypass any section and then come back later as you wish. Sometimes, you may just wish to read Thai sentences only and skip explanations and grammar explanations altogether. That way, you can facilitate your intuitive expression of the Thai language; you can also learn naturally unfamiliar words and language skills.

1. แล้ว แล้ว shares her wisdom

Listen to the audio several times and see if you can make the meaning clear to yourself what **แล้ว แล้ว** says. There are not any English translations in this section. However, we shall translate some words which can be helpful to you.

This is also an excellent exercise for those who wish to practise reading the Thai script. It has been made easier for you by writing each word separately.

You may wish to skip this exercise for the time being and concentrate on the sentences section. It is up to you, however!

Secret 7

จริง ๆ แล้ว – แล้ว คิด ว่า กาล ใน ภาษา ไทย ไม่ ค่อย ยาก – แล้ว เป็น คน ที่ เปลี่ยน ความ หมาย ตัว เอง ได้ ง่าย ๆ – แล้ว บอก ว่า – ฉัน ชอบ ปัจจุบันกาล มาก ที่ สุด – แต่ ว่า บาง ครั้ง เรา ต้อง คุย กัน เกี่ยว กับ เรื่อง อดีต กาล หรือ อนาคต กาล ด้วย – เพราะ ว่า พวก เขา มี ผล ต่อ ปัจจุบัน กาล – นั่น คือ ธรรมชาติ ของ ชีวิต

tsing-tsing lɛ́ɛu – *lɛ́ɛu* khít wâa kaan nai phaasǎa thai *mâi-khɔ̂i-yâak* – *lɛ́ɛu* pen khon thîi pliian *khwaam-mǎai* tuua-eeng dâai ngâai-ngâai – *lɛ́ɛu* bɔ̀ɔk wâa – tʃán tʃɔ̂ɔp pàt-tsùban-na-kaan mâak thîi-sùt – tɛ̀ɛ-wâa baang-khráng rau tông khui kan *kìiau-kàp* rûuang adìit-ta-kaan rʉ̌ʉ anaakhót-ta-kaan dûuai – phrɔ́-wâa phûuak-kháu *mii-phǒn-tɔ̀ɔ* pàt-tsùban-na-kaan – nân khʉʉ *tham-má-tʃâat* khɔ̌ɔng tʃiiwít

Words

tsing-tsing lɛ́ɛu	จริงๆ แล้ว	*actually*
mâi-khɔ̂i-yâak	ไม่ ค่อย ยาก	*not that difficult, not very difficult*
khwaam-mǎai	ความ หมาย	*meaning*
kìiau-kàp	เกี่ยว กับ	*about, concerning*
mii-phǒn-tɔ̀ɔ	มี ผล ต่อ	*to influence something*
tham-má-tʃâat	ธรรมชาติ	*nature*

2. Spoken sentences – *present, past* and *future*

Listen to the audio several times and see if you understand how the *completed actions* in the past, *present time* and *future time* are expressed in Thai. Here are some grammatical words and expressions which can be helpful.

lɛ́ɛu แล้ว as a *time indicator* with:

Present time:

tɔɔn-níi	ตอน นี้	*now*
pàt-tsùban	ปัจจุบัน	*nowadays*
yùu	อยู่	*state exists*
kamlang	กำลัง	*action in progress*

Past time:

mûua-waan	เมื่อ วาน	*yesterday*
mûua-kɔ̀ɔn	เมื่อ ก่อน	*before, previously*
khəəi	เคย	*used to, once*
phûng	เพิ่ง	*just, a moment ago*

Future time with:

phrûng-níi	พรุ่ง นี้	*tomorrow*
tsà	จะ	*will*
kamlang-tsà	กำลัง จะ	*just about*
yàak-tsà	อยาก จะ	*would like to*
thâa	ถ้า	*if*

3. Review of the *Thai time aspect* and léɛu แล้ว

In this Secret, we shall review the *Thai time aspect* – how Thai people express themselves in different situations. Thais talk rather about the *present time, completed actions* in the past and about the *future time*.

It is crucial for foreign language learners to grasp the intricacies of Thai *time aspects* and *language structure*. Once you have a firm grasp of grammar, learning to speak *intuitively* becomes easier, but it's a distinct skill. Understanding how the language functions must precede the ability to express yourself intuitively. This is because you might unintentionally impose the structure of your native language onto Thai, which is your second language; Thai follows a different *grammatical structure*.

After learning to make grammatically correct sentences, your language skills grow gradually stronger. Repeating words and phrases is the key; your *intuitive* feeling for Thai becomes gradually your second nature.

In Thai, the meaning is very much understood from the context. Whether the sentence refers to the *present, past* or *future*, depends on the type of main verb (Groups 1– 5) léɛu แล้ว is used with. We may also use *time words* or *tense markers* in order to make the meaning clear or place some extra emphasis.

The Thai way to talk about the *present, past* or *future* differs from English. English tenses do not help you understand the Thai language any better. Bringing English tenses into Thai may even make things more complicated. So, from the Secret 8 (Book II) onwards, we will leave the names of the English tenses out and concentrate on the Thai language and time aspect only.

Often, Thai people use only a *basic sentence* without *time words* or *tense markers*. Yet, there is not any difficulty in understanding whether the sentence refers to the *present, past* or *future time*. The meaning is understood from the context and from the type of main verbs (Groups 1–5) **lɛ́ɛu** แล้ว is used with.

Word order

When **lɛ́ɛu** แล้ว *already* is used as a time indicator, it normally comes at the end of the sentence.

In Thai, *time words* such as **tɔɔn-níi** ตอน นี้ *now* are often placed at the beginning of the sentence. Depending on the context, *time words* can also be placed at the end of the sentence before **lɛ́ɛu** แล้ว.

All *tense markers* such as **tsà** จะ *will* are always placed before the main verb.

Thai time aspect

In Thai, we normally talk about the three main time aspects as follows.

pàt-tsùbanna-kaan	ปัจจุบัน กาล	*present time, now* or *nowadays*
adìitta-kaan	อดีต กาล	*past time, completed actions*
anaakhótta-kaan	อนาคต กาล	*future time, future planning* or *prediction*

In this Secret, we shall review the *Thai time aspect*. The time aspect is understood *naturally* from the *context*. It can also be made clear by the *time words* or *tense markers: present, past* and *future.*

Natural time aspect

The *basic sentences,* which denote the *natural time aspect,* are translated into *English in italics.*

The term *natural time aspect* is understood as follows. When *basic sentences* are used without *time words* or *tense markers*, then the meaning is understood *naturally* from the context.

Usually, the *natural time aspect* refers to the *present time* or *completed actions* in the past. The outcome depends mainly on the *five verb groups,* **lέεu** แล้ว and from the *context.*

The *natural Thai time aspect* can be changed to reflect the *present, past* or *future* time by *time words* or *tense makers.*

English Tense

As we have already mentioned, English tenses are not very helpful in understanding the *Thai time aspect.*

English translations

Often there are two translations into English: one with *time words* or *tense markers* and one without them.

4. Overall meaning – the *Thai time aspect* and the *verb groups 1–5*

Try to make clear to yourself what overall meaning **lέεu** แล้ว plays in Secrets 1–7 as far as the *Thai time aspect* is concerned. Much depends on the context and the type of verbs **lέεu** แล้ว is used with. **lέεu** แล้ว makes the *bridge* between the *present state* and the *previous state* in the past or *future state.*

This is our last Secret when **lέεu** แล้ว is used as a *time indicator.* In Secrets 8–11 (Book II), **lέεu** แล้ว will be used as a *conjunction word.* Then, the grammatical function of **lέεu** แล้ว is very different.

It is important to understand that, in the *basic sentences,* the meaning in Thai is *naturally understood* from the context. The *natural time aspect* can differ depending on what *type of main verb*s

(Groups 1–5) lέεu ແล້ວ is used with. It is not the word lέεu ແล້ວ itself that determines the time aspect, but it makes the *natural time aspect* clear.

There are two types of verbs, *action verbs* and *non-action verbs*. However, we have divided the Thai verbs into *five different groups* in order to find out how the *Thai time aspect* is affected when lέεu ແล້ວ is placed at the end of the sentence. This is very important since the main verbs (Groups 1– 5) play a major role in how the sentences are understood.

When we wish to place some extra emphasis or change the focus in Thai, it can be done in two ways. First, by adding *time words (present, past* or *future)* into a sentence; then, the exact *timing of the action* is given, and the time aspect is clear.

Second, we may also use *tense markers* to emphasise the fact whether the action is happening *now*, has been *completed* in the past or *will happen* in the future.

In every language, there is a grammatical structure. However, it cannot be too heavily forced into the spoken language. Sometimes, the sentence is grammatically correct, but it does not sound good. Therefore, it is not used by native speakers.

This applies to lέεu ແล້ວ as well. In some context, it is better to leave it out or to replace it with some other indicator such as yùu อยู่ *state exists*. It depends on the feeling and usage of the language. In some context, lέεu ແล້ວ *already* is better translated into English as *now*.

There are only a few written grammar books in the Thai language. Most Thai grammar books are written in English by Westerners in cooperation with Thai professionals. Thais rely more on the intuitive usage of language.

However, as a foreigner, when you first learn to make grammatically correct sentences, your knowledge about the Thai language grows. Your intuitive expression will improve gradually. You become confident. Soon, you will speak like a Thai.

5. Spoken sentences translated and grammar explained

Study the details of each sentence in this Secret and make sure that you understand all the words and how Thai people express the *time aspect, present, past* and *future*.

Every sentence is translated into English with some grammatical explanations. We have also given "word-for-word" translations.

Transliterations, how words are pronounced in Thai, can be used alongside with the spoken audio file. You should be able to get the correct tone from the spoken audio file. It can also be checked from the transliterations since they have tone marks.

A. Sentences – *present, past* and *future*

1. Using basic sentences

lɛ́ɛu แล้ว *already*, as a time indicator, is commonly placed at the end of the sentence. When the time aspect is clearly understood from the context, there is no need for additional indicators.

In this section, there is only one translation into English because the *basic sentences* are used without *time words* or *tense markers*. Thai people understand the time aspect *naturally* from the context and types of verbs **lɛ́ɛu** แล้ว is used with.

Examples

1.1 Present

Question
   au ìik mái khá
   เอา อีก ไหม คะ
   take more "question" khá

Would you like to have some more?

Reply
   khɔ̀ɔp-khun khâ – *phɔɔ lɛ́ɛu* khâ
   ขอบ คุณ ค่ะ – พอ แล้ว ค่ะ
   thank-you – enough already khâ

Thank you! It is already enough. / It is enough now.

1.2 Past

Question
  khau pai năi *lέεu* khá
  เขา ไป ไหน แล้ว คะ
  he go where already khá

  Where did he go?

Reply
  pai duu năng *lέεu* khâ
  ไป ดู หนัง แล้ว ค่ะ
  go see movie already khâ

  He went to see a movie.

1.3 Future

Question
  khun hĭu mái khá
  คุณ หิว ไหม คะ
  you hungry question khá

  Are you hungry?

Reply
  hĭu khâ – *tɔ̂ng* pai kin-khâau *lέεu* khâ
  หิว ค่ะ – ต้อง ไป กิน ข้าว แล้ว ค่ะ
  hungry khâ – must go eat-rice already khâ

  Yes, I am hungry. I have to go to eat now.

Time aspect and basic sentences

- In the above sentences, there are not any *time words* or *tense markers*. Therefore, the time aspect is understood *naturally* from the context. That is called the *natural time aspect*.
- Comments below refer to the *replies* only!

Natural time aspect

- Sentence 1.1 reflects the *present time* since **phɔɔ** พอ *enough* is a *non-action verb* (Group 1).

- The English tense is the *Present Simple*.
- Sentence 1.2 reflects the *completed* action in the past since **lɛ́ɛu** แล้ว is used with *direction verb*s like **pai** ไป *to go* (Group 5).
- The English tense is *Past Simple*.
- Sentence 1.3 refers to the *future*. The *modal verb* **tɔ̂ng** ต้อง *must, have to* is normally associated with the *future time*.
- The same applies to the English language.

Notes
- **lɛ́ɛu** แล้ว is placed at the end of the sentence to emphasise the fact that a certain state or action has been *reached* or *must be reached*..
- Depending on the context, **lɛ́ɛu** แล้ว is sometimes better translated into English as *now* instead of *already*.

2. Using time words

In this section, the *time aspect* is made clear by the *time word*s such as **tɔɔn-níi** ตอน นี้ *now*, **mûua-waan** เมื่อวาน *yesterday* and **phrûng-níi** พรุ่ง นี้ *tomorrow* in order to tell when the action takes place.

When the *time words* and *tense markers* are omitted, the *Thai time aspect* normally changes.

The *basic sentences* denote the *natural time aspect*, which are translated into *English in italics*.

Examples

2.1 Present

Question
    kháu phûut phaasăa arai khá
    เขา พูด ภาษา อะไร คะ
    he speak language what khá
    What language does he speak?

Reply
>   **tɔɔn-níi** kháu phûut phaasǎa thai *lɛ́ɛu* khâ
>   ตอน นี้ เขา พูด ภาษา ไทย แล้ว ค่ะ
>   at-this he speak language Thai already khâ
>
>   **Now**, he already speaks Thai.
>   *He already speaks Thai.*

2.2 Past

Question
>   khun dâai-ráp wiisâa khun lɛ́ɛu rɯ̌ɯ-yang khá
>   คุณ ได้ รับ วีซ่า คุณ แล้ว หรือ ยัง คะ
>   you get-receive visa you already or-not khá
>
>   *Did you already get your visa or not?*

Reply
>   **mûɯa-waan** tʃán dâai-ráp *lɛ́ɛu* khâ
>   เมื่อวาน ฉัน ได้ รับ แล้ว ค่ะ
>   yesterday I get-receive already khâ
>
>   Yes, I received it already **yesterday**.
>   *Yes, I have already received it.*

2.3 Future

Question
>   **phrûng-níi** kháu pìt-thəəm *lɛ́ɛu* – tʃâi-mái khá
>   พรุ่ง นี้ เขา ปิด เทอม แล้ว ใช่ ไหม คะ
>   tomorrow he close-term already – "yes-question" khá
>
>   *Tomorrow, she will finish the school term, right?*

Reply
>   tʃâi khâ – **phrûng-níi** kháu pìt-thəəm *lɛ́ɛu* khâ
>   ใช่ ค่ะ – พรุ่งนี้ เขา ปิด เทอม แล้ว ค่ะ
>   yes khâ – tomorrow he close-term already khâ
>
>   Yes, she is going to finish her school term already **tomorrow**.
>   *Yes, she has already finished her school term.*

Time aspect and time words
- Comments below refer to the *replies* only!
- The *time aspect* is made clear by the *time words* **tɔɔn-níi** ตอน นี้ *now*, **mûua-waan** เมื่อวาน *yesterday* and **phrûng-níi** พรุ่งนี้ *tomorrow*.
- The English tenses are the *Present Simple, Past Simple* and *Future with going to*.

Natural time aspect
- If we omit the *future time words*, the *natural time aspect* refers to the *present time* in sentence 2.1 since **phûut** พูด *to speak* is a *general action verb* (Group 3).
- However, sentences 2.2–2.3 refer to the *completed actions* in the past since **dâai-ráp** ได้ รับ *to receive* is a *direction verb* (Group 5) and **pìt-thəəm** ปิด เทอม is a *specific action verb* (Group 4).
- The English tense is the *Present Perfect*.

Notes
- **lɛ́ɛu** แล้ว is placed at the end of the sentence to emphasise the fact that a certain state or action *has been reached* or *will be reached*.
- There is no *natural future time aspect* in Thai. The *natural time aspect* normally refers either to the *present time* or *completed action* in the past.
- In English, we can also talk about the future by using the *Present Simple*.

3. Using tense markers

In this section, the time aspect is made clear by the *tense markers* such as **kamlang** กำลัง *action in progress*, **yùu** อยู่ *state exists*, **khəəi** เคย *once, used to* and **tsà** จะ *will*.

When the *time words* and *tense markers* are omitted, the *Thai time aspect* normally changes.

The *basic sentences* denote the *natural time aspect,* which are translated into *English in italics.*

Examples

3.1 Present

Question
> kháu **kamlang** tham arai **yùu** khá
> เขา กำลัง ทำ อะไร อยู่ คะ
> he being do what be khá
>
> *What is he doing?*

Reply 1
> kháu **kamlang** tham-ngaan *lέεu* khâ
> เขา กำลัง ทำ งาน แล้ว ค่ะ
> he being do-work already khâ
>
> He is already work**ing**.
> *He is already working.*

Reply 2
> kháu tham-ngaan **yùu** khâ
> เขา ทำ งาน อยู่ ค่ะ
> he do-work be khâ
>
> He is work**ing**.
> *He is working.*

3.2 Past

Question
> khun **khəəi** pai thîiau pràthêet kamphuutʃaa mái
> คุณ เคย ไป เที่ยว ประเทศ กัมพูชา ไหม
> you once go trip country Cambodia "question"
>
> *Have you ever been to Cambodia?*

Reply
> tʃán **khəəi** pai *lɛ́ɛu* khâ
> ฉัน เคย ไป แล้ว ค่ะ
> I **once** go already khâ
>
> I **have** already been there.
> *I have already been there.*

3.3 Future

Question
> khun **tsà** tham man sèt mûɨa-rai khá
> คุณ จะ ทำ มัน เสร็จ เมื่อไร คะ
> you will do it finish when khá
>
> *When are you going to finish it?*

Reply
> **ìik-sǎam-wan tsà** sèt *lɛ́ɛu* khâ
> อีก สาม วัน จะ เสร็จ แล้ว ค่ะ
> more three day will finish already khâ
>
> **In three days**, it **will** already be finished.
> *It has already been finished.*

Time aspect and tense markers
- The focus can be made clear by *tense markers*.
- Comments below refer to the replies only!

Present time aspect
- Normally, the *present tense marker* **kamlang** กำลัง *action in progress* before the main verb denotes *actions* that happen at the *time of speaking*. Alternatively, the *present time indicator* **yùu** อยู่ *state exists* can be used.
- The English tense is the *Present Continuous*.

Past time
- **khəəi** เคย before the main verb denotes the fact that the action has happened *at least once* before now.
- The English tense is the *Present Perfect*.

Future time

- The *future time word* **iik-sǎam-wan** อีก สาม วัน *in three days* and the *future tense marker* **tsà** จะ *will* are used to make the *future time* clear.
- The English tense here is the *Future Simple*.

Natural time aspect

- Without *time words* or *tense markers*, replies 1 and 2 (sentence 3.1) would still refer to the *present time* since the main verb **tham-ngaan** ทำ งาน *to work* is a *general action verb* (Group 3).
- The English tense is the *Present Continuous*.
- The reply (sentence 3.2) would still refer to the *completed action* in the past since the main verb **pai** ไป *to go* is a *direction verb* (Group 5).
- The English tense is the *Present Perfect*.
- In sentence 3.3, the *natural time aspect* changes from the *future time* to refer to the *completed* action in the past since **sèt** ไป *to finish, to complete* is a *specific action verb* (Group 4).
- The English tense is the *Present Perfect*.

Notes

- **lɛ́ɛu** แล้ว is placed at the end of the sentence to emphasise the fact that a certain state or action *has been reached* or *will be reached*.
- There is no *natural future time aspect* in Thai. Normally, the *natural time aspect* refers either to the *present time* or *completed action in the past*.
- Therefore, when the sentences refer to the future, the *future time words* or *future tense markers* are often used to avoid misunderstanding.

4. Point of time – using **tâng-tɛ̀ɛ** ตั้ง แต่

   In this section, the point of time is made clear by the **tâng-tɛ̀ɛ** ตั้ง แต่ and by the *time phrases* such as the *present time word* **pii-níi** ปี นี้ *this year*, the *past time word* **yîisìp naa-thii thîi-kɔ̀ɔn** ยี่ สิบ นา ที ก่อน *twenty minutes ago* and from the *future time word* **dʉʉan-nâa** เดือน.

In addition, the *future tense marker* **tsà** จะ *will* is placed before the main verb.

When the **tâng-tɛ̀ɛ** ตั้ง แต่ *time phrases* and *tense markers* are omitted, the *Thai time aspect* normally changes.

The *basic sentences* denote the *natural time aspect*, which are translated into *English in italics*.

Examples

4.1 Present

Question
   pàt-tsùban-níi khwaam tə̀əp-too thaang sèet-thàkìt khɔ̌ɔng pràthêet-thai pen yang-ngai
   ปัจจุบัน นี้ ความ เติบ โต ทาง เศรษฐกิจ ของ ประเทศ ไทย เป็น ยังไง
   now-this matter excessively big way economy of country-Thai be how-many

   How is the economic situation in Thailand nowadays?

Reply
   dii khûn lɛ́ɛu – lɛ́ **tâng-tɛ̀ɛ pii-níi pen-tôn-pai** – kɔ̂ɔ **tsà** tsàrəən khûn yàang-rûuat-reu
   ดี ขึ้น แล้ว – และ ตั้ง แต่ ปี นี้ เป็น ต้น ไป – ก็ จะ เจริญ ขึ้น อย่าง รวด เร็ว
   good up already – and set-from year this be-start-go – also will flourish up as-speedy-fast

   It is already good, and **from this year onwards**, it **will** grow even faster.
   It is already good; it is growing even faster now.

4.2 Past

Question
 kháu ook-pai **tâng-tɛ̀ɛ mûua-rai** khráp
 เขา เลิก ไป ตั้ง แต่ เมื่อไร ครับ
 he out-go set-from when khráp
 When did he leave?

Reply
 kháu ɔ̀ɔk-pai **tâng-tɛ̀ɛ yîisìp naa-thii-kɔ̀ɔn** *lɛ́ɛu**
 เขา ออก ไป ตั้ง แต่ ยี่ สิบ นา ที ก่อน แล้ว
 he out-go set-from two-ten minute that-already
 He left **twenty minutes ago**.
 He has already left.

4.3 Future

Question
 khun **tsà** dâai khûn-ngən-duuan **mûua-rài** khá
 คุณ จะ ได้ รับ เงินเดือน เพิ่ม เมื่อไหร่ คะ
 you will get increase-money-month when khá
 When will you receive the salary increase?

Reply
 tsà dâai **lǎng-tsàak duuan-nâa pen-tôn-pai** *lɛ́ɛu* khâ
 จะ ได้ หลัง จาก เดือน หน้า เป็น ต้น ไป แล้ว ค่ะ
 will receive after-from month-next be-start-go already khâ
 I **am going** to receive it **after next month** already.
 I have already received it.

Point of time

- In the above sentences, the point of time is in the *present, past* and *future*.
- It is understood from the *present time word* **pii-níi** ปี นี้ *this year,* *past time word* **yîisìp naa-thii thîi-kɔ̀ɔn** ยี่ สิบ นา ที ที่ แล้ว *twenty minutes ago* and from the *future time word* **duuan-nâa** เดือน หน้า *next year.*

- **tâng-tèɛ** ตั้ง แต่ *since, from, onwards* is placed before the *point of time*.

Time aspect and the point of time

- Comments refer to the replies only!
- When the point of time is *now* or in the *future*, the sentence refers to the *future time*.
- In the sentences 4.1 and 4.3, the *future tense marker* **tsà** จะ *will* is used to emphasise the *future time aspect*.
- The English tenses are *Present Simple* and the *Future with going to*.
* In sentence 4.2, **yîisìp naa-thii thîi-kɔ̀ɔn** ยี่ สิบ นา ที ก่อน *twenty minutes ago*, **lɛ́ɛu** แล้ว is usually dropped.
- The sentence refers to the *completed action* in the past, and the *point of time* is in the *past*.
- The English tense is the *Past Simple*.

Natural time aspect

- Without *time phrases* or *tense markers* the reply in sentence 4.1 refers to the *present time* since **tsàrɔɔn** เจริญ *to grow, to flourish* is a *general action verb* (Group 3).
- The English tense is the *Present Continuous*.
- The sentences 4.2 and 4.3 refer to a *completed* action in the past since **ɔ̀ɔk-pai** ออกไป *to leave* and **dâai** ได้ *to receive, to get* are *direction verbs* (Group 5).
- The English tense is the *Present Perfect*.

Notes

- Often, **tâng-tèɛ** ตั้ง แต่ can be omitted and **pen-tôn-pai** เป็น ต้น ไป is used instead; it is placed after the *point of time*. The meaning is the same or very similar.
- **pen-tôn-pai** เป็น ต้น ไป is used only when the point of time is *now* or in the *future*.
- If the point of time is in the *past*, then **pen-tôn-maa** เป็น ต้น มา is used.

C. Language hints

lɛ́ɛu แล้ว *already* plays a much bigger role in grammatical terms than the English word *already*. This is because the Thai language has no tenses, and omitting **lɛ́ɛu แล้ว** may change the meaning of the sentence and the time aspect; the sentence may not be complete.

Even though **lɛ́ɛu แล้ว** *already* has a strong connection to the *present time*, it is also used in the sentences that refer to the *completed actions* in the past or even to the *future actions*.

The *time aspect* can be emphasised and made more clear by the *present, past* or *future time words*.

Examples

tɔɔn-níi	ตอน นี้	now
pàt-tsùban	ปัจจุบัน	nowadays
mûɯa-waan	เมื่อ วาน	yesterday
mûɯa-kɔ̀ɔn	เมื่อ ก่อน	before
phrûng-níi	พรุ่ง นี้	tomorrow

We may also use *tense markers* in order to focus on the *present, past* or *future time*.

Examples

kamlang	กำลัง	action in progress
yùu	อยู่	state exists
khəəi	เคย	once, used to
phûng	เพิ่ง	just, a moment ago
tsà	จะ	will

Point of time

The English meanings such as *since, from, onwards* may be expressed by the point of time and **tâng-tɛ̀ɛ ตั้ง แต่**.

We shall summarize **lɛ́ɛu แล้ว** as a *time indicator* in the following way.

a) **lɛ́ɛu แล้ว** brings the *past* into the *present*

In this language hints section, mostly *basic sentences* are used. Hence, the time aspect is *naturally* understood from the *context* and from the type of verbs (Groups 1–5) **lɛ́ɛu แล้ว** is used with.

In order to understand the *time indicator* **lɛ́ɛu แล้ว**, think in terms that it always has some connection to the *present state*. Depending on the context, we are "here and now" looking into the *present* (now) or into the *past* (previous state).

So, the term *natural time aspect* applies only to the *past* and the *present time*. The *present time* and the *past time* are something we know. Out of them, the *future* is born. However, the future time is not known. It can only be predicted.

When **lɛ́ɛu แล้ว** is used with *completed past time actions*, it creates the *bridge* between the *present* and the *past*. The action has happened *recently*.

We must give a few more examples here in order to clarify our standpoint. Consider the following expressions.

1. Present time

    When the *basic sentences* are used without *time words* or *tense markers*, the *natural time aspect* reflects normally the *present state of affairs*. The time aspect is understood from the type of verbs **lɛ́ɛu แล้ว** is associated with (Groups 1–3).

    In the following sections, there is only one translation into English since the *basic sentences* are used without *time words* or *tense markers*.

    Thai people understand the time aspect *naturally* from the context and types of verbs **lɛ́ɛu แล้ว** is used with.

Examples

1.1 *rót-tìt lέεu*
รถ ติด แล้ว
car-stuck already
There is already a traffic jam.

1.2 tʃán *tʃɔ̌ɔp* kháu *lέεu* khâ
ฉัน ชอบ เขา แล้ว ค่ะ
I like he already khâ
I already like him!

1.3 kháu *yùu* thîi-nîi *lέεu* khráp
เขา อยู่ ที่ นี่ แล้ว ครับ
he live place-this already khráp
He is staying here already.

1.4 kháu *tham-ngaan lέεu*
เขา ทำ งาน แล้ว
he do-work already
He is already working.

1.5 kháu *aasǎi* thîi lɔɔndɔɔn *lέεu*
เขา อาศัย งาน ที่ ลอนดอน แล้ว
he live at London already
He is already living in London.

Time aspect
- In the above sentences, there are not any *time words* or *tense markers*. Therefore, the time aspect is understood *naturally* from the context. That is called the *natural time aspect*.

Natural time aspect
- The focus falls *naturally* on the *present time* since **rót-tìt** รถ ติด *traffic jam* (to be car-stuck) and **tʃɔ̌ɔp** ชอบ *to like* are *non-action verbs* (Groups 1–2). **yùu** อยู่ *to live, to stay* and **tham-ngaan**

ทำ งาน *to work* and **aasǎi** อาศัย *to live* are *general action verbs* (Group 3).
- The English tenses are the *Present Simple* and *Present Continuous*.

Notes
- **lɛ́ɛu** แล้ว creates the *bridge* between the *present* and the *past*. *"It is true now." "Before, it was different."*
- The *natural time aspect* reflects the *present time*.

2. Recently completed actions
- When **lɛ́ɛu** แล้ว is used with *specific action verbs* or *direction verbs* (Groups 4–5), the sentences denote the *recently completed actions*. **lɛ́ɛu** แล้ว tells that it is *now done; it is already the case*.

Examples

2.1 tʃán *kin* kaafɛɛ *lɛ́ɛu*
    ฉัน กิน กาแฟ แล้ว
    I eat coffee already

    I have already been drinking coffee.

2.2 kháu *maa* lɛ́ɛu
    เขา มา แล้ว
    he come already

    He has already arrived.

2.3 kháu *pai* Udɔɔn *lɛ́ɛu*
    เขา ไป อุดร แล้ว
    he go Udon already

    He has already gone to Udon.

2.4 tʃán *sòng* phátsàdù *lɛ́ɛu*
    ฉัน ส่ง พัสดุ แล้ว
    I send parcel already

    I have sent the parcel already.

Time aspect

- In the above sentences, there are not any *time words* or *tense markers*. Therefore, the time aspect is understood *naturally* from the context. That is called the *natural time aspect*.

Natural time aspect

- The *natural time aspect* reflects the *completed actions* in the past since **kin** กิน *to eat* is a *specific action verb* (Group 4), and **maa** มา *to come,* **pai** ไป *to go* and **sòng** ส่ง *to send* are *direction verbs* (Group 5).
- The English tenses are the *Present Perfect Continuous* and *Present Perfect*.

Notes

- Even though the action has taken place before now, the focus of **lɛ́ɛu** แล้ว is on the *present time*. **lɛ́ɛu** แล้ว connects the action with the *present time*.
- **lɛ́ɛu** แล้ว makes the *bridge* between the *present* and the *past*. The action has been *completed*. It is *done now*. The action has happened *recently; it is already the case*.

So, what have we learned?

1. When **lɛ́ɛu** แล้ว is used as a *time indicator* after the main verb, it normally comes at the end of the sentence.

2. We have used here several English *tenses* for seemingly the same Thai structure. All English tenses have one common tense component *"present."* (Present Simple, Present Continuous, Present Perfect, Present Perfect Continuous).

3. Even though we should not try to understand the *time indicator* **lɛ́ɛu** แล้ว through the English tenses, we can try to understand English tenses with the help of **lɛ́ɛu** แล้ว. The action has already taken place, and **lɛ́ɛu** แล้ว makes the *bridge* between the *present* and the *past*.

It is often said that the above English tenses, used here, have a strong or at least some connection to the *present state;* even if the action has been *completed* in the past.

4. The *basic sentences* with **lɛ́ɛu แล้ว** are usually understood *naturally* by Thais as a *present* or *recently completed* action in the *past*. The overall conclusion is that we can conveniently express the *Thai time aspect* without *time words* or *tense markers*.

5. **lɛ́ɛu แล้ว** makes the action become a *state*, which refers to the *past* and *present*. The *natural time aspect* is determined by **lɛ́ɛu แล้ว** and by the verb groups 1–5.

b) Different ways to express the *present time* with **lɛ́ɛu แล้ว**

lɛ́ɛu แล้ว plays an important role when expressing the *present time* in Thai. We have mainly three main types of the *present time* activities:

1. Things which are *true now* with *non-action verbs* (Groups 1–2).
2. Actions that are happening *now*, at the time of speaking *with general action verbs* (Group 3).
3. *Ongoing actions* which have started earlier and are *still going on* (the duration of time).

When **lɛ́ɛu แล้ว** is used with the above three verb categories, it determines the *natural time aspect* in Thai.

1. Non-action verbs (Groups 1–2) are normally associated with actions, which are *true now*.

When **lɛ́ɛu แล้ว** is placed after *non-action verbs* (Groups 1–2), the sentence usually denotes the *Present Simple* in English.

In this section, there is only one translation into English since the *basic sentences* are used without *time words* or *tense markers*. Thai people understand the time aspect *naturally* from the context and type of verbs **lɛ́ɛu แล้ว** is used with.

Examples

1.1 Question
phûuan khun pen yang-ngai bâang
เพื่อน คุณ เป็น ยังไง บ้าง
friend you be like-how some

How is your friend?

Reply
sàbaai-dii lέεu khâ
สบาย ดี แล้ว ค่ะ
well-good-already khâ

He is already well (now).

1.2 Question
khun kháu-tsai mái khá
คุณ เข้า ใจ ไหม คะ
you enter-heart "question" khá

Do you understand?

Reply
khâu-tsai lέεu khâ
เข้า ใจ แล้ว ค่ะ
enter-heart already khâ

I understand already. / I understand now.

Time aspect
- Comments below refer to the replies only!
- In the above sentences, there are not any *time words* or *tense markers*. Therefore, the time aspect is understood *naturally* from the context. That is called the *natural time aspect.*

Natural time aspect
- The *natural time aspect* refers to the *present time* since **dii** ดี *good* (Group 1) and **khâu-tsai** เข้า ใจ (Group 2) *to understand* are *non-action verbs,* which are followed by **lέεu** แล้ว.
- The English tense is the *Present Simple.*

Notes

- Normally, when **lɛ́ɛu** แล้ว is placed directly after *non-action verbs* (Groups 1–2), the sentences are associated with the *present time* in relation to the *past*.
- **lɛ́ɛu** แล้ว makes the *bridge* between the *present* and the *past*.

2. General action verbs (Group 3) normally reflect actions that are happening *now, at the time of speaking* or *nowadays*.

   When **lɛ́ɛu** แล้ว is placed after *general action verbs* (Group 3), the sentences are usually expressed in English by the *Present Continuous*.

   - However, depending on the context, the *general action verbs* (Group 3) can sometimes also denote a *completed action* in the past.

Examples

2.1 Question
khun tham-ngaan rɯ̌ɯ-plàu
คุณ ทำ งาน หรือ เปล่า
you do-work or-not

Are you working or not?

Reply
khâ – tʃǎn *tham-ngaan* thîi ráan-aahǎan *lɛ́ɛu* khâ
ค่ะ – ฉัน ทำ งาน ที่ ร้าน อาหาร แล้ว ค่ะ
yes khâ – I do-work at shop-food already khâ

Yes, I am working at a restaurant nowadays.

2.2 Question
kháu sɔ̌ɔn phaasǎa arai *lɛ́ɛu* khá
เขา สอน ภาษา อะไร แล้ว คะ
he teach language what already khá

What language is he teaching?

Secret 7

Reply

    kháu *sɔ̌ɔn* phaasǎa-thai *lɛ́ɛu* khâ
    เขา สอน ภาษา ไทย แล้ว ค่ะ
    he teach language-Thai already khâ

    He is teaching Thai now.

2.3 Question

    khun yùu thîi-nîi mái khá
    คุณ อยู่ ที่ นี่ ไหม คะ
    you live place-this "question" khá

    Are you living here?

Reply

    khâ – tʃán *yùu* thîi-nîi *lɛ́ɛu* khâ
    ค่ะ – ฉัน อยู่ ที่ นี่ แล้ว ค่ะ
    yes – I live place-this already khâ

    Yes, I am living here already / now.

Time aspect

- Comments below refer to the replies only!
- In the above sentences, there are not any *time words* or *tense markers*. Therefore, the time aspect is understood *naturally* from the context. That is called the *natural time aspect*.

Natural time aspect

- The *natural time aspect* refers to the *present time* since **tham-ngaan** ทำ งาน *to work*, **sɔ̌ɔn** สอน *to teach* and **yùu** อยู่ *to live* are *general action verbs* (Group 3), which are followed by **lɛ́ɛu** แล้ว.
- The action is normally happening at the *time of speaking* or *nowadays*.
- The English tense is the *Present Continuous*.

Notes

- Normally, the *general action verbs* (Group 3) are associated with the *present time*.
- **lɛ́ɛu** แล้ว makes the *bridge* between the *present* and the *past*.

- However, depending on the context, the *general action verbs* (Group 3) can sometimes also denote a *completed* action in the past.

3. Ongoing actions which have started earlier and are *still going on* and the *duration of time*.

    When **lɛ́ɛu** แล้ว is placed after the *duration of time,* the sentence usually reflects the *Present Perfect Continuous* in English.

    In this section, the *duration of time* is made clear by the *time words* such as **sìi pii** สี่ ปี *four years* and **sǎam dʉʉan** สาม เดือน *three months* that are directly followed by **lɛ́ɛu** แล้ว.

    When the *duration of time phrases* and *tense markers* are omitted, the *Thai time aspect* normally changes.

    The *basic sentences* denote the *natural time aspect,* which are translated into *English in italics*.

Examples

3.1 Question
    khun yùu thîi krungthêep naan thâu-rai lɛ́ɛu khá
    คุณ อยู่ ที่ กรุงเทพ นาน เท่าไร แล้ว คะ
    you stay at Bangkok long how-many already khá

    How long have you been living in Bangkok?

Reply
    tʃán *yùu* thîi krungthêep **maa sìi pii** *lɛ́ɛu*
    ฉัน อยู่ ที่ กรุงเทพ มา สี่ ปี แล้ว
    I stay at Bangkok come four year already

    I have already been living in Bangkok **for four years**.
    I already live in Bangkok. / I live in Bangkok now.

3.2 Question

kháu khàp rót-théksîi naan thâu-rai *lɛ́ɛu* khá
เขา ขับ รถ แท็กซี่ นาน เท่าไร แล้ว คะ
he drive car-taxi long how-many already khá

How long has he already been driving a taxi?

Reply

kháu khàp rót-théksîi **maa sǎam duuan** *lɛ́ɛu* khâ
เขา ขับ รถ แท็กซี่ มา สาม เดือน แล้ว ค่ะ
he drive a car-taxi come three month already khâ

He has already been driving a taxi **for three months**.
He already drives a taxi. / He drives a taxi now.

Duration of time

- Comments below refer to the replies only!
- **sìi pii** สี่ ปี *four years* and **sǎam duuan** สาม เดือน *three months* are directly followed by **lɛ́ɛu** แล้ว here.
- The helping verb **maa** มา is placed before the duration of time to emphasise the fact that the action is *coming from the past*.

Time aspect

- The time aspect is understood *naturally* from the *context* (Group 3) and from the *duration of time*.
- The English tense is the *Present Perfect Continuous*.

Natural time aspect

- When the duration of time is dropped, the focus changes.
- The *natural time aspect* refers to the *present time* since **yùu** อยู่ *to live* and **khàp rót** ขับ รถ *to drive a car* are *general action verbs* (Group 3).
- The English tense is the *Present Simple*.

Notes

- In the above replies there are not any *time words* or *tense markers*.
- However, the *duration of time* affects the time aspect.

- When **lɛ́ɛu** แล้ว is placed directly after a *duration of time*, it usually denotes meanings like *up to now, so far, until now*, etc.
- **lɛ́ɛu** แล้ว makes a *bridge* between the *present* and the *past*.

c) Completed actions in the past

Often, Thai people understand the time aspect *naturally* from the context and types of verbs **lɛ́ɛu** แล้ว is used with.

We have shown in the above that when **lɛ́ɛu** แล้ว is placed after *non-action verbs* (adjectives and state verbs (Groups 1–2) or *general action verbs* (Group 3), the sentence *naturally* reflects the *present time aspect* in Thai.

When **lɛ́ɛu** แล้ว is placed after *specific verbs* or *direction verbs* (Groups 4–5), the sentences normally refer to the *past*. The English tense is the *Present Perfect*. This type of sentences *often* express actions, which have happened *recently*.

In this section, there is only one translation into English since the *basic sentences* are used without *time words* or *tense markers*. Thai people understand the time aspect *naturally* from the context and type of verbs **lɛ́ɛu** แล้ว is used with.

Examples

1. Question
    kin *lɛ́ɛu* rǔu-yang
    กิน แล้ว หรือ ยัง
    eat already-or-not

    Have you already eaten?

Reply
    kin lɛ́ɛu khâ
    กิน แล้ว ค่ะ
    eat already khâ

    Yes, I have already eaten.

2. Question
khun hěn mái
คุณ เห็น ไหม
you see "question"

Have you seen it?

Reply
hěn lɛ́ɛu khâ
เห็น แล้ว ค่ะ
see already khâ

Yes, I have seen it.

3. Question
khun bɔ̀ɔk kháu *lɛ́ɛu* rǔɯ-yang
คุณ บอก เขา แล้ว หรือ ยัง
you tell he already-or-not

Have you already told him?

Reply
bɔ̀ɔk lɛ́ɛu khâ
บอก แล้ว ค่ะ
tell already khâ

Yes, I have already told him.

Time aspect
- Comments below refer to the replies only!
- In the above sentences, there are not *time words* or *tense markers*. Therefore, the time aspect is understood naturally from the context. That is called the *natural time aspect*.

Natural time aspect
- The *natural time aspect* refers to the *completed* actions in the past since **kin** กิน *to eat* and **hěn** เห็น *to see* are *specific action verb*s (Group 4) and **bɔ̀ɔk** บอก *to tell* is a *direction verb* (Group 5).

- The *Thai time aspect* is understood from the context and from the type of action verbs lέεu แล้ว is used with.
- The English tense is the *Present Perfect*.

Notes

- The *natural time aspect* normally refers to the *recently completed* action in the past.
- lέεu แล้ว makes the *bridge* between the *present* and the *past*.

d) More examples about expressing Thai time aspect

In this section, there is only one translation into English since the *basic sentences* are used without *time words* or *tense markers*.

Thai people understand the time aspect *naturally* from the context and types of verbs lέεu แล้ว is used with.

Examples

1. Question
   khun yàak tham arai khá
   คุณ อยาก ทำ อะไร คะ
   you want do what khá

   What would you like to do?

   Reply
   mâi yàak tham arai – tʃán nùuai lέεu khâ
   ไม่ อยาก ทำ อะไร – ฉัน เหนื่อย แล้ว ค่ะ
   no want do what – I tired already khâ

   I don't want to do anything. I am already tired.

2. Question
   rót-fai tsà maa mûua-rai
   รถ ไฟ จะ มา เมื่อไร
   car-fire will come when

   When is the train coming?

Reply
pai lɛ́ɛu khâ
ไป แล้ว ค่ะ
go already khâ
It has gone already.

3. Question
aakàat tsà yen *lɛ́ɛu* – tʃâi mái khá
อากาศ จะ เย็น แล้ว – ใช่ ไหม คะ
weather will cold already – yes "question" khá
The weather is already getting cold, right?

Reply
tʃâi khâ – tông hăa sûɯa-kan-năau *lɛ́ɛu* khâ
ใช่ ค่ะ – ต้อง หา เสื้อ กัน หนาว แล้ว ค่ะ
yes khâ – must search cloth-protect-cold already khâ
Right! We must look for our overcoats now.

Time aspect
- Comments below refer to the replies only!
- In the above replies, there are not any *time words* or *tense markers*. Therefore, the *time aspect* is understood *naturally* from the context. We call it the *natural time aspect*.

Natural time aspect
- The reply in sentence 1 refers to the *present time* since **lɛ́ɛu** แล้ว is placed after the *non-action verb* **nùuai** เหนื่อย *to be tired* (Group 1).
- The English tense is the *Present Simple*.
- The reply in sentence 2 reflects *naturally* the *completed action* in the past since **lɛ́ɛu** แล้ว is used with the *direction verb* **pai** ไป *to go* (Group 5).
- The English tense is the *Present Perfect*.
- The reply in the sentence 3 reflects the *present time plan* since the *modal verb* **tông** ต้อง *must* is placed before the main verb **hăa** หา *to find*.

- The second action happens because of the first action.
- The modal verb *must* has no tense in English. It emphasises the necessity of doing something.

Notes

- The *modal verb* **tôñg** ต้อง *must, have to* is normally associated with the *future time*.

e) Anticipated future actions

In the previous sections, the *present time* and the *past time* is expressed without *time words* or *tense markers*. The time aspect is understood *naturally* from the verb groups and **lέεu** แล้ว.

The term *natural time aspect* does not directly apply to the *future actions*. Hence, Thai people like to use the *future time words* or *future tense marker* **tsà** จะ *will* when talking about the *future*.

However, when the future tense is clearly understood from the context, there is no need for any additional indicators.

In this section, there are two translations into English. The future time aspect is made clear by the *future time words* such as **ìik-sǎam-wan** อีก สาม วัน *in three days*, **duuan-nâa** เดือน หน้า *next month* and **phrûng-níi** พรุ่งนี้ *tomorrow* and by the *future tense marker* **tsà** จะ *will*.

When the *time words* and *tense markers* are omitted, the *Thai time aspect* normally changes.

The *basic sentences* denote the *natural time aspect,* which are translated into *English in italics*.

Examples

1. Question
khun tsà tham man sèt mûua-rai khráp
คุณ จะ ทำ มัน เสร็จ เมื่อไร ครับ
you will do it finish when khráp

   When are you going to finish it?

Reply
ìik-sǎam-wan tsà sèt *lɛ́ɛu* khâ
อีก สาม วัน จะ เสร็จ แล้ว ค่ะ
more-three-day will finish already khâ

It **will** be finished **in three days.**
It has already been finished.

2. Question
khun súu rôt-mài lɛ́ɛu mái khá
คุณ ซื้อ รถ ใหม่ แล้ว ไหม คะ
you buy car-new already question khá

Have you already bought a car?

Reply
yang – duuan-nâa tʃán **tsà** súu *lɛ́ɛu* khâ
ยัง – เดือน หน้า ฉัน จะ ซื้อ แล้ว ค่ะ
not-yet – month-next I will buy already khâ

Not yet. I **will** buy it **next month.**
I have already bought it.

3. Question
tsəə-kan phrûng-níi dâai mái khá
เจอ กัน พรุ่งนี้ ได้ ไหม คะ
meet-together tomorrow can "question" khá

Shall we meet tomorrow?

Reply
mâi-dâai khâ – **phrûng-níi tsà** pai tàang-tsangwàt *lɛ́ɛu* khâ
ไม่ ได้ ค่ะ – พรุ่งนี้ จะ ไป ต่าง จัง หวัด แล้ว ค่ะ
no-can khâ – tomorrow will go different-province already khâ

It is not possible. **Tomorrow**, I am **going to** go to the countryside.
It is not possible. I have already gone to the countryside.

Future time aspect
- Comments below refer to the replies only!

- The *future time words* **ìik-sǎam-wan** อีก สาม วัน *in three days,* **duuan-nâa** เดือน หน้า *next month* and **phrûng-níi** พรุ่งนี้ *tomorrow* are used to give the exact timing of the action.
- The *future tense marker* **tsà** จะ *will* is placed before the action verb to *emphasise* the *future time aspect*.
- The English tenses are the *Future Simple* and the *Future with going to*.

Natural time aspect

- If we drop the *time words* and the *future tense marker* in the above sentences, the *natural time aspect* would refer to *completed* actions in the past since the main verbs **sèt** เสร็จ *to finish* and **súu** ซื้อ *to buy* are *specific action verbs* (Group 4) and **pai** ไป *to go* is a *direction verb* (Group 5).
- The English tense is the *Present Perfect*.

Notes

- **lɛ́ɛu** แล้ว makes the *bridge* between the *present, past* and the *future time*.
- There is not any *natural future time aspect* in Thai. However, sometimes *future actions* are understood from the context. Then, the *future time words* or *future tense markers* are normally omitted.

f) Using **tâng-tɛ̀ɛ** ตั้ง แต่ – present, past and future

1. The point of time in the present time, *now*

   In this section, there are two translations into English. **tâng-tɛ̀ɛ** ตั้ง แต่ is placed before the point of time, such as **wan-níi** วัน นี้ *today*. In addition, the *modal verb* **nâa-tsà** น่า จะ *should* is placed before the main verb.

   When the point of time is in the *present*, we can use **pen-tôn-pai** เป็น ต้น ไป *from now onwards* after the *point of time* to place some extra emphasis.

   When the **tâng-tɛ̀ɛ** ตั้ง แต่ *time phrases* and *tense markers* are omitted, the *Thai time aspect* normally changes.

The *basic sentences* denote the *natural time aspect,* which are translated into *English in italics.*

Examples

Question
tɔɔn-níi khun sàbaai dii lɛ́ɛu – tʃâi mái khráp
ตอน นี้ คุณ สบาย ดี แล้ว – ใช่ ไหม ครับ
at-this you well good already – yes "question" khráp
Now, you are already well, right?

Reply
mâi nɛ̂ɛ-tsai – khít wâa **tâng-tɛ̀ɛ wan-níi pen-tôn-pai** – tʃán nâa-tsà hăai lɛ́ɛu
ไม่ แน่ ใจ – คิด ว่า ตั้ง แต่ วัน นี้ เป็น ต้น ไป – ฉัน น่า จะ หาย แล้ว
no sure-heart – think that set-from day-this be-start-go – I should-will well already

I am not sure. I think **from today onwards**, I should be fine.
I am not sure. I think I should be fine now.

Time aspect
- Comments below refer to the replies only!
- The point of time is expressed by the *present time word* **wan-níi** วัน นี้ *today.*
- **tâng-tɛ̀ɛ** ตั้ง แต่ *from* is placed before the point of time.
- We have also used **pen-tôn-pai** เป็น ต้น ไป to emphasise the fact that the point of time is from *today onwards.*
- The starting point is at the *present time, now.*
- However, the second clause is going to happen in the *future.*
- The English tense is the *Present Simple.*

Natural time aspect
- If the **tâng-tɛ̀ɛ** ตั้ง แต่ *time phrase* is omitted, then the *natural time aspect* refers to the *present time* since **hăai** หาย *to be cured* is a *non-action verb* (Group 2).
- The English tense is the *Present Simple.*

Notes

- We may drop **tâng-tɛ̂ɛ** ตั้ง แต่ and use **pen-tôn-pai** เป็น ต้น ไป *from, onwards* instead, which is placed after the *point of time*, and the meaning is the same or very similar.
- **lɛ́ɛu** แล้ว is placed at the end of the sentence to emphasise the fact that a certain state or action *will be reached*.

2. The point of time in the past – *ongoing action "up to now"*

- When the point of time is in the past, and the action is still going on, we can use **pen-tôn-maa** เป็น ต้น มา *until now* to give the statement some more emphasis.

Examples

2.1 khun riian phaasǎa thai tâng-tɛ̂ɛ mûua-rai
คุณ เรียน ภาษาไทย ตั้ง แต่ เมื่อไร
you study language Thai set-from where

Since when have you been studying Thai?

Reply 1

phǒm riian phaasǎa thai **tâng-tɛ̂ɛ pii-kɔ̀ɔn pen-tôn-maa** *lɛ́ɛu*
ผม เรียน ภาษา ไทย ตั้ง แต่ ปี ก่อน เป็น ต้น มา แล้ว
I study language Thai set-from year-before be-start-come already

I have already been studying Thai **since last year**.
I am already studying Thai.

Reply 2

phǒm riian phaasǎa thai **tâng-tɛ̂ɛ pii-kɔ̀ɔn** *lɛ́ɛu*
ผม เรียน ภาษา ไทย ตั้ง แต่ ปี ก่อน แล้ว
I study language Thai set-from year-before already

I have already been studying Thai **since last year**.
I am already studying Thai.

Reply 3

    phǒm riian phaasǎa thai **pii-kɔ̀ɔn pen-tôn-maa** *lɛ́ɛu*
    ผม เรียน ภาษา ไทย ปี ก่อน เป็น ต้น มา แล้ว
    I study language Thai year-before be-start-come already

    I have already been studying Thai **since last year**.
    I am already studying Thai.

Time aspect
- Comments below refer to the replies only!
- The above sentences can be translated into English the same. The difference is only on the emphasis.
- The starting point of time in the past is expressed by **pii kɔ̀ɔn** ปี ก่อน *last year*.
- **tâng-tɛ̀ɛ** ตั้ง แต่ *since* is placed before the point of time.
- **pen-tôn-maa** เป็น ต้น มา *until now* after the point of time is optional.
- **lɛ́ɛu** แล้ว is placed at the end of the sentence to emphasise the fact that a certain state or action *has been reached, "up to now"*.
- The English tense is the *Present Perfect Continuous*.

Natural time aspect

    If **tâng-tɛ̀ɛ** ตั้ง แต่ *time phrases* and **pen-tôn-maa** เป็น ต้น มา *until now* are omitted, the *natural time aspect* refers to the *present time* since **riian** เรียน *to study* is a *general action verb* (Group 3).

Notes
- We may drop **tâng-tɛ̀ɛ** ตั้ง แต่ and use **pen-tôn-maa** เป็น ต้น มา *until now* instead, and the meaning is the same or very similar.

3. The point of time in the past – *action completed*

3.1 Question
    kháu ɔ̀ɔk-pai tâng-tɛ̀ɛ mûua-rai khráp
    เขา ออก ไป ตั้ง แต่ เมื่อไร ครับ
    he out-go set-from when khráp

    When did he leave?

Reply 1

kháu ɔ̀ɔk-pai **tâng-tɛ̀ɛ yîisìp naathii kɔ̀ɔn** *lɛ́ɛu* khráp
เขา ออก ไป ตั้ง แต่ ยี่ สิบ นาที ก่อน แล้ว ครับ
he out-go set-from two-ten minute before already khráp

He left **twenty minutes ago**.
He has already left.

Reply 2

kháu ɔ̀ɔk-pai **yîisìp naathii kɔ̀ɔn** *lɛ́ɛu* khráp
เขา ออก ไป ยี่ สิบ นาที ก่อน แล้ว ครับ
he out-go two-ten minute before already khráp

He left **twenty minutes ago**.
He has already left.

Time aspect
- Comments below refer to the replies only!
- The point of time is expressed by the **yîisìp naa-thii kɔ̀ɔn** ยี่ สิบ นาที ก่อน *twenty minutes ago*
- **lɛ́ɛu** แล้ว is placed at the end of the sentence to emphasise the fact that a certain state or action *has been reached, "up to now"*.
- The English tense is the *Past Simple*.

Natural time aspect
- If the *time phrases* are omitted, the *natural time aspect* still refers to the *completed* action in the past since **ɔ̀ɔk-pai** ออก ไป *to leave* is a *direction verb* (Group 5).
- The English tense is the *Present Perfect*.

Notes
- **tâng-tɛ̀ɛ** ตั้ง แต่ can be dropped. **yîisìp naa-thii kɔ̀ɔn** ยี่ สิบ นาที ก่อน would be enough, and the meaning is the same or very similar.
- **tâng-tɛ̀ɛ** ตั้ง แต่ cannot be translated into English here as *since*. We need to use the adverb *ago* in English because the action has been completed.

4. The point of time in the *future*

When the point of time is in the *future*, we can use **pen-tôn-pai** เป็น ต้น ไป *from, onwards* to place some extra emphasis on the *future time*.

4.1 Question

khun tham man sèt dɯɯan-nâa dâai mái khá
คุณ ทำ มัน เสร็จ เดือน หน้า ได้ ไหม คะ
you do it finish month-next can "question" khá

You are going to finish it next month, right?

Reply 1

mâi-dâai khâ – **tâng-tɛ̀ɛ aathít-nâa pen-tôn-pai** – tʃán tsà klàp tàang-tsangwat *lɛ́ɛu*
ไม่ ได้ ค่ะ – ตั้ง แต่ อาทิตย์ หน้า เป็น ต้น ไป – ฉัน จะ กลับ ต่าง จังหวัด แล้ว
no can khâ – set-from week-next be-start-go – I will return different-province already

It cannot be done; **from the next week onwards**, I **will** already have returned to the countryside.
It cannot be done. I have already returned to the countryside.

Reply 2

mâi-dâai khâ – **aathít-nâa pen-tôn-pai** – tʃán tsà klàp tàang-tsangwat *lɛ́ɛu*
ไม่ ได้ ค่ะ – อาทิตย์ หน้า เป็น ต้น ไป – ฉัน จะ กลับ ต่าง จังหวัด แล้ว
no can khâ – week-next be-start-go – I will return different-province already

It cannot be done; **from the next week onwards**, I **will** already have returned to the countryside.
It cannot be done. I have already returned to the countryside.

Reply 3

mâi-dâai khâ – **aathít-nâa** – tʃán **tsà** klàp tàang-tsangwat *lɛ́ɛu*
ไม่ ได้ ค่ะ – อาทิตย์ หน้า – ฉัน จะ กลับ ต่าง จังหวัด แล้ว
no can khâ – week-next – I will return different-province already

It cannot be done. **Next week,** I **will** already be in the countryside.
It cannot be done. I have already returned to the countryside.

Reply 4

mâi-dâai khâ – **phrɔ́-wâa aathít-nâa pen-tôn-pai** – tʃán **tsà** klàp tàang-tsangwat *lɛ́ɛu*
ไม่ ได้ ค่ะ – เพราะ ว่า อาทิตย์ หน้า เป็น ต้น ไป – ฉัน จะ กลับ ต่าง จังหวัด แล้ว
no can khâ – because-that week-next be-start-go – I will return different-province already

It cannot be done **because from the next week onwards,** I **will** already have returned to the countryside.
It cannot be done because I have already returned to the countryside.

Reply 5

mâi-dâai khâ – **phrɔ́-wâa-tâng-tɛ̀ɛ aathít-nâa pen-tôn-pai** – tʃán **tsà** klàp tàang-tsangwat *lɛ́ɛu*
ไม่ ได้ ค่ะ – เพราะ ว่า ตั้ง แต่ อาทิตย์ หน้า เป็น ต้น ไป – ฉัน จะ กลับ ต่าง จังหวัด แล้ว
no can khâ – because-that-set-but week-next be-start-go – I will return different-province already

It cannot be done **because/since from the next week onwards,** I **will** already have returned to the countryside.
It cannot be done because I have already returned to the countryside.

Time aspect

- Comments below refer to the replies only!

- The point of time is expressed by the *future time word* **aathít-nâa** อาทิตย์ หน้า *next year*.
- We have also used the *future tense marker* **tsà** จะ *will* in the second clause (replies 1–5).
- **lɛ́ɛu** แล้ว is placed at the end of the sentence to emphasise the fact that a certain state or action *will be reached*.

Natural time aspect

- If the *time phrases* and *future tense marker* **tsà** จะ are omitted, the *natural time aspect* refers to a *completed action* in the past since **klàp** กลับ *to return* is a *direction verb* (Group 5).

Notes

- Reply 1: **tâng-tɛ̀ɛ** ตั้ง แต่ *from* is a time related conjunction word. It is used here with the point of time **aathít-nâa** อาทิตย์ หน้า *next week*. **pen-tôn-pai** เป็น ต้น ไป *onwards* is optional.
- Reply 2: **tâng-tɛ̀ɛ** ตั้ง แต่ has been dropped and **pen-tôn-pai** เป็น ต้น ไป *onwards* is used after the point of time. This reply emphasises the fact that from **aathít-nâa** อาทิตย์ หน้า *next week onwards* it will be like that.
- Reply 3: Both **tâng-tɛ̀ɛ** ตั้ง แต่ and **pen-tôn-pai** เป็น ต้น ไป have been dropped. The point of time **aathít-nâa** อาทิตย์ หน้า *next year* is used alone. This is a simple sentence without emphasis.
- Reply 4: **phrɔ́-wâa** เพราะ ว่า *because* emphasises the cause. It points out why the action cannot happen. **pen-tôn-pai** เป็น ต้น ไป *onwards* is optional.
- Reply 5: **phrɔ́-wâa-tâng-tɛ̀ɛ** เพราะ ว่า ตั้ง แต่ *because-from* emphasises both the time and the cause. **pen-tôn-pai** เป็น ต้น ไป *onwards* is optional.

The difference between the above replies is very subtle. Thai people see the obvious difference in meaning between the replies 1 and 4. **tâng-tɛ̀ɛ** ตั้ง แต่ refers to *time only* even though there is a causative connotation in the sentence.

However, in English we can express causation with the conjunction words *since* and *because*. *Since* in English refers to *time* and to *causation* while *because* refers only to causation. *Since* in English expresses milder *causation*.

The question may be asked: can **tâng-tɛ̀ɛ** ตั้ง แต่ be used as a *causative conjunction* in Thai? Perhaps the answer is no. However, when the sentence is written in such a way that there is a causative relation, then the translation into English can be *since* or *because*.

A piece of advice would be to use **phrɔ́-wâa** เพราะ ว่า *because* for the causative sentences in Thai. **tâng-tɛ̀ɛ** ตั้ง แต่ is used for the sentences that refer to the *time only*. However, if you wish to emphasise that there is a causative and time connotation, **phrɔ́-wâa-tâng-tɛ̀ɛ** เพราะ ว่า ตั้ง แต่ may be used. That would be translated into English as *since*.

5. Grammatical summary of **tâng-tɛ̀ɛ** ตั้ง แต่

The conjunction **tâng-tɛ̀ɛ** ตั้ง แต่ has a wide semantic usage in Thai. It can be translated into English as *from, since, onwards, ago...*

When the **tâng-tɛ̀ɛ** ตั้ง แต่ *time phrases* and *tense markers* are omitted, the *Thai time aspect* normally changes.

The *basic sentences* denote the *natural time aspect*, which are translated into *English in italics*.

Examples

5.1 **tâng-tɛ̀ɛ kháu yáai-pai kràbìi** – tʃán mâi dâai tsəə kháu ìik-ləəi
ตั้ง แต่ เขา ย้าย ไป กระบี่ – ฉัน ไม่ได้ เจอ เขา อีก เลย
set-from she move-go Krabi – I no can meet she more-beyond

Since she moved to Krabi, I have not met her anymore.
I have not met her anymore.

5.2 tʃán mâi dâai tsəə kháu ìik-ləəi – **tâng-tɛ̀ɛ kháu yáai-pai kràbìi**
ฉัน ไม่ได้ เจอ เขา อีก เลย – ตั้ง แต่ เขา ย้าย ไป กระบี่
I no can meet she more-beyond – set-from she move-go Krabi

I have not met her at all **since she moved to Krabi.**
I have not met her at all.

Notes
- Both sentences, 5.1 and 5.2 are correct.
- However, **tâng-tɛ̀ɛ** ตั้ง แต่ clause is normally placed at the beginning of the sentence in Thai.
- Depending on the context, it can also be placed at the end of the sentence.

5.3 Question
kháu pen nák-thúrákìt tâng-tɛ̀ɛ mʉ̂ʉa-rai khráp
เขา เป็น นักธุรกิจ ตั้ง แต่ ตั้ง แต่ เมื่อไร ครับ
he be person-business set-from when khráp

Since when has he been a business person?

Reply 1
kháu pen nák-thúrákìt **tâng-tɛ̀ɛ pii 2018 pen-tôn-maa** *lɛ́ɛu*
เขา เป็น นักธุรกิจ ตั้ง แต่ ปี 2018 เป็น ต้น มา แล้ว
he be person-business set-from year 2018 be-start-come already

He has been a business person **since 2018.**
He is already a business person.

Reply 2
kháu pen nák-thúrákìt **pii 2018 pen-tôn-maa** *lɛ́ɛu*
เขา เป็น นักธุรกิจ ปี 2018 เป็น ต้น มา แล้ว
he be person-business year 2018 be-start-come already

He has been a business person **since 2018.**
He is already a business person.

Notes
- Often **tâng-tɛ̀ɛ** ตั้ง แต่ can be omitted as in the reply 2, and the translation into English would be the same or very similar.

5.4 Question
thammai khun mâi bɔ̀ɔk
ทำไม คุณ ไม่ บอก
why you no tell

Why did you not tell?

Reply
mâi bɔ̀ɔk – **phrɔ́-wâa** khun mâi thăam
ไม่ บอก – เพราะ ว่า คุณ ไม่ ถาม
no tell because you no ask

*I did not tell you **because/since** you did not ask.*

- This is an obvious case when **tâng-tɛ̀ɛ** ตั้ง แต่ is not used.
- When there is a clear causative relationship, it is best expressed by **phrɔ́-wâa** เพราะ ว่า *because* in Thai.
- Depending on the emphasis, in English we can use either *since* or *because*. *Because* is stronger than *since*.

Overall conclusions
- **tâng-tɛ̀ɛ** ตั้ง แต่ is a very important conjunction word in Thai. It is frequently used by Thais to refer to the *point of time* in the *present, past* and *future*.
- **tâng-tɛ̀ɛ** ตั้ง แต่ can be translated into English as *since, from, onwards,* etc. It refers to the time.
- Commonly used words to replace **tâng-tɛ̀ɛ** ตั้ง แต่ are:

pen-tôn-pai	เป็น ต้น ไป	*from now onwards*
pen-tôn-maa	เป็น ต้น มา	*until now*
lăng-tsàak	หลัง จาก	*after*

D. Conclusion

Key: Place **lɛ́ɛu** แล้ว *already* at the end of the sentence to express the fact that a certain state *has been reached, obtained* or *attained*. The meaning is the similar to the phrase *it is already the case.* **lɛ́ɛu** แล้ว

makes the *bridge* between the *present state* and the *previous state* in the past or the *future time*.

The *Thai time aspec*t can be expressed in several ways. **lέεu** แล้ว can be conveniently used in the *present, past* or *future* time sentences. The *natural time aspect* is very much understood from the context. Whether the sentence refers to the *present time* or *completed actions* in the past, depends on the context and the type of main verbs (Groups 1–5) **lέεu** แล้ว is used with.

We have divided Thai verbs into *five groups*. Each group is special. When the time indicator **lέεu** แล้ว is used in connection with them, the verb group determines what the *natural time aspect* is. That means that the main verb plays an important role, whether the sentence refers *naturally* to the *present time* or a *completed* actions in the past.

Sometimes, **lέεu** แล้ว is referred to as a kind of *past tense marker* or *action completed*. More accurate term would be to describe it as a time indicator, *state reached* or *attained; it is already the case*. One way to understand **lέεu** แล้ว is to compare it with the English word *already*. They are used in the similar way. However, **lέεu** แล้ว is a far more important word in Thai than *already* is in English. Depending on the context, **lέεu** แล้ว is sometimes better translated into English as *now*.

In order to understand the *time indicator* **lέεu** แล้ว and the *natural Thai time aspect,* just think in terms that it always has some connection to the *present state*. Depending on the context, we are *"here and now"* looking into the *present* (now) or to the *past* (completed action). So, **lέεu** แล้ว makes the bridge between the *present* and the *past*. With **lέεu** แล้ว, the *natural time aspect* becomes clear.

As far as the *future time* is concerned, we normally need to add the *future time words* or the *future tense marker* **tsà** จะ *will* to make the *future time aspect clear.*

In English, we can drop the adverb *already*, and the tense remains usually the same. If **lέεu** แล้ว is *dropped* in Thai, the *time focus* can change.

Unfamiliar expressions

Expressing the *time aspect*, the *point of time* and the *duration of time* correctly in Thai can sometimes be challenging.

Examples

a) **pai** ไป **maa** มา and **tâng-tɛ̀ɛ** ตั้ง แต่

> 1. khǎu pen nák-thúrákìt **pai tâng-tɛ̀ɛ** *pii 2018 lɛ́ɛu*
> เขา เป็น นักธุรกิจ ไป ตั้ง แต่ ปี 2018 แล้ว
> he be person-business go set-from year 2018 already
>
> *He has been a business person since 2018.*

- This sentence is grammatically correct but...
- The helping verb **pai** ไป is placed before **tâng-tɛ̀ɛ** ตั้ง แต่ and the *point of time* **pii** ปี *2018, year 2018.*
- The sentences has a negative connotation.

2. khǎu pen nák-thúrákìt **maa tâng-tɛ̀ɛ** *pii 2018 lɛ́ɛu*
เขา เป็น นักธุรกิจ มา ตั้ง แต่ ปี 2018 แล้ว
he be person-business come set-from year 2018

He has been a business person since 2018.

- This sentence is correct.
- The helping verb **maa** มา is placed before **tâng-tɛ̀ɛ** ตั้ง แต่ and the *point of time* **pii** ปี 2018, *year 2018*.
- The sentence sounds good. **maa** มา has a neutral connotation.

3. khǎu pen nák-thúrákìt **tâng-tɛ̀ɛ** *pii 2018 lɛ́ɛu*
เขา เป็น นักธุรกิจ ตั้ง แต่ 2018 แล้ว
he be person-business set-from year 2018 already

He has been a business person since 2018.

- This sentence is correct.
- **pai** ไป and **maa** มา have been dropped.
- Place only **tâng-tɛ̀ɛ** ตั้ง แต่ *since* or **lǎng-tsàak** หลัง จาก *after* before the *point of time* in the past, and the sentence is correct and sounds good.

b) **pii-thîi-lɛ́ɛu** ปี ที่ แล้ว *last year* or **pii-kɔ̀ɔn** ปี ก่อน *last year*

> 1. phŏm riian phaasăa thai tâng-tɛ̀ɛ **pii-thîi-lɛ́ɛu** *lɛ́ɛu**
>   ผม เรียน ภาษา ไทย ตั้ง แต่ ปี ที่ แล้ว แล้ว
>   I study language Thai set-from year-that-already *already*
>
>   *I have already been studying Thai since last year.*

- This sentence is grammatically correct, but...
- Some natives think that the above sentence sounds unnatural.
- The reason being that **lɛ́ɛu** แล้ว is used as a *time indicator* and repeated at the end of the sentence; it has two different grammatical functions.

2. phŏm riian phaasăa thai **tâng-tɛ̀ɛ pii-kɔ̀ɔn** *lɛ́ɛu**
   ผม เรียน ภาษา ไทย ตั้ง แต่ ปี ก่อน แล้ว
   I study language Thai set-from year before already

   I have already been studying Thai since last year.

- This sentence is grammatically correct.
- For some Thais, this sentence is a better option since **lɛ́ɛu** แล้ว plays only one grammatical function.
- **pii-kɔ̀ɔn** ปี ก่อน is used instead of **pii-thîi-lɛ́ɛu** ปี ที่ แล้ว. Both are translated into English as *last year.*

3. phŏm riian phaasăa thai **tâng-tɛ̀ɛ pii-kɔ̀ɔn**
   ผม เรียน ภาษา ไทย ตั้ง แต่ ปี ก่อน
   I study language Thai set-from year before

   I have already been studying Thai since last year.

- This sentence is grammatically correct.
- **lɛ́ɛu** แล้ว as a *time indicator* at the end of the sentence is dropped.
- This sentence is translated into English the same as the sentences 1 and 2.
- However, there is a slight change in the meaning. The adverb **lɛ́ɛu** แล้ว *already* is missing now.

4. phǒm riian phaasǎa-thai **tâng-tɛ̀ɛ pii-thîi-lɛ́ɛu**
   ผม เรียน ภาษา ไทย ตั้ง แต่ ปี ที่ แล้ว
   I study language-Thai set-from year-that-already

   I have been studying Thai since last year.

- This sentence is grammatically correct.
- This sentence is translated into English the same as the sentences 1, 2 and 3.
- **pii-thîi-lɛ́ɛu** ปี ที่ แล้ว is used instead of **pii-kɔ̀ɔn** ปี ก่อน. Both are translated into English as *last year*.
- **lɛ́ɛu** แล้ว as a *time indicator* is normally dropped in the sentences like this. The sentence sounds better without it.

E. Simple advice

In this Secret, we have summarised the *Thai time aspect*. We have concentrated mainly on the *natural time aspect*. If the *natural time aspect* is understood well, then everything follows easily. To express the *Thai time aspect, present, past* and *future* with *time words* and *tense markers* is relatively simple.

You may find that the last Language hints section D is slightly overwhelming. However, if you can comprehend it, you are on the way to understand how Thais use the *time indicator* **lɛ́ɛu** แล้ว and express themselves while communicating with each other every day. **lɛ́ɛu** แล้ว is used as a bridge *between* the *present state*, the *previous state* and the *future state*.

For Thai people, the language is often related to *feelings*. Whenever **lɛ́ɛu** แล้ว is used in the sentence, there is a change in a state. *Now, it is like this, before it was different* or *in the future, it will be different*.

To understand how words are positioned in a sentence is important. It is the basis for the successful Thai language learning since everything in Thai is in *basic form*. You may call it the *grammar, structure* or the *Thai way*, but you need to learn how Thai people use the language intuitively. Make clear to yourself what the term *natural time aspect* means. With **lɛ́ɛu** แล้ว, the *natural time aspect* normally becomes clear.

The *time aspect* can be changed or emphasised by the *time words* and *tense markers*. Normally, the *natural time* refers to the *present time* or *completed actions* in the past.

However, since there is not any *direct natural time aspect* for the *future*, the *future tense marker* **tsà** จะ *will* is often used to make the *future time clear*.

In fact, Thai people do not think in terms of tenses at all. It would make more sense to understand the role that **lɛ́ɛu** แล้ว plays for Thai people in different situations. **lɛ́ɛu** แล้ว expresses meanings such as a state *reached* or a condition *obtained; it is already the case*. These sentences have a strong connection to the *present time*, even if the action has taken place before now.

In Book II (Secrets 8–11), where **lɛ́ɛu** แล้ว is used as *conjunction word*, there will be many more interesting expressions with **lɛ́ɛu** แล้ว. Do not miss it!

Examples

lɛ́ɛu-kɔ̂ɔ	แล้ว ก็	*and*
lɛ́ɛu-yang	แล้ว ยัง	*and in addition*
lɛ́ɛu-lǎng-tsàak-nán	แล้ว หลัง จาก นั้น	*after that*
lɛ́ɛu-lǎng-tsàak-níi	แล้ว หลัง จาก นี้	*after this*
lɛ́ɛu-ləəi	แล้ว เลย	*and then, after that*
lɛ́ɛu-kɔ̂ɔ-ləəi	แล้ว ก็ เลย	*and then, after that*
lɛ́ɛu-ìik-yàang	แล้ว อีก อย่าง	*and one more thing*
lɛ́ɛu-nɔ̂ɔk-tsàak-nán	แล้ว นอก จาก นั้น	*and besides that*
lɛ́ɛu-phrɔ́-tʃànán	แล้ว เพราะ ฉะ นั้น	*consequently*
lɛ́ɛu-tsung	แล้ว จึง	*so, therefore*
lɛ́ɛu-khɔ̂i	แล้ว ค่อย	*and then, shortly*
lɛ́ɛu-dǐiau	แล้ว เดี๋ยว	*soon, in a moment*
lɛ́ɛu-ìik-mâi-naan	แล้ว อีก ไม่ นาน	*and soon after that*
sèt-lɛ́ɛu	เสร็จ แล้ว	*and after finished*
rîiap-rɔ́ɔi-lɛ́ɛu	เรียบ ร้อย แล้ว	*and when ready*
lɛ́ɛu-thǔng	แล้ว ถึง	*and when done*

etc.

One more thing

In fact, we have only *this moment* in our hands. Our *most precious time* is the *present time;* it belongs to the realm of *feelings* and *intuition*. The rest of our life lies in the *past;* the *future* offers us endless possibilities. **lέεu แล้ว** brings the *past* and the *future* into the *present time.*

ABC of the Thai language

A) Essential features of the Thai language

In every language, we must be able to make sounds in such a way that other people understand what we are saying. We also need to put words together in such a way that sentences make sense and sound right.

As an adult learner, this requires some conscious and active effort on your part. When you are learning a foreign language as a child, you are growing into it. Learning a foreign language as an adult is an unfamiliar process. The learning process is not that intuitive anymore. Your brain also wants to understand what you are learning. If the correct way is not readily available to you, your mind will understand things in the old way. It makes assumptions, right or wrong, from the point of view of your own native language.

Since the syntax of the Thai language differs from English and many other languages, the assumptions you make may not be valid. You need to think the way Thai people do in order to speak Thai fluently.

In this book, much emphasis is placed on verbs and *verb groups*. The list of verbs given on the following pages is not complete by all means. It can be used as an example of verbs in different group categories.

We take the verbs first since they play a major role in how the *natural time aspect* is determined when there are not any *time words* or *tense markers* in the sentence.

There are two types of verbs: *non-action verbs*, sometimes also called *state verbs* and *action verbs*, sometimes also called *dynamic verbs*.

State verbs describe a state that normally lasts for some time. Some common examples are: *to be (He is tall), to have (I have fever), to feel (I feel good)*.

Action verbs are verbs that express actions you can do, such as *to run, to work, to dance, etc.*

When the first three verb groups 1–3 are used with **lɛ́ɛu** แล้ว, the *natural time aspect* normally refers to the *present time*. When the verb groups 4–5 are used, the *natural time aspect* normally refers to a *completed action* in the past.

1. The verb groups of the Thai language

When **lɛ́ɛu** แล้ว is used as a *time indicator*, it is normally placed at the end of the sentence. The Thai verbs can be divided into five groups as follows.

1.1 Non-action verbs

The *time indicator* **lɛ́ɛu** แล้ว can be used together with *non-action verbs* (also called state verbs) (Groups 1–2) to express the *present time conditions* that have been *attained* or *reached*.

1.1.1 Adjectives (Group 1) as non-action verbs

Adjectives as *state verbs* describe a state or condition. Adjectives in Thai can play the role of a verb.

When **lɛ́ɛu** แล้ว is used with *adjectives,* the focus is normally on the *present time*.

The situation is expressed in English by the *Present Simple Tense* – *She is beautiful now*.

Examples

dii	ดี	to be good
yɛ̂ɛ	แย่	to be bad, terrible
leeu	เลว	to be bad, evil
nàk	หนัก	to be heavy
sànùk	สนุก	to be fun
tsèp	เจ็บ	to be hurt
aai	อาย	to be shy
kluua	กลัว	to be scary
kèng	เก่ง	to be skilled, talented, efficient
tʃàlàat	ฉลาด	to be clever, smart

yûng	ยุ่ง	to be busy
wâang	ว่าง	to be free
moo-hŏo	โมโห	to be angry
tsing	จริง	to be honest, real
nɛ̂ɛ	แน่	to be sure, certain
sòot	โสด	to be single
arɔ̀i	อร่อย	to be delicious
phèt	เผ็ด	to be spicy
khem	เค็ม	to be salty
lék	เล็ก	to be small
yài	ใหญ่	to be big
sĭi-dɛɛng	แดง	to be red
sĭi-lɯ̆ɯang	เหลือง	to be yellow
etc.		

1.1.2 State verbs (Group 2) as non-action verbs

State verbs describe a state or condition. When **lɛ́ɛu** แล้ว is used with *state verbs*, the focus is normally on the *present time*.

The situation is expressed in English by the *Present Simple Tense* – *I understand now.*

Examples

khâu-tsai	เข้าใจ	to understand
rúu	รู้	to know
mii	มี	to have
wái-tsai	ไว้ใจ	to trust
rák	รัก	to love
tsam-dâai	จำได้	to remember
rúu-sɯ̀k	รู้สึก	to feel
tʃɔ̂ɔp	ชอบ	to like
hĕn-dûuai	เห็นด้วย	to agree
dâai-yin	ได้ยิน	to hear
dâai-klìn	ได้กลิ่น	to smell
tʃɯ̂ɯa	เชื่อ	to believe

sŏngsăi	สงสัย	*to doubt*
klìiat	เกลียด	*to hate*
yɔɔm	ยอม	*to agree* (usually against one's will)
wăng	หวัง	*to hope*
sŏng-săi	สง สัย	*to suspect*
etc.		

1.2 Action verbs

Action verbs are more *dynamic* than state verbs. There are three kinds of action verbs. Action verbs are used when something happens or when somebody is performing an action.

1.2.1 General action verbs (Group 3)

General action verbs may be conveniently used together with **lέεu** แล้ว. When **lέεu** แล้ว is used with *general action verbs* (Group 3), the focus usually falls on the actions which are happening at the *time of speaking* or *nowadays*.

With **lέεu** แล้ว, there was a state which *did not exist before*; now, the state has been *attained*.

The situation is normally expressed in English by the *Present Continuous Tense – He is already working*.

Examples

tham-ngaan	ทำ งาน	*to work*
yùu	อยู่	*to stay, to live*
aasăi	อาศัย	*to live*
riian	เรียน	*to study*
nɔɔn	นอน	*to sleep*
khàp	ขับ	*to drive*
sài	ใส่	*to wear*
pràtʃum	ประชุม	*to hold a meeting*
khum	คุม	*to take care, to watch over*
duu-lεε	ดูแล	*to take care*
khɔɔi	คอย	*to wait*

rɔɔ	รอ	*to wait*
bin	บิน	*to fly*
khǐian	เขียน	*to write*
nâng	นั่ง	*to sit*
dəən	เดิน	*to walk*
etc.		

1.2.2 Specific action verbs (Group 4)

When **lɛ́ɛu** แล้ว is used with *specific action verbs* (Group 4), the focus is normally on *completed actions* in the *past*.

The situation is expressed in English by the *Present Perfect Tense* – *I have already eaten*.

Examples

kin	กิน	*to eat*
dùum	ดื่ม	*to drink*
tham	ทำ	*to do*
khui	คุย	*to chat*
triiam	เตรียม	*to prepare, to make ready*
lə̂ək	เลิก	*to cease, to stop*
yɛ̂ɛk	แยก	*to separate*
wîng	วิ่ง	*to run*
hǎai	หาย	*to disappear, to recover*
ɔ̀ɔk-kamlang-kaai	ออก กำลังกาย	*to exercise*
rə̂əm	เริ่ม	*to start*
plìian	เปลี่ยน	*to change*
ráksǎa	รักษา	*to heal*
tìt-tɔ̀ɔ	ติด ต่อ	*to contact, to communicate*
tsəə	เจอ	*to meet*
tsàai	จ่าย	*to pay*
khɔ̌ɔ	ขอ	*to ask*
kə̀ət-khûn	เกิด ขึ้น	*to happen*
pháyaayaam	พยายาม	*to try*
fàak	ฝาก	*to deposit*

sămrèt	สำเร็จ	*to succeed*
kɛ̂ɛ-khăi	แก้ไข	*to fix*
trùuat-sɔ̀ɔp	ตรวจ สอบ	*to check, to investigate*
thaa	ทา	*to paint*
long-thun	ลง ทุน	*to invest*
etc.		

1.2.3 Direction verbs (Group 5)

When **lέεu** แล้ว is used with *direction verbs* (Group 5), the statement usually refers to *completed actions* in the *past*.

The situation is normally expressed in English by the *Present Perfect Tense – He has already gone*. In Thai, we simply say **kháu-pai-lέεu** เขา ไป แล้ว *he go already*.

Examples

pai	ไป	*to go*
maa	มา	*to come*
sòng	ส่ง	*to send*
hâi	ให้	*to give*
dâai	ได้	*to get*
ráp	รับ	*to receive*
ɔ̀ɔk	ออก	*to leave*
thoo	โทร	*to call (to phone)*
rîiak	เรียก	*to call out*
khâu	เข้า	*to enter*
bɔ̀ɔk	บอก	*to tell*
athíbaai	อธิบาย	*to explain*
yáai	ย้าย	*to move*
wέ-yîiam	แวะ เยี่ยม	*to visit*
thíng	ทิ้ง	*to throw away*
yuum	ยืม	*to borrow*
khuun	คืน	*to return*
nam-maa	นำ มา	*to bring*
nam-khâu	นำ เข้า	*to import*

mɔɔng	มอง	*to look at*
tìt-taam	ติด ตาม	*to follow*
etc.		

2. The Thai time aspect

The grammar rules in Thai are straightforward. For instance, the verbs are not conjugated, there are no tenses for verbs, there are no plural forms for nouns and no genders or articles like a, an or the. In Thai, the *time aspect* is made clear by words. It is normally understood from the *context* or made clear by the *time words* and *tense markers*.

Thais talk rather about the *present time*, *completed actions* in the past and about the *future time*.

- **pàt-tsùbanna-kaan** ปัจจุบัน กาล *present time, now* or *nowadays*
- **adìitta-kaan** อดีต กาล *past time, completed actions*
- **anaakhótta-kaan** อนาคต กาล *future time, future planning* or *prediction*

2.1 Time words and tense markers

The Thai time aspect can be changed by time words such as **tɔɔn-níi** ตอน นี้ *now*, which are often placed at the beginning of the sentence. Depending on the context, *time words* can also be placed at the end of the sentence. All tense markers such as **tsà** จะ *will* are always placed before the main verb.

2.2 Natural time aspect

When *basic sentences* are used without *time words* or *tense markers*, the meaning is normally understood *naturally* from the context. Usually, the *natural time aspect* refers to the *present time* or *completed actions* in the past. The outcome depends mainly on the *five verb groups*, **lɛ́ɛu** แล้ว and from the context.

The *natural Thai time aspect* can be changed to reflect the *present*, *past* or *future* time by time *words* or *tense makers*.

2.3 English tenses

The term tense in English is used to describe tenses such as *past, present* and *future*. The semantic meaning of the word *tense* is that the verbs change form when different tenses are used in English. In Thai, everything is in a *basic form*.

B) Parts of speech

When describing the structure of the Thai language, we need to know a few basic terms, usually called parts of speech in English. The sentences are normally constructed by using *verbs, nouns, adjectives, adverbs, pronouns* and *conjunctions*.

1. Verbs

In this book, verbs play an important role. They are reviewed in the above Section A.

2. Nouns

Nouns can be classified in Thai as:

2.1 Common nouns

The word common noun is a word used for things such as *dogs, cats, cars, computers*. They have a physical form and they can be touched.

2.2 Abstract nouns

An abstract noun is a word used for things like *luck, beauty* and *effectiveness*. These nouns do not have a physical form and cannot be touched.

2.3 Personal pronouns

In Thai, personal pronouns such as I, he and we are used pronouns such as I, he and we, are used in a wider semantic sense than in English. They may refer to age, gender, social status and the context.

2.4 Classifiers

Thai count nouns are called classifiers. In English we also have classifiers: *bottles of milk, head of cattle*, a *glass of beer*. Perhaps, the more accurate term for these types of nouns is "measure words". The difference compared to English is that in Thai, it is compulsory to use classifiers for all nouns when counting. For example, you cannot say in Thai, *two cars*. You must say a *car two vehicles*. A vehicle would be a classifier in Thai.

3. Adjectives

3.1. Adjectives

Adjectives in Thai can be used as adjectives as we understand them in English. Adjectives usually answer the question "what kind?" Examples: *good, beautiful, happy...*

3.2 Adjectives as verbs

Adjectives in Thai can also play the role of a verb. For the sentence to be complete, all you need is a subject and an adjective. There is no need for any verb. A similar structure is not possible in English. In Thai, we can say that *she beautiful*, but in English you need to say that *she is beautiful*.

3.3. Adjectives as adverbs

Adjectives in Thai can be used as adverbs. In Thai, when an adjective follows an action verb, *good* becomes *well*, *beautiful* becomes *beautifully* and *slow* becomes *slowly*. In Thai, we can say that *she walk slow*, but in English, we need to say that *she walks slowly*. See the list of adjectives above.

4. Adverbs

4.1 Adverbs of time

Adverbs of time tell us when the action happened, will happen or perhaps it is happening right now. Examples: *yesterday, two days ago, tomorrow, now...* In this book, we usually call adverbs of time "*time words*".

4.2 Adverbs of frequency

Adverbs of frequency are used to tell us how often the action happens. Examples: *often, regularly, always...*

4.3 Adverbs of place

Adverbs of place are used to tell us where the action happens. Examples: *far, near, inside...*

4.4 Adverbs of manner

Adverbs of manner are used to tell us how and in what way the action happens. Examples: *slowly, well, gently...*

5. Prepositions

Both Thai and English use prepositions such as *in, to, above, for, etc...*

6. Conjunctions

Conjunction words are also called linking words. They are used to connect *words, phrases* and *sentences*. Examples: *and, then, after that, therefore...* Conjunction words are reviewed in the Book II, Secrets 8–11.

C) Making sentences

In order to make correct sentences, there are a few basic terms which may be helpful to know while learning Thai.

1. Simple subject

The simple subject is a noun or a pronoun. It is a person or thing that actively performs the action, the one who is in charge.

2. Simple predicate

The simple predicate is a verb, which describes or tells something about the subject. In Thai, an *adjective* can be both a *predicate* and an *adjective* at the same time. No separate verb, as we understand it in English, is needed.

3. Object

3.1 Direct object

The term direct object is used for something which is given.

3.2 Indirect object

The term indirect object is used for the person to whom the direct object is given.

3.3 Subject-verb-object in the sentence

The word order of *subject-verb-object* is normally the same as in English. However, in Thai, the *subject* or the *object* can be dropped if understood from the context. Even the *verb*, as we understand it in English, can be dropped, if an adjective is used as a verb.

4. Word order of **lɛ́ɛu** แล้ว

   When **lɛ́ɛu** แล้ว *already* is used as a *time indicator* (Book I) after the main verb, it normally comes at the end of the sentence. When **lɛ́ɛu** แล้ว is used as a *linking word* (Book II), it normally is placed as the first element in the second clause, and the meaning is *and then.*

5. Context

   The context can be verbal or social or both. In this book, the word context is used abstractly.

   The speaker takes into account the surroundings in which the conversation takes place and adapts her or his language to suit that context. Therefore, much is already understood, and not everything needs to be spoken out.

   Much care has been taken in explaining what the context means in practical terms. The verb groups 1–5 play a major role in how the sentences are understood in Thai.

6. Idiomatic expressions

   Idiomatic expressions are informal ways to convey meanings. An idiomatic phrase may have a different meaning than the words in it. Idiomatic expressions give some juice to the expression. Many idiomatic expressions are included in Book III.

7. Gerund

   Gerund is a grammatical term used in English for nouns that are formed from verbs by the ending **-ing** such as giv**ing**. This kind of noun (gerund) can be a subject or an object in a sentence. In Thai, we form nouns from verbs by placing the prefix **kaan** การ before the verb. **kaan-dâai** การได้ is translated into English as *getting*.

8. Genitive/possessive form

   The term genitive is used to show possession. In Thai, the possessive form is created by the word **kɔ̌ɔng** ของ *of* before the possessor or just placing a noun directly before the possessor. So, *my car* in Thai is expressed as *car I* or *car of I.*

9. Polite particles

In Thai, polite particles are used frequently. The most common are **khâ** ค่ะ (for men) and **khráp** ครับ (for women). They are not very easy to translate into English. Therefore, we have not given an exact English translation for them in our "word for word" translations. Their usage and "semantic boundaries" are wide.

10. Syntax

Syntax is concerned with the structure of the language, how the words are put together in the sentence. This is important since the Thai language uses a different type of syntax from English.

11. Semantics

Semantics is concerned with the meaning of words and sentences. This is important since one word can have different semantic meanings. **lέεu** แล้ว *already* is an excellent example of this type of word.

12. Semantic boundary

We use the term semantic boundary to describe the fact that we need to use different English words in order to define the meaning of **lέεu** แล้ว *already*. We must use English words such as *already, now, and, and then, etc.* to grasp the correct meaning when it is placed in diverse positions in a sentence. That is because **lέεu** แล้ว has a wide *semantic boundary*, and much depends on the context.

13. Phonetics

When you speak Thai, you need to know how to pronounce the words. It does not matter how many words you know or how well you understand the Thai grammar, but if you mispronounce Thai words, you are not understood by Thais. The English language normally forgives non-native speakers even if the pronunciation is not perfect or the choice of words is not right. Thai people are smiling and very generous, but as far as the Thai language is concerned, they are strict.

Phonetics is concerned with the sounds of the language. This is quite important since English sounds cannot be directly transferred into Thai. This is true particularly with the vowel sounds. If you want to be understood by Thais, you should be able to produce correct Thai sounds.

Transliteration is a way to write Thai sounds with western letters and international phonetic symbols. This helps you to get the sounds right. After all, reading the Thai script can be challenging.

If you feel that you need help with *"how to pronounce the Thai sounds and tones right"*, you can find the comprehensive explanation of Thai sounds in the following books:

22 Secrets of Learning Thai – Sounds of the Thai Language

Book I – Basic Sounds, ISBN 978-952-6651-32-3

Book II – Advanced Sounds, ISBN 978-952-6651-33-0

www.thaibooks.net

www.amazon.com

Bibliography

Becker, Benjawan Poomsan. Thai for Beginners.
Paiboon Publishing, California, 1995.

Becker, Benjawan Poomsan. Thai for Intermediate Learners. Paiboon Publishing, California, 1998.

Becker, Benjawan Poomsan. Thai for Advanced Learners. Paiboon Publishing, California, 2000.

Burusphat Somsonge. Reading and Writing Thai.
Institute of Language and Culture for Rural Development,
Mahidol University, Bangkok, 2006.

Dhyan, Manik. 22 Secrets of Learning Thai – Complete Guide to Sounds, Tones and Thai Writing System, Dolphin Books, Helsinki, 2014.

Dhyan, Manik. 22 Secrets of Learning Thai – Learning Thai with hâi ให้. Dolphin Books, Helsinki, 2016.

Dhyan, Manik. 22 Secrets of Learning Thai – Learning Thai with dâai ได้ Book I. Dolphin Books, Helsinki, 2017.

Dhyan, Manik. 22 Secrets of Learning Thai – Learning Thai with dâai ได้ Book II. Dolphin Books, Helsinki, 2018.

Dhyan, Manik. Learning Thai Quickly and Easily – Learning Thai with Original Thai Words. Dolphin Books, Helsinki, 2019.

Dhyan, Manik. Learning Thai Quickly and Easily – Learning Thai Language and Grammar. Dolphin Books, Helsinki, 2020.

Dhyan, Manik. 22 Secrets of Learning Thai – Sounds of the Thai Language Book I – Basic Sounds, Secrets 1–15. Dolphin Books, Helsinki, 2020.

Dhyan, Manik. 22 Secrets of Learning Thai – Sounds of the Thai Language Book II – Advanced Sounds, Secrets 16–22. Dolphin Books, Helsinki, 2021.

Higbie, James & Thinsan Snea. Thai Reference Grammar: The Structure of Spoken Thai. Orchid Press, Bangkok, 2003.

James, Helen. Thai Reference Grammar.
D.K. Editions & Suk's Editions, Bangkok, 2001.

Kanchanawan, Nitaya & Eynon, Matthew J. Learning Thai – A Unique and Practical Approach. Odeon Store, Bangkok, 2005.

Ponmanee, Sriwilai. Speaking Thai for Advanced Learner. Thai Studies Center, Chiang Mai Universtity, Chiang Mai, 2001.

Smyth, David. Thai: An Essential Grammar.
Routledge, London and New York, 2002.

Smyth, David. Teach Yourself Thai.
Hodder Headline, London, 2003.

Our books can be obtained from the following bookshops in Thailand:

DK today
www.dktoday.co.th

Asia Books
www.asiabooks.com

Kinokuniya
www.kinokuniya.com

Chulalongkorn University Book Center
www.chulabook.com

Thammasat University Bookstore
www.bookstore.tu.ac.th

Chiang Mai University Bookstore
http://www.cmubook.com

Naiin Bookstore
www.naiin.com

Sounds of the Thai Language
Basic Sounds

Book I – Secrets 1–15

ISBN 978-9526651323, 182 pages

Sounds of the Thai Language (Book I) teaches you all the basic sounds used in spoken and written Thai. It includes 20 consonant sounds and 18 pure vowel sounds. It points out the main obstacles for learners, for example which Thai sounds are most difficult for an English speaker to produce. It then gives you handy tips to help overcome these difficulties. Much care has been taken to describe each sound in phonetic as well as in practical terms so that everyone should be able to grasp the correct way to produce Thai sounds.

The book has been designed so that it can be used by all levels of Thai learners. It contains a special exercise section, which teaches you in a step by step manner how to learn to read Thai script.

The book includes MP3 download spoken by native speakers to give you examples of how the words are produced in practice. In addition to individual words, the audio features many of the most common expressions used by Thai people in everyday conversation. This book is suitable for self-study and can also be used as an aid in the classroom. It contains a vast number of tips to assist you in learning Thai and understanding some of the crucial cultural aspects of the language.

This book and audio will set you on the road to confident Thai language learning.

Sounds of the Thai Language Advanced Sounds

Book II – Secrets 16–22

ISBN 978-9526651330, 178 pages

Book II teaches you the advanced sounds of the Thai language such as consonant clusters, rare consonants, vowel combinations, final sounds and tones rules.

It includes the audio file spoken by native speakers to give you examples of how the special words are pronounced in practice. In addition to individual words, the audio features many of the most common expressions used by Thai people in everyday conversation.

This book is suitable for self-study and can also be used as an aid in the classroom. It contains a vast number of tips to assist you in learning Thai and understanding some of the crucial cultural aspects of the language. This book and audio will set you on the road to confident Thai language learning.

If you are a beginner, it is recommended that you first read Book I – Basic sounds. It gives you an overall understanding of the basic sounds used in spoken and written Thai and includes all 20 consonant sounds and 18 pure vowel sounds.

Much care has been taken to describe each sound in phonetic as well as in practical terms so that everyone should be able to grasp the correct way to produce Thai sounds.

The free MP3 audio files can be downloaded from the address: www.thaibooks.net

Learning Thai with hâi ให้

ISBN 978-9526651156, 296 pages

hâi ให้, along with words like dâai ได้, lέεu แล้ว and kɔ̂ɔ ก็, is one of the most important words in the Thai language.

When speaking Thai, it is important to understand the correct usage of the verb hâi ให้ in everyday speech.

One simple way to use the verb hâi ให้ is *to give something to someone*. It is used in a similar manner as the English verb *to give*.

In addition, hâi ให้ is used as a causative verb which has several different meanings depending on the situation, and the way it is spoken. It can be translated into English as *to let, to allow, to make* and even *to order* or *to force someone to do something*.

In some situations hâi ให้ is better translated into English as the preposition *for*, as in *for you, for me*, etc. It is also often used in idiomatic phrases where it carries no meaning itself but denotes only the sense of a command.

Thais use the verb hâi ให้ in an intuitive way in a variety of situations in order to express feelings, wishes, commands and nuances of meaning while communicating with each other every day.

If you learn this word well, you will be rewarded.

Learning Thai with dâai ได้

Book I – Secrets 1–14

ISBN 978-9526651200, 283 pages

Whether you are a beginner or an advanced learner, you certainly want to learn to speak Thai fluently. This book will take you a long way towards your goal.

dâai ได้ is one of the most common words in Thai. It is a multifunctional helping verb and is used by Thais in several different ways. It has many distinct meanings depending on where it is placed in a sentence and which other words are used with it. With this book you won't just learn how to use dâai ได้ but will also acquire a deeper knowledge of the Thai language in general.

Included are:
- complete and informative written examples
- audio spoken by native speakers
- highlights and explanations of dâai's ได้ usage
- sections of simple and easy to understand advice
- useful hints and tips on dâai ได้ and the spoken Thai language

Furthermore, you will get to see the language "through the eyes of dâai ได้". Study this book and you will be rewarded; your Thai friends will be amazed at your deep understanding of the subtleties of their language.

Learning Thai Tenses with dâai ได้

Book II – Secrets 15–22

ISBN 978-9526651408 , 278 pages

Whether you are a beginner or an advanced learner, you will surely want to learn to speak Thai fluently. In order to do this, it is vital to use time words and tense markers correctly.

The English term *tense* is also a handy way to talk about past, present and future activities in Thai, even though there are no *tenses* as such in the Thai language. When compared to English, Thai tenses are expressed very differently.

It is often said that dâai ได้ denotes a past tense. However, it would be better not to think of dâai ได้ as the past tense marker since it can also be used to refer to present or future events.

To help you speak Thai fluently the Book II includes:
- complete and informative written examples
- audio spoken by native speakers
- highlights and explanations of dâai's ได้ usage
- sections of simple and easy to understand advice
- useful hints and tips on dâai ได้ and the spoken Thai language

Books I and II complement each other. However, each book has a different focus. In Book I, Secrets 1–14, we introduced dâai ได้ and explained where it should be placed in sentences. dâai ได้ has several grammatical functions; hence, it also has several meanings depending on the context. In Book II, Secrets 15–22, we focus on tenses.

Have fun while you study them both; then, you will understand how Thais express themselves in everyday life!

Learning Thai with Original Thai Words

ISBN 978-9526651439, 320 pages

Do you want to learn to speak Thai as naturally as Thais do? Thai is not as difficult as you may think! If you follow the guidelines of this book, you will acquire a basic knowledge of the language in just a few weeks.

Students, usually, face several obstacles when studying Thai. In this book, we shall explain clearly what these obstacles are and how to overcome them. We shall also point out what you need to know and what you may ignore when learning to speak Thai. This will ensure your time and effort is focused on the things that really matter. You will be in a position to make an informed decision on how to proceed and deepen your language skills.

We use a simple and direct method which is easy to comprehend. You don't have to master the complex Thai writing system in order to speak Thai fluently. In this book, we concentrate on "original Thai words" which form a very important part of the Thai vocabulary and are used by Thais every day in conversation.

The book is designed in such a way that it can be used by both beginners and by those who have already reached intermediate level.

Included are:

• written examples and sentences • audio spoken by native speakers
• highlights, explanations and examples on "how the language works"
• simple and easy to understand advice • hints and tips on spoken Thai language • "Take it further" section which includes many more tips on how to proceed with your studies

Now, you can tell all your friends that learning Thai can be easy. Read this book and you will discover how!

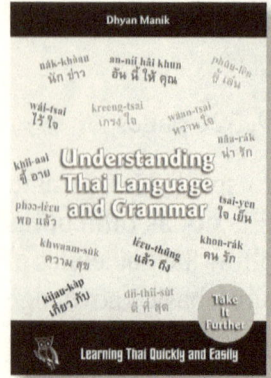

Understanding Thai Language and Grammar

ISBN 978-9526651460, 264 pages

Understanding the structure and grammar of the Thai languge is very important since it may differ considerably from your own language

Included are:
- Original Thai words compared to foreign origin words
- Personal pronouns and family members
- Days, weeks, months, seasons and numbers
- Telling time – 24-hour clock compared to the Thai style
- Foods, drinks and spices
- Travelling, places, buildings and countries of the world
- Names of animals and insects
- Health words and personal items
- Adjectives, adverbs and verbs
- Thai question words, prepositions and conjunction words
- Classifiers and prefixes
- tsai ใจ heart -word
- Summary of the Thai tenses
- Words of wisdom

Learning Thai Quickly and Easily

- Learning Thai with Original Thai Words (2019)
- Learning Thai Language and Grammar (2020)
- Learning Thai with English Words (coming 2024)
- ABC of Thai Language and Grammar (coming 2025)
- Learning Thai with Foreign Words – Pali, Sanskrit, Khmer, Chinese... (coming 2026)

22 Secrets of Learning Thai

- Learning Thai with hâi ให้ (2016)
- Learning Thai with dâai ได้ Book I, Secrets 1–14 (2018)
- Learning Thai Tenses with dâai ได้ Book II, Secrets 15–22 (2018)
- Sounds of the Thai Language Book I – Basic Sounds, Secrets 1–15 (2020)
- Sounds of the Thai Language Book II – Advanced Sounds, Secrets 16–22 (2021)
- Mastering Thai Grammar and Tenses with lɛ́ɛu แล้ว Book I, Secrets 1–7 (2023)
- Mastering Thai Grammar and Conjunction Words with lɛ́ɛu แล้ว Book II, Secrets 8–11 (coming 2024)
- Mastering Thai Language and Grammar with lɛ́ɛu แล้ว and Her Friends Book III, Secrets 12–22 (coming 2026)
- Learning Thai with kɔ̂ɔ ก็ (coming 2027)

For more information

www.thaibooks.net
www.facebook.com/22secrets

www.ingramcontent.com/pod-product-compliance
Lightning Source LLC
La Vergne TN
LVHW091631070526
838199LV00044B/1014